FABRICATING EVIDENCE

Drug Set-up/Cover-up of a Correctional Whistleblower

Britton Mosley, Sr.

Fabricating Evidence: Drug Set-Up/Cover-Up Of A Correctional Whistleblower. Copyright © 2015 by Britton Mosley, Sr. All rights reserved.

Published by
Mighty Monarch Publishing
P.O. Box 2036
Woodbridge, Virginia 22195
Email: fabevidence@gmail.com

No part of this book may be reproduced in any form or by any means including electronic, mechanical or photocopying or stored in a retrieval system without permission in writing from the publisher except by a reviewer who may quote brief passages to be included in a review.

ISBN: 978-0-9860909-0-5

Library of Congress Control Number: 2015902897

Manufactured and Printed in the United States of America

If you purchased this book without a cover, you should be aware that this book is stolen property. It is reported as "unsold and destroyed" to the publisher, and neither the author nor the publisher has received any payment for this "stripped" book.

DEDICATION

I dedicate this book to...

The people in America who were wrongfully convicted on nonviolent drug charges. I hope this book will show how evidence can be deliberately fabricated by law enforcement personnel, falsely imprisoning targeted Americans.

The families who are striving to recover from the emotional and financial hardship created by judicial injustice and the prison industrial complex.

There is a need for a bold step in the right direction for people victimized by the failed "war on drugs" unjust incarceration and extraordinarily long prison sentences for nonviolent, drug-related offenses.

TABLE OF CONTENTS

From the Author 7

Preface 9

Introduction 19

Chapter 1: Set-up the Whistleblower 28

Chapter 2: Mississippi Department of
  Corrections Investigation... 58

Chapter 3: County District Attorney
  Investigation 86

Chapter 4: The Office of the Attorney General
  Investigation 97

Chapter 5: Mississippi Highway Patrol
  (Criminal Investigation Bureau) Investigation 117

Chapter 6: Congressional Inquiry 141

Chapter 7: U.S. Department of Justice
Investigation 162

Chapter 8: Britton Mosley, Sr. vs. Mississippi
Department of Corrections 198

Chapter 9: Attorney Mike Cooke 237

Chapter 10: The Appeal Process 261

Chapter 11: National Association for the
Advancement of Colored People (Mississippi
State Conference) 270

Chapter 12: Protecting the Whistleblower 281

Conclusion 288

About the Author 299

FROM THE AUTHOR...

Miriam-Webster defines *terrorism* as *the use of violent acts to frighten the people in an area as a way of trying to achieve a political goal.*

Growing up in Mississippi in the forties, fifties and sixties, I became accustomed to terrorism because of the color of my skin. However, as a citizen of the United States in the nineteen century, never would I have imagined that terrorism would come from law enforcement and political figures right here in these United States of America.

There is a new generation of terrorism in Mississippi that state and local government support—wrongful convictions based on fabricated evidence.

While working as a correctional officer at South Mississippi Correctional Institute in Leakesville, Mississippi, I saw firsthand the disproportionate incarceration of people of color for petty, nonviolent offenses.

As a Black man, born and raised in the Jim Crow era in Mississippi, the fear of going to prison was always present in my mind. Fabricating evidence by law enforcement personnel and going to prison was common in Mississippi. Motivation, in most cases, was racial hate, and the fact that they could get away with it almost happened to me.

PREFACE

Incarceration in the United States of America is one of the main forms of punishment, rehabilitation, or both for the commission of felony and other offenses. The United States has the largest prison population in the world, and the second-highest per-capita incarceration rate, behind **Seychelles** (in Africa, which has a total prison population of 786 out of a population of 90,024). In 2012, 707 adults were incarcerated per 100,000 population.

The U.S. Bureau of Justice Statistics stated that 2,266,800 adults were incarcerated in U.S. federal and state prisons, and county jails at year-end 2011—about 0.94% of adults in the U.S. resident population. Additionally, 4,814,200 adults at year-end 2011 were on probation or on parole. In total, 6,977,700 adults were under correctional supervision (probation, parole, jail, or prison) in 2011 – about 2.9% of adults in the U.S. resident population.

Wikipedia.org states, "The United States has the highest documented incarceration rate in the world at 754 per 100,000 (as of 2009)." Louisiana ranks number 1, followed by Mississippi ranking number 2 in the United States with the highest number of inmates housed in its facilities. Mississippi incarcerates more people than those in developing countries.

Fabricating Evidence: Drug Set-up/Cover-up of a Correctional Whistleblower could not be timelier as the former Mississippi Corrections Commissioner, Chris Epps, was indicted on 49 federal counts, and accepting hundreds of thousands of dollars in bribes on November 6, 2014.

Having worked in the prison and seeing the disparity in the inmate population where Blacks were 80% of the inmates, it angers and saddens me to see Chris Epps, being a fellow African American, in this situation. Mississippi is known for its historic injustice against African Americans, and for Chris Epps—although he's innocent until proven guilty—to use his high-ranking position to allegedly profit off fellow African Americans.

What's equally disheartening is that in 2002, Chris Epps reviewed and approved the Mississippi Department of Corrections Policy: General Standards of Professional Conduct (ACA Standards: 3-3068, 3-3069, 3-4067 and ACRS-3A-07).

Writing this book has been very difficult for me. To relive the injustice I endured has taken an emotional toll on me.

My experience with the DOC gave me the mindset that prisons in Mississippi were the new form of slavery.

Fabricating Evidence

On the heels of the Chris Epps indictment is the impromptu resignation of Johnny Denmark, who was appointed South Mississippi Correctional Institution Superintendent in 2013 by Chris Epps. Under Denmark's watch, there were inmate-on-inmate crimes, which resulted in inmate deaths. Also under his watch, the prison was on lockdown after seven officers were assaulted.

The importance of this subject is timely and necessary for the only thing the so-called "war on drugs" in the United States has achieved is filling up the nations prisons and becoming number one in the nation in incarceration. The United States has millions of its citizens behind bars; two-thirds of them are people of color. And, people of color are not limited to African Americans. Hopefully, this book will show how evidence can be deliberately fabricated by law enforcement personnel in order to falsely imprison and target African American men. My goal is to focus on the mass incarceration of people of color and the prison industrial complex.

The United States criminal justice system is building an entire economy around the unjust incarceration of its citizens. Many are people of color. This concept became common knowledge to me in the '90s when I worked as a Correctional Officer with the Mississippi Department of Corrections (MDOC). I wrote this book in an attempt to expose the corruption and injustice I experienced while working at the South Mississippi Correctional Institute (SMCI).

In 1991, I started working as a Correctional Officer at SMCI in Leakesville, Mississippi. My job performance was excellent, and I worked well with the inmates. Often times, I was the voice for the inmates who were abused by Correctional Officers. Unfortunately, two months after my wife filed an Equal Employment Opportunity Commission (EEOC) discrimination charge against the Mississippi Department of Corrections, my supervisors and fellow officers conspired to plant drugs on me on two separate occasions, using inmates as their perpetrators. The inmates were promised an early release, if successful.

Soon thereafter, I was interviewed by the Mississippi FBI field office, the Attorney General's office, which represented the MDOC on court cases, never investigated my allegations.

This book explores the actual tactics law enforcement personnel use to incarcerate African American men in America, and damage the family unit in the Black community. Written in a manner that will cover as many topics in the criminal justice system as clearly and detailed as possible, my goal is to focus on the new method of slave-making techniques and how these techniques are covered up.

The United States has millions of its citizens behind bars—two-thirds of them are people of color, one-quarter of them are incarcerated for a drug-related offense.

Fabricating Evidence

I was trained at the MDOC to help rehabilitate inmates and the implementation of the many Standard Operating Procedures (SOPs), and it almost cost me my freedom. My sole intentions are to help bring this corruption to the forefront, and to show how the criminal justice system of the United States is building an entire economy around the incarceration of its citizens. Prisons and penitentiaries are no longer a place of rehabilitation, but a huge money-making machine.

All allegations are backed up by newspaper articles, legal documentation and audio recording.

BUSINESS JOURNAL

Byrd succeeds Denmark as SMCI superintendent
by Associated Press
Published: November 17, 2014

LEAKESVILLE — Raymond T. Byrd has been named superintendent at South Mississippi Correctional Institution in Leakesville.

Byrd succeeds Johnnie Denmark, who announced his retirement on Oct. 31. Byrd has more than 30 years of correctional experience with both private and state prisons not only in Mississippi but also in Texas, Louisiana, Arkansas and Washington, D.C.

Byrd most recently was a warden at Central Mississippi Correctional Facility and SMCI.

SMCI, established in 1989, sits on 360 acres in Greene County, and has the capacity for 3,082 beds. It currently has 2,806 inmates.

http://msbusiness.com/blog/2014/11/17/byrd-succeeds-denmark-smci-superintendent/

Fabricating Evidence

Leakesville prison on lockdown after 7 officers assaulted, 5 attackers identified

By GulfLive.com staff
on September 22, 2014 at 8:09 PM, updated September 22, 2014 at 8:13 PM

LEAKESVILLE, Mississippi -- Seven correctional officers at South Mississippi Correctional Institution were assaulted Monday afternoon as they were leaving a housing unit following a shakedown at the prison in Leakesville.

All of the officers were treated and released at the local hospital, suffering head and facial bruises. None of the injuries appears life-threatening.

Five inmates had been identified Monday evening as being among the attackers, and were moved to another prison. The investigation continues, and all inmates involved in the assault will face charges.

"We do not know at this time what provoked these inmates to assault our officers," Corrections Commissioner Christopher B. Epps said. "At no time was the public at risk nor was the security, custody, control and care of other staff and inmates."

— NEXT PAGE —

PAGE 2

The disturbance occurred around 1:30 p.m. at SMCI Area II, A 2 building, which can house a capacity of 200 inmates who require close supervision and observation. The unit held 193 close custody inmates at the time of the disturbance. Other SMCI staff responded to the unit when an officer radioed for assistance.

SMCI Area II is the same location where an officer was assaulted Thursday but in a different unit. The officer was in Unit A1 when an inmate struck him with a bread tray and the officer fell and struck his head on the floor. The officer, whose condition has been improving, remains hospitalized.

"Regardless of the reason for these assaults, I intend to see that all these inmates are prosecuted," Epps said. "These assaults illustrate the type of inmates we are dealing with these days. I am committed to ensuring that our prisons are appropriately staffed, as SMCI was in these two cases, and our officers are able to go home each day."

SMCI remained on lockdown Monday evening.

http://blog.gulflive.com/mississippi-press-news/2014/09/leakesville_prison_on_lockdown.html

Fabricating Evidence

Inmate stabbed to death at Leakesville correctional facility

By April M. Havens | ahavens@al.com
on August 02, 2014 at 5:15 PM, updated August 02, 2014 at 5:22 PM

LEAKESVILLE, Mississippi -- An inmate at the South Mississippi Correctional Institution in Leakesville was fatally stabbed today by a fellow inmate, according to the Mississippi Department of Corrections.

Merlin Littleton, 37, was pronounced dead at the prison infirmary at 3:37 p.m.

He was attacked with a sharp instrument in Unit 8 of the prison, authorities said.

Littleton was serving a 30-year sentence for two convictions of armed robbery from Hinds and Madison counties.

Offender Terrance Bridges, 24, was identified by prison officials as the assailant and is being questioned by investigators with MDOC.

No correctional officer was injured.

PAGE 2

"An initial investigation revealed policy and procedure were not followed," Commissioner Christopher B. Epps said. "We will take the necessary disciplinary action upon completion of our investigation."

Bridges is serving a 10-year sentence for aggravated assault and possession of a controlled substance with intent out of Jefferson Davis County.

Since his incarceration, Bridges has received 10 disciplinary actions, including for destroying property, abusive or threatening language, assaulting other inmates and possessing contraband to include sharpened instruments and cell phones.

"What charges will be filed depends on the outcome of the investigation," MDOT Criminal Investigation Division Director Sean K. Smith said.

http://blog.gulflive.com/mississippi-press-news/2014/08/inmate_stabbed_to_death_at_lea.html

INTRODUCTION

I completed the training academy at the Mississippi State Penitentiary, also known as Parchman Farm. Its history, during the civil rights movement, and how it housed freedom riders lends it a notorious legacy toward Blacks; horror stories of mistreatment at Parchman Farm. Even after completing the academy, I was reluctant about working in law enforcement because of the history between law enforcement and the Black community.

At the graduation ceremony, high-ranking Black officials within the Mississippi Department of Corrections (MDOC) spoke, and one of them was Chris Epps, the longest serving Commissioner of MDOC in Mississippi's history. He, along with others, talked about making corrections a profession, and how rewarding and fulfilling it had been for them. Therefore, they sold me on the idea. *Hey, maybe this might not be too bad*, I thought, as I began my journey as an MDOC Correctional Officer.

However, there's a saying: "*The chickens have come home to roost*," and boy did they come home! On November 4, 2014, a federal judge set a $25,000 bond for former Mississippi Corrections Commissioner Chris Epps, who is accused, along with a Rankin businessman, in a bribery and kickbacks case. Emily Le Coz, of *The Clarion-Ledger*, reported in her November 10, 2014 article that, "*One of Mississippi Department of Corrections' largest contractors confirmed claims in a 49-count federal indictment against former Corrections Commissioner Chris Epps and Rankin County businessman Cecil McCrory.*" The article went to state that, "*Utah-based Management & Training Corporation said in a lengthy statement issued Monday that immediately after winning contracts to run three Mississippi prisons in the summer of 2012, Epps recommended the company hire McCrory as a $12,000-per-month consultant. The men allegedly then split those payments as part of a massive kickback scheme in which McCrory paid Epps nearly $1 million in exchange for nearly $1 billion in contracts benefiting his various business interests, according to the indictment. Epps and McCrory both pleaded not guilty Thursday in federal court. Each could face more than 200 years behind bars if convicted.*" For more information, view the *Clarion-Ledger* at http://www.clarionledger.com/story/news/local/2014/11/10/mtc-confirms-indictment-claims/18822479/.

My assignment was at South Mississippi Correctional Institute (SMCI) in Leakesville, Mississippi, which was a different type of culture from what I learned in the academy.

I discovered some of the personnel hadn't gone through the academy process and instead received on-the-job training. It was confusing; they were doing things contrary to the academy. Therefore, I complained and questioned the "unethical" behavior of fellow correctional officers and staff. The Department of Corrections instills that we are about correcting people, and security, custody and control is the goal. It is a correctional officer's obligation to assist inmates with their rehabilitation process, but that wasn't happening.

A correctional officer's job is very challenging and deals with a lot of biases and prejudices. At the onset of my employment, inmates wore ID badges listing the crimes they had committed, which was a struggle for me as I tried to be professional with murderers, child molesters and rapists. To ensure constant professionalism, I had to dig deep within. I was elated when they stopped that procedure. It affected the culture of the prison, incarcerating inmates *as punishment* and not *for punishment*. It was uncomfortable knowing some officers were more racially biased than crime biased. I saw a trend of how Black inmates received differential treatment that was more subjected to brutal beatings than Whites inmates, which was a great disparity.

Early in my career, I sensed I had become a target. Fellow officers not trained at the academy criticized my approach, as I operated according to the rules and regulations of the academy.

My background was in constructing nuclear submarines, which was a policy and detailed-oriented environment. The submarine had to do things in order and by the book. The Department of Corrections had proper Standard Operating Procedures not followed by staff.

I wrote this book to expose and correct corruption within the correctional and judicial systems, specifically law enforcement. I believe in accountability, so I am not against imprisonment. However, nonviolent drug offenders are receiving very harsh penalties. I want to bring about change from a grassroots perspective. Most accomplishments in America started from the bottom up and not the top down. This book is beneficial to what is happening now, where the results of the so-called "war on drugs" has incarcerated a lot of young, African Americans—in staggering numbers—whose lives are forever ruined for something former Presidents of the United States had done themselves.

Before he resigned as United States Attorney General, I was in support of Eric Holder, and what he was doing on the federal level, but it should trickle down to the state level. I know that it is a problem, and it concerns me.

I am not an authority on prison operations across the United States. My experience is based on my employment with the Mississippi Department of Corrections South Mississippi

Correctional Institute facility, the injustices I've witnessed, and the discrimination I've endured. I'm not writing this for fortune or fame, but for change...mass incarceration affects us all.

Many inmates had told me they were in prison because of being set-up with drugs, but I didn't believe it until it happened to me. This is why I am adamant that nonviolent drug offenders should be released and their records expounded, especially in the Mississippi prison system.

Britton Mosley, Sr.

MDOC contractor fires McCrory, confirms claims

By Emily Le Coz, The Clarion-Ledger
7:13 p.m. CST November 10, 2014

One of Mississippi Department of Corrections' largest contractors confirmed claims in a 49-count federal indictment against former Corrections Commissioner Chris Epps and Rankin County businessman Cecil McCrory.

Utah-based Management & Training Corporation said in a lengthy statement issued Monday that immediately after winning contracts to run three Mississippi prisons in the summer of 2012, Epps recommended the company hire McCrory as a $12,000-per-month consultant.

The men allegedly then split those payments as part of a massive kickback scheme in which McCrory paid Epps nearly $1 million in exchange for nearly $1 billion in contracts benefiting his various business interests, according to the indictment.

Epps and McCrory both pleaded not guilty Thursday in federal court. Each could face more than 200 years behind bars if convicted.

"We deeply regret that in this case we didn't have any idea that improprieties may have taken place, especially in light of the significant allegations in the indictment," MTC spokesman Issa Arnita said in the statement.

According to the indictment, "Epps had personally negotiated McCrory's consulting fee, telling McCrory later, 'I got us $12,000 per month.' "

Arnita confirmed that "MTC paid Mr. McCrory $12,000 per month for his work, after Mr. Epps told us that is what others had been paying him." The company ended its relationship with McCrory last week, Arnita said.

Epps signed his first contract with MTC to operate Marshall County Correctional Facility, effective Aug. 13, 2012, according to documents obtained by The Clarion-Ledger.

Eight days later, the indictment states, McCrory wired $34,000 from his bank to Wells Fargo Home Mortgage to pay down the loan on Epps' beachfront condo in Biloxi.

Less than a month after that payment, Epps signed another contract with MTC, on Sept. 14, 2012, to operate East Mississippi Correctional Facility. Eleven days later, McCrory wired $14,000 from his bank to Well Fargo.

And on Oct. 18, Epps signed yet another contract with MTC, this time to operate East Mississippi Correctional Facility.

Although Epps recommended MTC hire McCrory, he did not mandate nor require it, Arnita said.

"MTC hired Mr. McCrory as a consultant because of his many years of experience working in the state," Arnita said. "Mr. McCrory had been working with the previous prison contractor and other vendors so MTC felt his services would be beneficial given his knowledge and experience."

Arnita also said MTC won the contracts through a "competitive procurement process where multiple companies were invited to tour facilities and submit bids."

The first payment to McCrory was sent in July 2012, Arnita said, adding that although the contracts were executed later in the summer, they actually were awarded in early June. From July 2012 through early November, McCrory and Epps would have split $336,000.

MTC won a fourth contract in July 2013 to operate Wilkinson County Correctional Facility, just five months after yet another wire transfer from McCrory — this time for $40,000 to Epps' Edward Jones investment account.

Altogether, the state Department of Corrections has paid MTC

$114,643,308 since August 2013, according to the state's transparency website and SeeTheSpending.org, a website operated by the Mississippi Center for Public Policy that tracks the spending of public dollars.

It's unclear how much longer the company will retain its contracts, though. Even before Gov. Phil Bryant's announcement on Thursday that the state would rebid all contracts held by firms cited in the indictment, Epps already had ordered MTC's contracts to be rebid.

Epps had said in an August news release that the four facilities required more security staff and that he was rebidding the contracts, which would go into effect Dec. 1. MTC and New Jersey-based Community Education Centers both had bid, but Bryant suspended the process.

MTC continues to run the four facilities in the meantime.

"We fully support the government's investigation to learn what happened and to take appropriate action," Arnita said. "We also believe the state of Mississippi made the right decision in reviewing all current corrections contracts including suspending the procurement process for the four private prison contracts which we hold."

Contact Emily Le Coz at elecoz@jackson.gannett.com or (601) 961-7249. Follow @emily_lecoz on Twitter.

FULL STATEMENT FROM MTC:

We're saddened, surprised and disappointed by the allegations against former Commissioner Chris Epps. MTC was hired in 2012 to operate three prisons for the state after a competitive procurement process where multiple companies were invited to tour facilities and submit bids. MTC was brought in with the primary objective of improving the overall operations of these facilities. In 2013, we submitted a proposal to operate a fourth prison for the state during an open and competitive procurement (RFP 13-005) with the same mission.

MTC worked very closely with Mr. Epps over the last two years in implementing changes to these facilities that would improve security and the treatment of offenders. He was very involved in the management of our four contracts. He knew of the challenges we faced and was working closely with us to overcome them. In partnership with the state and with their support, MTC has made significant improvements at all four facilities and continues to make great strides.

Soon after being awarded the contracts in 2012, Mr. Epps recommended MTC work with Cecil McCrory to provide services within the state of Mississippi. Mr. Epps also made us aware of the fee McCrory had charged in the past to other contractors. MTC hired Mr. McCrory as a consultant because of his many years of experience working in the state. Mr. McCrory had been working with the previous prison contractor and other vendors so MTC felt his services would be beneficial given his knowledge and experience. MTC paid Mr. McCrory $12,000 per month for his work, after Mr. Epps told us that is what others had been paying him. MTC hires consultants in every state where we provide services to the state. Mr. McCrory's services included working with counties to explore possible business opportunities, coordinating with local and state officials to strengthen MTC's relationship within the state, and networking at various industry conferences. He worked at length to investigate a potential bid for a federal corrections contract in Mississippi. At no time did Mr. Epps instruct or mandate MTC to hire Mr. McCrory. In light of the indictment, MTC cancelled its contract with Mr. McCrory last week.

Each month, MTC received an invoice from Mr. McCrory and paid it in full just as we would any other invoice. MTC was not aware of any alleged inappropriate relationships between Mr. Epps and Mr. McCrory or that Mr. Epps was allegedly a participant in any way in the contract with McCrory.

We fully support the government's investigation to learn what happened and to take appropriate action. We also believe the state of Mississippi made the right decision in reviewing all current corrections contracts including suspending the procurement process for the four private prison contracts which we hold. The integrity of contracting is of paramount importance to the state as well as to MTC. All MTC employees are required to take ethics training and are held to the highest standards of ethical conduct. We deeply regret that in this case we didn't have any idea that improprieties may have taken place, especially in light of the significant allegations in the indictment.

http://www.clarionledger.com/story/news/local/2014/11/10/mtc-confirms-indictment-claims/18822479/

CHAPTER ONE

Set-up the Whistleblower

There is an old adage that history is forever repeating, but I never gave it much thought until September 1991, while working as a correctional officer at South Mississippi Correctional Institute (SMCI) in Leakesville, Mississippi when I experienced a series of events that took me on a stroll down Memory Lane, evoking disheartening feelings within me.

Born in Moss Point, Mississippi in 1948, I grew up in the Jim Crow era that was first enacted in the 1880s by lawmakers who were bitter about their loss to the North and the end of slavery; the statutes separated the races in all walks of life. As a Black child, I experienced and saw a lot of hatred toward Black people; hated by people who knew nothing about us. Hated because of the color of our skin. Murdering Blacks at alarming rates was the norm in Mississippi.

On August 28, 1955, a White mob brutally murdered a Black, fourteen-year-old boy because he reportedly flirted with a White woman is one example. His name was Emmett Louis

Till from Chicago, Illinois. He was visiting family in Money, Mississippi.

On June 12, 1963, a member of the White Citizens' Council by the name of Byron De La Beckwith assassinated Medgar Wiley Evers, a Black civil rights activist involved in efforts to overturn segregation.

Weeks later, on June 24, 1963, members of the Mississippi White Knights of the Ku Klux Klan shot, at close range, three American civil rights' workers: James Earl Chaney, Andrew Goodman, and Michael "Mickey" Schwerner. The three were working on the "Freedom Summer" campaign, attempting to register Blacks to vote.

Black people met their demise at the bottom of the Pearl River that runs from Mississippi to Louisiana, weighted by chains. The evening news broadcast showed a Black man dragged from the Pearl River, wrapped in chains with a padlock. When asked about the Black man pulled from the Pearl River, the sheriff said, "This is the damndest case of suicide I'd ever seen in my life." For as long as I live, I will never forget that news broadcast, as well as countless other because of senseless murders of people of color.

Yet, growing up in Mississippi was bittersweet. I learned how to survive and how not to become a statistic, how to not end up in the Pearl River, how to not dangle by a tree. It's unfortunate that people had to live in fear, and teach their children how to live in fear, because of the color of their skin.

In 1968, I graduated high school, was looking forward to starting college in the fall, and Martin Luther King, Jr. was assassinated on April 4 on the balcony of the Lorraine Hotel in Memphis, Tennessee while protesting civil rights for Black people. His death affected me beyond measure. The murder of the most active and important Black American civil rights activist was devastating, but it didn't stop there.

Two months later, on June 6, the same night I traveled to Washington, DC to visit my older brother, twenty-two-year-old Palestinian Sirhan Sirhan assassinated Senator Robert Kennedy at the Ambassador Hotel in Los Angeles, California after winning the California presidential primary, immediately after announcing to his cheering supporters that the country was ready to end its fractious divisions.

Kennedy's assassination was also the night before the Poor People's Campaign (also known as the Solidarity March), which was a 1968 effort to gain economic justice for poor people in the United States. It was organized by Martin Luther King, Jr. and the Southern Christian Leadership Conference, and carried out in the wake of King's assassination.

That was a rough time for me. The assassinations of two major figures in the civil rights era overshadowed my celebration of my achievement of graduating high school and attending college in the fall. The movement took a blow and the mindset of Black people was that of defeat. The civil rights community, especially Black folks, began to lose hope. People who weren't raised in the civil rights era are without that damage, unlike those of us raised in the middle of it. We are forever scarred.

Police officers are supposed to protect and serve all people, but Black parents had to instill the fear of the police in their children. Jim Crow paralleled apartheid. It was two worlds: Black and White. Fear was definitely instilled in me. I had to walk past a White-only high school to attend a Black high school, where we were given outdated books from the White high school. So, over the years, Black people lived their lives with the fear of random acts of violence against them for only one reason: the color of their skin. So understandably, taking a job with the Department of Corrections was a tough decision that took a lot of soul searching. I had to support my family, so I decided to try it.

My wife and I applied for the positions of correctional officer (CO). After attending and successfully completing six weeks of training in Parchman, Mississippi, we were assigned to SMCI in Leakesville, Mississippi as correctional officer trainees. We were assigned the third shift (11:00 p.m. to 7:00 a.m.). My job title was zone officer.

All my life I've been an advocate for civil and human rights. So, the idea of rehabilitating inmates resonated with me. The concept of corrections is to maintain custody, security and control of the inmates. The duties of a zone officer are to make sure these three concepts are implemented. I was stationed inside a zone with two hundred inmates per zone at a time. There are A and B Zones. The tower officer and zone officer are in charge of four hundred inmates. There is an open bay area where inmates are allowed to roam freely, which is nothing like what is portrayed on television or the movies, where inmates are kept in separate cells. Not at SMCI. There are rows of bunk beds in the open bay.

Many inmates had severe mental problems, and should have been in a mental institution. Eventually, I had gained the trust of the inmates. I was in my forties and had become a father figure to many of them. After getting to know them and learning their stories, I encouraged them to let the time serve them by taking advantage of the opportunities that were available to them, and to get their GED and a marketable vocation. Inmates confided in me and always interacted with me. I worked in Unit 9, which was called the Throw Away Unit that housed inmates that weren't doing anything but doing out their time. Once I realized the positive impact I had on the inmates, I started liking the job. Often I saw inmates on the street after their release, and they would tell me how well they were doing. That made me proud.

Fabricating Evidence

It made me feel good to know I had helped with an inmate's rehabilitation.

Although it didn't pay a lot of money, knowing I had a positive impact on men who were at their lowest moment, made it worth it.

Then, the dark side of the job reared its ugly head when CO Johnny Denmark came around at night, wanting to take inmates up to the gymnasium and beat them, calling it discipline. In order for an inmate to leave the Zone, that inmate had to be signed out by the officer. So the tower officer was ordered not to log out the inmate, so there wouldn't be a record of taking out inmates. The next morning, when the inmates complained about the "discipline," there would be no record of them leaving the Zone.

On one particular night, I was assigned the duties of yard officer. I noticed smoke coming from the Recreation Area of Unit 10. When I reached the area, an inmate was standing outside in his underwear, trembling. His prison uniform was in a burning heap on the ground. He told me that CO Johnny Denmark had beaten him and had set his uniform on fire. I was dumbfounded by the actions of a CO.

After working there for a couple years, I started to see my whole life flash before me. Everything I experienced and read during Jim Crow I witnessed personally at SMCI. It was evident that the Willie Lynch Doctrine was the marching orders at this prison. Many of the younger inmates didn't realize what was going on, as they had not experienced the effect of Jim Crow or Willie Lynch. I became vocal about what was happening. Inmates were being beaten for looking a White officer in the eye, which they called "eye fucking." Inmates were beaten for being accused of masturbating in front of White female officers, who made it a routine to watch inmates shower. Inmates were beaten for not saying "Yes, sir." This made me furious, and I spoke out about it. SMCI's claim was that inmates "came off the wall and force was needed."

On one occasion, an inmate was preparing to be released the following day, a CO provoked an incident, and the inmate was given five more years in prison.

Frequently I complained to upper management about this type of behavior, and no action was taken. Soon, I was labeled the "inmate lover." I called Lieutenant Mike Kelley, the instructor at the training academy, and informed him that what was taught at the academy wasn't being utilized at SMCI. I told him that inmates were being beaten, and it was a turnaround from what I was taught, and I didn't sign up for this type of brutality. I was not going to be a part of falsifying records. Then, I became a target. I was accused of all kinds of illegal doings because inmates were talking to me and I was not partaking in their callous behavior toward inmates.

CO Johnny Denmark had become hostile toward me. He started spreading rumors that I was doing illegal activities and that I was bringing in drugs, and other crooked things simply because I interacted with the inmates.

In the academy, I was taught that I was supposed to help inmates with their rehabilitation process, and I was driven by that, and that's what I did. Because of my "doing the right thing," a bull's eye was smacked on my back. I was their next target.

Some inmates were telling me that COs were trying to recruit inmates to set me up. Although I had no proof, inmates were bringing this to me. Currency is not allowed in the prison, so it didn't make any sense for a person to bring in drugs to an environment where currency isn't allowed. There were no secrets in the prison system, especially at SMCI. Inmates often told me what CO Johnny Denmark was attempting to do, and he was trying to recruit inmates to do his dirty deed.

THE FIRST SET-UP ATTEMPT

It all began on November 4, 1996, at approximately 7:15 a.m., when CO Michael Miller and Inmate Mandell Walker (#78206) approached me at the side gate of the prison yard of

SMCI while I was in the process of picking up maintenance inmates.

CO Miller and Inmate Walker inquired about the policies and procedures of my bringing a pair of shower shoes into the prison to Inmate Walker. At approximately 2:30 p.m., on that same day, I was taking an inmate to Greene County High School on a work detail. CO Miller approached me at the entrance of SMCI and asked me if I were leaving for the day. I told him I was not leaving, but I was en route to Greene County High School.

At approximately 3:00 p.m., when I returned from the high school and entered the Maintenance Building, Sergeant Daniel Paff told me that CO Miller had left a black, zipper bag for me in my office. Sergeant Paff continued to tell me that CO Miller was acting suspicious, and that I needed to search the zipper bag. CO Harold James assisted me with searching the black, zipper bag. Inside were a pair of size 8 shower shoes and a bottle of hair moisturizer for Inmate Walker, which instantly drew suspicion. Inmate Walker wore a size 14 and had a baldhead. Also inside the bag was a large container of baby powder. When I opened it, two ounces of marijuana in a plastic bag, wrapped in black tape, was inside.

CO James and I worked ten-hour day shifts, however our supervisors—Captain Johnny Denmark, who had since been promoted from CO to captain, and Lieutenant Victor Brewer—worked eight-hour shifts, and routinely parked their vehicles in front of the Maintenance Building. This all took place after 3:00 p.m., which meant their shift had ended, their offices were closed and their vehicles were not parked in front of the Maintenance Building.

Immediately, I contacted the watch commander to conduct an investigation on the alleged marijuana set-up. After waiting several minutes for the watch commander, I walked to the west end of the Maintenance Building near Captain Denmark and Lieutenant Brewer's office. The door to their office was locked, and the main lights were off. However, the bathroom lights were on. I looked inside the office window and saw movement. That's when I started banging on the office door repeatedly after which Lieutenant Brewer finally opened it. After turning on the lights inside their office, Captain Denmark and Lieutenant Brewer were acting very suspicious when I started telling them about the approximately two ounces of marijuana found in a black, zipper bag near my desk inside the Maintenance Building.

Typically, Captain Denmark and Lieutenant Brewer would have shown excitement when a drug bust took place inside the prison. However, they were hostile toward me. There was a red flag moment when Lieutenant Brewer told me "not to write an incident report about the marijuana bust." Incident reports were standard operating procedure at SMCI and most prisons.

Captain Denmark used the office phone to inform Chief Investigator Malcolm McClendon that marijuana was found inside the Maintenance Building. After Captain Denmark completed his call with Chief Investigator McClendon, Lieutenant Brewer called CO Michael Miller at home, informing him of what had just taken place with him, Captain Denmark and Chief Investigator McClendon, which was so profound. What was his purpose of calling CO Michael Miller? He wasn't my superior and did not work directly with me or in the Maintenance Building.

After leaving the Central Security Office, I returned to my desk inside the Maintenance Building. CO James and I were in a state of disbelief at what we had just experienced.

Captain Denmark, Lieutenant Brewer and I had worked at SMCI as correctional officers for several years, and even went on fishing trips together. This failed attempt of a drug set-up was one of the darkest experiences of my life. If the plan had been successful, I would have been wrongfully convicted of drug possession inside a correctional institution, which would have carried a very long prison sentence.

Chief Investigator McClendon never attempted to interview me.

Cosmetically, the Jim Crow era had ended; the "White Only" signs were gone, but the concept still existed in the state of Mississippi.

LEONARD DAVIS, JR. VERSUS STEVE PUCKETT

I was a member of the Emergency Response Team (ERT). The duties of the ERT are to restore order in the prison if riots or gang violence happens inside the prison. On the evening of November 21, 1996, I was at home when I received a call to come to SMCI. I was informed that we were going to participate in an exhibit of "show of force" in Unit 9. When I arrived at the prison, members of the Mississippi Highway Patrol Riot Unit were dressed in riot gear, toting all types of equipment. I was told we were just doing a show of force. There were no riots, so it was more of a drill. Superintendent David Turner (now deceased) had requested the services of the Mississippi Highway Patrol, and I was informed that the inmates "had been acting up."

When I went to the unit where I worked and had established myself as trustworthy and honest with the inmates, we all entered the building, and the members of the Mississippi Highway Patrol and the ERT commenced to beating inmates for no apparent reason. Inmates were forced out of their beds. Many inmates took strong, psychiatric medications that left them heavily sedated, so when those inmates did not respond to the harassment by the officers, they were beaten badly. During this whole process, Superintendent David Turner was filming the activities. Black and White officers participated. After the inmates were beaten, they were forced outside in their underwear. I was blown away. I was hurt. I was disappointed. I was a ball of emotions. How the inmates looked at me was devastating, as I had earned their trust, and surely, they felt betrayed by me. While I didn't participate in any of the cruelty, I was an unwilling bystander. I escorted the inmates outside and advised them not to resist. The look in their eyes simply tore at my soul, as I'm sure they assumed I was a part of it.

Following the barbaric beatings, the inmates' belongings were emptied onto the floor in the middle of the unit; everything from family pictures to legal documents to letters from family. It was truly an extremely dark moment. It reminded me of Selma, Alabama on Sunday, March 7, 1965, when six hundred marchers crossed the Edmund Pettus Bridge over the Alabama River en route to Montgomery, Alabama. Just short of the bridge, they found their way blocked by Alabama State Troopers and local police who had ordered them to turn around. When the protesters refused, the officers threw teargas and waded into the crowd, beating *nonviolent* protesters with batons and ultimately hospitalizing more than fifty people. That day was called

"Bloody Sunday," and was televised around the world. Seeing the Mississippi Highway Patrol officers beat up on those inmates reminded me of how Alabama police officers had beaten up on Congressman John Lewis and protestors marching for voters' rights in 1965. Being a witness to such brutality still haunts me to this day. The next day, I resigned from ERT, but still worked in maintenance at SMCI.

On September 30, 1997, a civil action suit was filed by Leonard Davis, Jr. (an inmate at SMCI) against Steve Puckett (*now former* commissioner) in the United States District Court for the Southern District of Mississippi, Jackson Division. Davis alleged that on November 21, 1996, while he was incarcerated at SMCI in Leakesville, Mississippi, a practice drill was executed by the prison officials. According to Davis, members of the Mississippi Highway Patrol, ERT, and K-9 stormed into Unit-9 B Zone, dressed with helmets and ski masks. Davis alleged that one of the officers, whom he believed was a Mississippi Highway patrolman, had beaten him as well as other prisoners. He also lost property in the raid. Davis asserted that Steve Puckett was liable for the actions of the officers because Puckett had approved the drill. The court advised Davis that he could call any free world witnesses, but that it would be his responsibility to secure any free world witnesses' presence at the trial. Davis requested the presence of three inmates, who were incarcerated at SMCI at the time of the complaint, and me. Even though the testimony from his witnesses and the evidence was overwhelming, Davis lost his court case.

THE SECOND SET-UP ATTEMPT

In July 1997, Inmate Marvin Thomas (#79517) approached me inside the Maintenance Building at SMCI. Inmate Thomas told me that CO II Louis Kittrell (now lieutenant) and Internal Audit Division Investigator Jerry Dettman conspired to get Inmate Thomas to plant drugs in my office. By cooperating with officials, Inmate Thomas was promised an early release from prison, however he did not participate. But, to assist me, he agreed to wear a wire to expose their plot against me. Inmate Thomas wore the wire and recorded a conversation between him and Lieutenant Louis Kittrell, one of the co-conspirators. *To review the transcript or listen to the audiotape, visit my website at www.brittonmosleysr.com.*

Once the correctional personnel gained knowledge of Inmate Thomas' cooperation with me, they threatened his life and used his prior prison record to deny him parole on October 15, 1997.

Had this second attempt been successful, another innocent Black man would have been sent to prison by a group of White racists from Mississippi. Their motive was to have me fired from my job, permanently damage my reputation and put a burden on my family by sending me to prison.

I've never been big on heroes, but Marvin Thomas is a hero in my eyes. He put his life on the line for by wearing the wire and helping me to prove my case against MDOC. I never really thanked him the way I should have. I don't know where he is today, but I truly want to thank him for his heroic effort. Marvin Thomas was incarcerated on a nonviolent offense, and did not have to risk his life or chances of parole, but he did. For that, I am forever humble, thankful and grateful to Marvin Thomas.

This "above the law" behavior by MDOC staff has absolutely no place in rehabilitating inmates.

Britton Mosley, Sr.

☐ Parchman	☐ CMCF	☒ SMCI	☐ CWC

INCIDENT REPORT   Page   of   Pages

FILE TITLE: Security Operations   CASE STATUS:

BY: CO II Britton Mosley
WITNESS(ES)
CO II Harold James
Sgt. Danial Paff

AT 1520 Hours

RELATED FILES:
( )
( )
( )
( )
( )

DATE 11-4-96

REPORT RE: Package containing what appeared to be marijuana.

On the above date at approximately 0715 hours, I CO II Britton Mosley was approached by Ofc. Michael Miller and Inmate Mandell Walker, #78206, about allowing a package to enter the compound containing shower shoes and personal hygiene items. I told Ofc. Miller that I would have to first get it cleared from the Watch Commander. At approximately 1445 hours, as I was leaving Entry Point, Ofc. Miller approached this writer again and asked if I was leaving for the day? I informed Ofc. Miller that I was on my way to Green co. High to escort an inmate. At approximately 1520 hours, Sgt. Danial Paff informed me as I arrived back to the maintenance complex that Ofc. Miller had left a package with him for this writer to give to Inmate Walker. Sgt. Paff suggested that I should search the content in the package. I, COII Britton Mosley, made a search of the contents inside of the black zipped bag. While searching the baby power, this writer discovered what appeared to be marijuana in a clear plastic bag wrapped with black electrical tape. At this time, I notified fellow Officer Harold James about the discovered content. I then informed Capt. Denmark and Lt. Brewer of this incident. Investigator McLendon was notified of the incident. The marijuana and other items inside the bag was left with Capt. Denmark, Lt. Brewer and Investigator McLendon.
*************************END OF REPORT*************************

SIGNATURE OF OFFICER	APPROVED NAME TITLE	DATE
Britton Mosley		11/5/96

INSTIT-SEC-INCIDENT REPORT NO.30 Tsu (2. (Rev-1-1)

Fabricating Evidence

IN THE UNITED STATES DISTRICT COURT
FOR THE SOUTHERN DISTRICT OF MISSISSIPPI
JACKSON DIVISION

SOUTHERN DISTRICT OF MISSISSIPPI
FILED
SEP 3 0 1997
J. T. NOBLIN, CLERK
BY _____ DEPUTY

LEONARD DAVIS, JR.   PLAINTIFF

VS.   CIVIL ACTION NO. 3:97-CV-304BN

STEVE PUCKETT   DEFENDANT

OMNIBUS ORDER

The parties appeared and participated in an omnibus hearing before the undersigned United States Magistrate Judge on the 25th day of September, 1997, at the James O. Eastland Courthouse in Jackson, Mississippi. The plaintiff appeared *pro se*, and the defendant was represented by counsel, Hon. Leonard Vincent and Hon. John Clay. The court scheduled this hearing for the combined purposes of conducting a *Spears*[1] hearing; a scheduling/case management hearing; a discovery conference; and, a pretrial conference. The court conducted this hearing in an attempt to insure the just, speedy and inexpensive determination of this *pro se* prisoner litigation. After due consideration of the issues involved in this case and the requests for discovery, the court does hereby find and order as follows:

1. **JURISDICTION AND SUMMARY OF CLAIMS**

Jurisdiction of this case is based up on 42 U.S.C. §1983. The plaintiff alleges that on November 21, 1996, while he was incarcerated at the South Mississippi Correctional Institute in Leakesville, Mississippi, a practice drill was executed by the prison officials. According

---

[1] *See, Spears v. McCotter*, 766 F.2d 179 (5th Cir. 1985).

to the plaintiff, members of the Mississippi Highway Patrol, E.R.T. [Emergency Response Team], and K-9 stormed into his Unit-9 B Zone, dressed with helmets and ski masks on. The plaintiff alleges that one of the officers, whom he believes was a Mississippi Highway Patrolman, beat him as well as other prisoners. He also lost property in the raid. Plaintiff asserts that the defendant Puckett is liable for the actions of the officers because Puckett approved of the practice drill.

2. **DISCOVERY ISSUES and PENDING MOTIONS**

The defendant's attorney is directed to provide copies at trial of the plaintiff's M.D.O.C. file, including any reports regarding the incident complained of.

The defendant shall also furnish plaintiff and the court within 30 days from entry of this order (1) any written report promulgated by any M.D.O.C. official regarding the incident which occurred on November 21, 1996, at SMCI; (2) any rules and policies of M.D.O.C. regarding practice drills or emergency response plans.

The defendant shall investigate the incident complained of by the plaintiff and attempt to determine the identity of the persons involved in the drill as to the zone occupied by the plaintiff. Specifically, the defendant shall attempt to determine the identity of the highway patrolman, or other officer, who allegedly beat the plaintiff and/or other inmates. The defendant shall report to the court within 30 days from date as to the results of the investigation. If the identity of that person can be determined, the court shall allow the plaintiff to amend his complaint to name the individual who allegedly beat him.

The defendants shall also provide at trial the medical records of the plaintiff from his M.D.O.C. files. The parties shall stipulate as to the authenticity of the records without the necessity of physician testimony.

There are no other discovery matters pending at this time, except for those set forth herein. The discovery matters set forth herein will fairly and adequately develop the issues to be presented to the court, and no other discovery is deemed reasonable or appropriate considering the issues at stake in this litigation. *See* Federal Rules of Civil Procedure 26(b)(1).

3. **TRIAL WITNESSES**

The plaintiff has requested that the following persons, thought to be incarcerated in the South Mississippi Correctional Institute, be brought to the trial of this cause to give testimony in support of his claims:

   1. CARLOS MORRIS
       #17886
       South Mississippi Correctional Institute
       Leakesville, MS

   2. CURTIS CLAYTON
       #78825
       Mississippi Correctional Institute
       Leakesville, MS

   3. JOHNNY COVAN
       #34637
       South Mississippi Correctional Institute
       Leakesville, MS

Britton Mosley, Sr.

The court orders that subpoenas *ad testificandum* issue for these persons for the trial of this cause, as long as they are still in the custody of MDOC at that time. The court advises the plaintiff that he may call any free world witness, but that it will be his responsibility to secure any free world witnesses' presence at the trial of this cause.

4. **PRETRIAL CONFERENCE, PRETRIAL ORDER, AND TRIAL SETTING**

This conference shall stand in lieu of a pretrial conference, and this order shall stand in lieu of a pretrial order. All parties have consented to proceed before the undersigned United States Magistrate Judge in accordance with the provisions of 28 U.S.C. 636(c) and Rule 73 of the Federal Rules of Civil Procedure.

IT IS HEREBY ORDERED AND ADJUDGED that the trial of this cause is set before the undersigned on January 26, 1998, at 9:30 A.M. in Courtroom No. 4 in the James O. Eastland Federal Courthouse, Fifth Floor, 245 E. Capitol Street, Jackson, Mississippi.

SO ORDERED, this the 30th day of September, 1997.

s/ Alfred G. Nicols, Jr.
_____
UNITED STATES MAGISTRATE JUDGE

October 28, 1997

Mr. Mosley;

    I hope everything is going O.K. for you. As for me I am scheduled for Court January 26, 1998. I am enclosing a copy of the order. According to the Judge, I must make arrangements to suppoena free world witnesses. In order to do so I need an address for <u>you</u>, Officer Wayne Dearman and Bennie Ashley. If you can help me I would appreciate it and any advice which might be helpful. Tell the Mrs. hello and God bless the two of you. Covon made Parole.

                        Sincerely,
                        L. Davis

☐ Parchman	☐ CMCF	☒ SMCI	☐ CWC

INCIDENT REPORT Page 1 of 1 Pages

FILE TITLE: Security Operations   CASE STATUS:

BY: CoII Britton Mosley
AT SMCI maintenance Complex
DATE July 25, 1997

WITNESS(ES):
CoII Necole Pearson
CoII Danny Woodard
Sgt. John Graham

RELATED FILES:
(✓) Incident Report November 4, 1996
( )
( )
( )

REPORT RE: CoII Louis Kittrell Conspiring with Inmate Marvin Thomas, 79517, to set this writer up with drug possession

On July 25, 1997, at approximately 1230 hours, I, CoII Britton Mosley, was able to confirm that a conspiracy to set this writer up with drugs possession was planned by MDOC staff and upper management at the maintenance Complex at SMCI.

An audio tape recording of the details was obtained on this date. This is the second attempt within a year. (See attachment 1st incident 11-4-96). The action that took place on July 25, 1997, has caused me to seek medical help for anxiety disorder. A copy of the audio can be furnished upon request from U.S. Representative Gene Taylor's office or the U.S. Justice Department, Civil Rights Division.

— — — — — END OF REPORT — — — — — —

SIGNATURE OF OFFICER: Britton Mosley
APPROVED NAME TITLE:
DATE: 10/3/97

Fabricating Evidence

On July 25, 1997 Ofc. Nicole Person was working at SNNCI-I perimeter tower #9 at approximately 12:15 p.m. Afternoon this writer observed Inmate Marvin Thomas #79517 at the fence behind the maintenance shop standing around waiting on what I don't know. At 12:17 I saw road gang in common labor Ofc. Price Kittrell go to the fence where Inmate Marvin Thomas #79517 was standing. It appeared that Ofc. Price Kittrell had given Inmate Marvin Thomas #79517 something through the fence. At 12:30 p.m. Ofc. Price Kittrell and Inmate Marvin Thomas #79517 exited the fence. Inmate Marvin Thomas #79517 rushed from the fence and went into the gray building behind the maintenance shop and then came out and entered into the maintenance shop. At 12:40 p.m. Inmate Marvin Thomas #79517 came back to the fence and gave something to another Inmate that was in Ofc. Lewis Kittrell work crew.

End of Report

Nicole Person

This a report Pertain to a Set-up on a Officer

This all start the Reed Boys had been talking to Off. Kitchen had told all of the Reeds that he could help them get out if they help him. So Willie Reed was a Mason so was Off. Kitchen and he decide to help him set up Officers that was bring in dope or who they thought was. So they first went at Off. Jackson and he got fire. but I believe he went on and Quite. Timothy Reed told me that they would help me to but what he did not know that I was already telling with Inv. Mc Cleod on Off. Mose trying to set him up but that was not me so I gave them the run around alot the problem they had. But they did give me a $120.00 dollars to set up Mose but I told Mose what was going on with him. So then they start asking me about Off. percy because they could not set Mose up and I told her so they chill out for awhile and that's when Off. Kitchen start talking to me every day I would meet him at the front gate and he was asking me about Off. Mosley but I did not know anything about Off. Mosley if he say I said any thing it was a lie.

So around Aug. I was move to Mont. to work were Officer Mosley wah sight was so the first day I was out there Off. Kitchens call me off to the side and talk to me about setting Off. Mosley up for them. I said yes and then I went back to Off. Mosley and talk with him about the matter and he could not believe that. So later that day I was call to the front to talk with Mr. MC clean about setting up off. Mosley and he state that if I set up off. Mosley that Dave's Turner the Warden will sing the peppers for me to be released. So that's when I told him I had to see it in black and white. And he then state that they know Off. Mosley was bring dope in. But he said that they will give me some dope and put it out at Mont. And say he brought it to me. So me and Off. Kitchens had a talk and he said that he want to be a the next meeting we have so I would not get mess around like W. Reed & A. Reed. So I had a tape record and tape Off. Kitchens talking about setting off. Mosley up. They had already stole about they miss him the first time when they busted Off. Michael Miller it suppose to been Off Mosley too. But they sought the wrong one up. There was other people they want me to set up but it just wasn't me they even gave me money to set up ~~different~~ office but I never did it they video me with money. the video come in well Mr. Doven, & there were other ~~Captains~~ Captains that knew dat this. End of report.

Mr. Mosley I need you to send me a little change if you can I fagot to ask you when I was on the phone. If ya can't don't worry about it. Money order.

By MARVIN Thomas79517
ElK A2

Fabricating Evidence

TRANSCRIPTION OF TAPE   PAGE 1 OF 6

INMATE MARVIN THOMAS-IMT
UNKNOWN INMATE-UI
OFFICER LOUIS KITTRELL-OLK
SGT. JOHN GRAHAM-SJG

THE TAPE STARTS WITH AN UNKNOWN INMATE ASKING INMATE THOMAS FOR A CIGARRETTE AND INMATE THOMAS SAYS, I'LL GET YOU ONE IN A MINUTE.

IMT HEY, HOLLER AT OFFICER KITTRELL FOR ME

UI   OFFICER KITTRELL

IMT HEY OFFICER KITTRELL

OLK HOLD ON JUST A MINUTE

IMT JULY 24, 1997, CONFERENCE WITH OFFICER KITTRELL

IMT YOU SHOULD HAVE BOUGHT THAT WITH YOU

OLK UH

IMT YOU SHOULD HAVE BOUGHT THAT WITH YOU

OLK

IMT LAUGHTER

SJG YOU WANT THIS ONE (THEY WERE TALKING ABOUT THE WEAPON)

IMT ALL SGT, YOU KNOW I'LL MESS YOU

OLK YOU BEEN UP THERE YET?

IMT YEAH YEAH I WAS HOPING YOU BE UP THERE THOUGH

OLK I COULDN'T BE THERE

IMT CAUSE I, I WAS TELLING HIM ABOUT IT... YOU KNOW WHAT I'M SAYING MAN THE ONLY THANG IT IS NOW, I CAN GET THE DUDE TO BRING ME THE DOPE IN, THAT WON'T, THAT WON'T BE NO PROBLEM. BUT THE THING IS, I DON'T WANT TO BE LIKE THOSE REED BOYS.

OLK YEAH

IMT HE LOOKED AT ME LIKE-LOOKED AT ME LIKE WHERE THEY KNOW WHAT I'M SAYING... THEY IN RANKIN COUNTY. SO AH, I WAS FEN TO ASK HIM LIKE WELL OFFICER KITTRELL, HE WAS THE ONLY ONE BEING STRAIGHT UP WITH ME... YOU KNOW WHAT I'M TALKING ABOUT...

OLK YEAH

IMT SO AH, HE GOT TO TALKING ABOUT WELL, IF YOU CAN GET IT, IF YOU CAN GET THE DOPE... YOU KNOW WHAT I'M SAYING... JUST GET IT AND PUT IT UP. YOU KNOW WHAT I'M SAYING...

OLK THAT AINT WORTH A GOT DAMN...

IMT YEAH, SO I WAS MORE LIKE, I WAS MORE LIKE JUST TELLING HIM

IMT   I CAN DO IT, IT WON'T BE NO PROBLEM YOU KNOW, I WAS TELLING HIM WOULD IT BE GUARANTEED THAT I CAN GET OUT... YOU KNOW WHAT I'M SAYING... OR WERE YOU GOING TO HELP ME GET AWAY FROM HERE, HE WASN'T REALLY SAYING NOTHING.

OLK   HE DIDN'T SAY NOTHING?

IMT   THAT'S WHY I WAS HOPING YOU'LL BE UP THERE

OLK   AH, ALL I COULDN'T BE THERE

IMT   I WAS SITTING THERE TALKING ABOUT OFFICER KITTRELL, OFFICER KITTRELL, YOU KNOW WHAT I'M SAYING... THEN I TOLD HIM WELL, TALKED WITH OFFICER KITTRELL ABOUT THAT TIME

OLK   THAT'S NOT WHAT WE WANT... YOU DONT NEED TO PUT IT UP, THEY NEED TO, THEY NEED TO HAVE IT READY FOR HIM TO GET IT PUT ON HIM, OR EITHER KNOW WHEN HE'S GOING TO GET IT TO YOU AND BE THERE. THEY NEED TO HAVE YOU WIRED SOME WAY OR ANOTHER.

IMT   RIGHT THAT'S WHAT, THAT'S WHAT I TOLD HIM, I'LL WEAR A WIRE.

OLK   RIGHT

IMT   YOU KNOW WHAT I'M SAYING, I SAY WELL OFFICER MOSLEY, HE'S BEEN DOING IT FOR A WHILE. HE WAS IN CONNECTION WITH... WHAT'S THAT...

CHAPTER TWO
Department of Corrections Investigation

Because of two failed drug set-up attempts, I became very hostile and angry. It was disheartening to know that people I worked so closely with would set me up by fabricating evidence that would have possibly caused my incarceration. I was a ball of emotions. I was hurt, I was devastated, and I felt betrayed. Knowing what coworkers had attempted made my work environment very hostile, which caused me mental anguish and instability. I didn't believe it until it happened to me, which led me to realize that there were inmates who had more integrity than some prison officials.

While on medical leave, Larry Smith, an Integrity Investigator with the Mississippi Department of Corrections Internal Audit Division (IAD), called and asked if I would meet with him. He asked to meet IAD at the visitor's trailer on the SMCI compound where he could conduct an investigative interview with me in the presence of Investigator Johnny Covington of IAD. During that interview, he offered me a bribe.

"The commissioner wants to know what you want to make this go away," he said, referring to Commissioner Steve Puckett.

"What do you mean what do I want?" I asked him, perplexed.

"What position at the prison do you want that will make this go away?"

With a number of false criminal allegations against me, I was insulted by his bribery. It would have been a great injustice for me to accept a job I wasn't qualified for just to appease the commissioner and "make this all go away." I also felt it would give them a third opportunity to set me up, so I angrily declined.

"I have a job, and I want these people to be held accountable for their actions," I told him.

"Good luck," he replied.

Not only was this attempt wrong, but it was unlawful. Fabricating evidence is a crime, and by them planting marijuana in my office, they committed the crime. I was assuming they were interviewing me to gather information on the drug set-ups, and bring those responsible parties to justice, as well as protecting my Fourteenth Amendment right. But instead, insult was added to injury with a bribe, and I abruptly ended the interview. There were several violations of the Mississippi Department of Corrections Policy Number 03.1 General Standards of Professional Conduct, and I lost respect for law enforcement, the system and the investigative process by the IAD. I also left the meeting finding it hard to believe that Larry Smith's title was Integrity Investigator. Where was his "integrity" when he offered me that bribe?

Following my meeting with Larry Smith, and my refusal to accept his offer, an investigation by the IAD ensued.

It is a culture of corruption in how staff members and inmates at SMCI described the IAD. Inmates informed me of the actual tactics that IAD used, which included fabricating evidence on targeted staff members.

It was alleged by staff members and inmates that former Commissioner Steve Puckett had a "target list" of staff members he did not like and used IAD to carry out gestapo type of tactics against targeted staff members. Inmates informed me that these tactics happened in the streets and in the prison system.

Before Steve Puckett was appointed commissioner, he was the superintendent at SMCI. It is alleged that he befriended CO Michael Moore, Lieutenant Victor Brewer and Captain Johnny Denmark. Staff members alleged they played golf together, especially at the 1996 M.A.P.C. Awards Banquet Golf Tournament. Steve Puckett, CO Michael Miller, K-9 CO Hal Walley and K-9 CO Greg Howard, who were assigned to the K-9 unit, and had direct access to marijuana used to train dogs, were teammates.

Fabricating Evidence

The two ounces of marijuana CO Michael Miller planted at my desk were wrapped in black tape inside a plastic bag, which was used by SMCI's K-9 officers as a method to train drug dogs. IAD tried to make its investigation appear as if I had busted CO Miller attempting to bring marijuana inside the compound to Inmate Mandell Walker, who worked for CO Miller on landscaping detail. CO Miller could have easily given the drugs to Inmate Walker. I worked inside the Maintenance building, which was located in a different area outside the prison gates, with inmates who had no contact with Inmate Walker on a day-to-day basis. Working as Maintenance CO, I had never met or worked with CO Miller. Going on the compound was not a requirement, and I would have had to get permission from the watch commander to enter the compound. However, CO Miller had direct access to the compound and all inmates, including Inmate Walker.

The evidence shows CO Miller, Lieutenant Victor Brewer and Captain Denmark conspired to plant marijuana at my desk. IAD did not conduct an interview with Lieutenant Victor Brewer or Captain Johnny Denmark.

In 2000, after former Commissioner Steve Puckett retired, former Governor Ronald Musgrove appointed Robert L. Johnson as MDOC commissioner. At that time, by Commissioner Robert Johnson being an African American, I was encouraged to seek his assistance. Morris Hill, supervisor of Beat #2 Greene County, met with Commissioner Robert L. Johnson pertaining to my case. At that time, Commissioner Johnson requested my information. On April 22, 2000, I wrote to Commissioner Johnson, sending him a package of documents and evidence pertaining to my case, showing the corruption at SMCI, in hopes that he would re-open the investigation or at least talk with me. Seven days later, on April 28, I received communication from Commissioner Robert L. Johnson, declining to reopen my case and expressing his unwillingness to meet with me.

    I never expected to have a painful experience like this at SMCI.

Fabricating Evidence

MISSISSIPPI DEPARTMENT OF CORRECTIONS POLICY		DOC. 03-01
GENERAL STANDARDS OF PROFESSIONAL CONDUCT	ACA STANDARDS: 3-3068, 3-3069, 3-4067 & 4-ACRS-3A-07	
§ 97-3-97, House Bill 59 (1998)		RESTRICTED
EFFECTIVE DATE: 10-01-02	INITIAL DATE: 12-01-82	PAGE 1 of 3

POLICY:

It is the policy of the Mississippi Department of Corrections (MDOC) that all employees will conduct themselves, and perform their duties, in a professional manner.

DEFINITIONS:

Employees – Paid employees of MDOC, contract workers, volunteers, and consultants.

Immediate Family – Spouse, parent, stepparent, sibling, child, stepchild, grandchild, grandparent, son-in-law, daughter-in-law, mother-in-law, father-in-law, brother-in-law, or sister-in-law (child means a biological, adopted or foster child, or a child for whom the individual stands or stood in loco parentis).

PRECEPTS:

The MDOC Director of Personnel will ensure that a written code of ethics prohibits employees from using their official position to secure privileges for themselves or others and from engaging in activities that constitute a conflict of interest. A copy of this code of ethics will be available to all employees.

This written code of ethics will include, but not be limited to the following:

- Employees will protect the civil, legal, and applicable constitutional rights of all offenders.

- Employees are expected to conduct themselves in a dignified, honest and professional manner.

- No employee will use his official position to secure special advantage for himself, any offender, or any other person(s).

- Employees responsible for personnel actions will not use their position to hire, appoint, promote, or dismiss any person on the basis of either person's personal or political interest.

- Information pertaining to offenders and obtained under the color of office will be considered confidential and will not be released to anyone not authorized to receive it.

- Any public statement related to the affairs of MDOC will be worded to indicate that the statement is either a personal or official MDOC statement.

MISSISSIPPI DEPARTMENT OF CORRECTIONS POLICY		DOC. 03-01
GENERAL STANDARDS OF PROFESSIONAL CONDUCT	ACA STANDARDS: 3-3068, 3-3069, 3-4067 & 4-ACRS-3A-07	
§ 97-3-97, House Bill 59 (1998)		RESTRICTED
EFFECTIVE DATE: 10-01-02	INITIAL DATE: 12-01-82	PAGE 2 of 3

- Employees will report any unethical, corrupt, or criminal behaviors occurring within the department to their supervisor, Internal Audit Division, or the Director of Personnel.

- No employee will accept from or provide to any offender or their immediate family any item not authorized by the MDOC, nor will any employee accept from or provide to any offender or their immediate family any item in a manner not authorized by MDOC.

- No employee will establish close friendships or fraternize with offenders or their immediate family, agent or other representative.

Any employee who becomes aware of any offender with whom he has had any previous or existing relationship, whether a kinship relationship (by blood or marriage, adoption, common law) or not, the employee will immediately report this in writing to his Supervisor or Department Head and the Superintendent or Community Corrections Director. The Superintendent or Community Corrections Director will immediately report this information in writing to the respective Deputy Commissioners who in turn will report this information to the Commissioner.

House Bill 59, signed by the Governor on March 26, 1998, states - "It will be unlawful for any jailer, guard, employee of the Department of Corrections, sheriff, constable, marshal, or other officer to engage in any sexual penetration as defined in Section 97-3-97, Mississippi Code of 1972, with any offender, with or without the offender's consent, who is incarcerated at any jail or any state, county or private correctional facility. Any person who violates this section will be guilty of a felony and upon conviction will be fined not more than Five Thousand Dollars ($5,000) or imprisoned for a term not to exceed five (5) years, or both."

Employees will not discriminate against any individual because of race, gender, creed, national origin, religious affiliation, age or any other type of prohibited discrimination.

REPORTS REQUIRED:

As required by this policy and through the chain of command.

Fabricating Evidence

MISSISSIPPI DEPARTMENT OF CORRECTIONS POLICY		DOC. 03-01
GENERAL STANDARDS OF PROFESSIONAL CONDUCT	ACA STANDARDS: 3-3068, 3-3069, 3-4067 & 4-ACRS-3A-07	
§ 97-3-97, House Bill 59 (1998)		RESTRICTED
EFFECTIVE DATE: 10-01-02	INITIAL DATE: 12-01-82	PAGE 3 of 3

ENFORCEMENT AUTHORITY		
All SOPs and/or other directive documents related to the implementation and enforcement of this policy will bear the signature of and be issued under the authority of the Director of Personnel and Commissioner.		
Reviewed and Approved for Issuance	General Counsel	9-26-02 Date
	Commissioner	09/27/02 Date

Mississippi Department of Corrections

CONFIDENTIAL

REPORT OF INTERVIEW
Internal Audit Division

Britton (NMN) Mosely, Correctional Officer II at South Mississippi Correctional Institution (SMCI) in Leakesville, MS. provided the following statement in reference to the alleged attempt of Officer Miller bringing contraband into the institution.

Mosely is a black male, born September 30, 1948, social security number   and has been employed with Mississippi Department of Corrections (SMCI), since September 13, 1991.

At approximately 0715 hours on November 04, 1996, Officer Michael Miller and Inmate Mandell Walker, #78206 approached him at the side gate of the yard of SMCI I. Mosely was in the process of picking up maintenance inmates at the time they approached.

The conversation consisted of Miller and Walker wanting him to bring some shower shoes in to Walker. Mosely told them they would have to get it approved by the Watch Commander.

At the time of the conversation Mosely said he did not know Miller's name. He was familiar with Walker.

At approximately 1430 hours the same date he said he was in the process of taking an inmate to the Greene County High School. Officer Miller approached him at the entrance building of SMCI-I and asked him if he was leaving for the day. He advised him he was not leaving but was enroute to the Greene County High School.

At approximately 1500 hours when he returned from Greene County High School, Sgt. Daniel Paff told him that Miller had left a package for him. When he looked in the package it contained shower shoes and personal items. Sgt. Paff told him he needed to search that package. He told Paff that is what he was going to do. He started searching the package and when he got to the baby powder, he discovered what appeared to be some type of contraband. There were two items wrapped in black tape inside a plastic bag.

Date of Interview: December 03, 1996	File Number: SMCI-19-96
Interviewing Officer: Michael J. Ballard	Place of Interview: Internal Affairs, SMCI

OFFICIAL USE ONLY
MDOC INTERNAL AUDIT DIVISION

This report is the property of the Mississippi Department of Corrections.
Neither it, nor its contents may be disseminated outside the agency to which it is loaned.

Page 7

Fabricating Evidence

Mississippi Department of Corrections

CONFIDENTIAL

REPORT OF INTERVIEW
Internal Audit Division

Daniel Clayton Paff, Correctional Administrator I, at South Mississippi Correctional Institution (SMCI) in Leakesville, MS., provided the following statement in reference to the allegations of attempting to bring contraband into the institution by Officer Miller.

Paff is a white male, born November 22, 1963, social security number   and has been employed with the Mississippi Department of Corrections, (SMCI), since April 3, 1989.

On November 04, 1996, he was working at the security desk at the maintenance building when he was approached by an officer he identified in my office as Officer Michael Miller. Miller brought a black zipper bag to him and told him to give it to Officer Mosely.

Paff identified the bag in my possession as the bag that Miller gave him. After the bag was left by Miller he (Miller) left the maintenance building and he did not see him anymore.

When Mosely returned to the maintenance building he gave the bag to him. Mosely opened the bag in front of him and he (Paff) described the contents of the bag. Mosely told him there was not supposed to be anything in the bag except shower shoes.

MVM/bkr

Date of Interview: November 05, 1996	File Number: SMCI-19-96
Interviewing Officer: M.V. McLendon	Place of Interview: Internal Affairs, SMCI

OFFICIAL USE ONLY
MDOC INTERNAL AUDIT DIVISION

This report is the property of the Mississippi Department of Corrections.
Neither it, nor its contents may be disseminated outside the agency to which it is loaned.

Page 4

Mississippi Department of Corrections

CONFIDENTIAL

REPORT OF INTERVIEW
Internal Audit Division

Michael Calvin Miller, Correctional Officer Trainee, at South Mississippi Correctional Institution (SMCI), in Leakesville, MS., provided the following statement in reference to the allegations of attempting to bring contraband into the institution.

Miller is a white male, born November 08, 1973, social security number   and has been employed with the Mississippi Department of Corrections (SMCI) since January 04, 1996.

Miller was advised of his Miranda rights and acknowledged understanding by signing.

Miller said he received a package from Inmate Mandell Walker's, #78206B, mother on October 29, 1996. He told Walker he would try to get it to him. On November 04, 1996, he discussed this with Walker and told him he would try to get it in to him that date. Walker told him to give it to Officer Britton Mosely and he would get it to him.

Miller said that the reason he had not brought the package in before was that he had been recently transferred to the wood crew.

When he got off work on November 04, 1996, he clocked out and then went to his truck and got the package and carried it to the maintenance shop where Mosely worked. Mosely was away from the institution at this time on a detail. He gave the package to Sgt. Daniel Paff with the instruction to give it to Mosely.

Date of Interview: November 05, 1996	File Number: SMCI-19-96
Interviewing Officer: M.V. McLendon	Place of Interview: Internal Affairs, SMCI

OFFICIAL USE ONLY
MDOC INTERNAL AUDIT DIVISION

This report is the property of the Mississippi Department of Corrections.
Neither it, nor its contents may be disseminated outside the agency to which it is loaned.

Page 5

Fabricating Evidence

```
REPORT OF INTERVIEW
Page 2
SMCI-19-96
```

Miller stated that he did not know the package contained drugs. He was only trying to help Walker get some personal items in. He acknowledged that his correctional officer training in the academy taught him not to bring anything into an inmate. He said he knew he was wrong when he did this.

Miller provided the following personal information:

```
Name:           Miller, Michael Calvin
Position:       Correctional Officer Trainee
Race:           White
Sex:            Male
Height:         5'8"
Weight:         155 lbs
Date of birth:  November 08, 1973
Employment:     MS Dep of Corrections (SMCI)
Address:        ███████████████████████
Education:      High School
Marital Status: Married
```

MVM/bkr

Page 6

Britton Mosley, Sr.

Mississippi Department of Corrections

CONFIDENTIAL

REPORT OF INTERVIEW
Internal Audit Division

Mandell Walker, Inmate #78206B, born September 19, 1969, social security number ███████, assigned to General Population, South Mississippi Correctional Institution (SMCI), Leakesville, MS. Walker provided the following statement in reference to the allegations of attempting to bring contraband into the institution by Officer Michael Miller.

Walker is a black male, serving twenty six (26) years for three (3) counts of cocaine sale out of Newton County.

Miller worked in Unit 10 where Walker was housed before he (Miller) was moved to Common labor approximately one week ago. During this time Miller had brought him food and items of that nature. He told Miller that he needed some shower shoes, powder and other items and would he bring them into him. Miller told him on October 29, 1996 that he had the items, but would have to wait until later to bring them in.

On November 04, 1996, Miller told him he would bring the package in at lunch time, which he did not do. Walker saw Officer Britton Mosely at the gate with Miller and he told Mosely to let Inmate Joseph Robinson bring the package into him. Mosely told him he would get it into him. Walker denied that he had any knowledge of any drugs in the package.

MVM/bkr

Date of Interview: November 04, 1996	File Number: SMCI-19-96
Interviewing Officer: M.V. McLendon	Place of Interview: Internal Affairs, SMCI

OFFICIAL USE ONLY
MDOC INTERNAL AUDIT DIVISION

This report is the property of the Mississippi Department of Corrections. Neither it, nor its contents may be disseminated outside the agency to which it is loaned.

Fabricating Evidence

Mississippi Department of Corrections

REPORT OF INVESTIGATION
Internal Audit Division
C O N F I D E N T I A L

CASE TITLE: Michael Calvin Miller, CO-Trainee, South Mississippi Correctional Institution (SMCI) - Suspect.

TYPE INVESTIGATION	CASE STATUS	
CRIMINAL __X__	ACTIVE __X__	FILE NUMBER: SMCI-19-96
ADMINISTRATIVE __X__	CLOSED ___	DATE: December 30, 1996
APPLICANT ___	OTHER ___	PAGE _1_ OF _8_ PAGES
REPORTING OFFICER: M.V. McLendon		

Offense Summary: Michael Miller, CO-Trainee, attempting to have delivered a package to Inmate Mandell Walker that contained approximately two (2) ounces of marijuana.

SYNOPSIS:

This investigation was initiated as a result of allegations that C.O.-Trainee Michael Miller attempted to have delivered to Inmate Mandell Walker, #78206B a package that contained approximately two (2) ounces of marijuana.

Officer Miller admitted that he received the package at his residence from Walker's mother and he brought it in with the intention of getting it to Walker.

Officer Miller delivered this package to Sgt. Daniel Paff with the instructions to give it to Officer Britton Mosely.

Officer Mosely received the package, inspected it and found what appeared to be approximately two (2) ounces of marijuana.

DISTRIBUTION:	SIGNATURE (Officer)	
D.A. Dale Harkey		
Roger Cook, Supt., SMCI	*M.V. McLendon*	
Gene Hill, Chief, Internal Audit DV.	APPROVED (Name and Title)	DATE
File		12-30-96

OFFICIAL USE ONLY
MDOC INTERNAL AUDIT DIVISION

REPORT OF INVESTIGATION
Page 2
SMCI-19-96

ADMINISTRATIVE

LEADS

Will review with District Attorney Dale Harkey for a possible prosecution for Section 47-5-193 Mississippi Code, i.e. bringing illegal drugs on the property belonging to the Mississippi Department of Corrections.

DETAILS

PREDICATION

This investigation initiated as a result of Captain Johnny Denmark notifying this writer that he had in his possession a package that contained approximately two (2) ounces of what appeared to be marijuana. This package was believed to have been brought on Mississippi Department of Correction grounds by CO-Trainee Michael Miller.

INTERVIEWS   PAGE

Name: Walker, Mandell, Inmate #78206B   3
Date of Interview: November 04, 1996

Name:- Paff, Daniel Clayton, Correctional-   4
Administrator I, Date of Interview:
November 05, 1996

Name: Miller, Michael Calvin, CO-Trainee   5-6
Date of Interview: November 05, 1996
Suspect

Name: Mosely, Britton, Correctional Officer II   7-8
Date of Interview: December 03, 1996

Fabricating Evidence

Mississippi Department of Corrections

CONFIDENTIAL

REPORT OF INTERVIEW
Internal Audit Division

LENT RICE, Special Agent, FBI, formerly assigned to the Pascagoula Office of the FBI and now assigned to the Oxford Office, telephone (601) 234-1713, contacted Internal Audit Division (IAD) on October 23, 1997, relating to Britton Mosley, Correctional Officer, South Mississippi Correctional Institution (SMCI), Leakesville, MS.

Rice was recently contacted by the U. S. Attorney's Office, Biloxi, MS, as a result of a letter Mosley wrote to U. S. Attorney General Janet Reno, alleging a conspiracy against him by Mississippi Department of Corrections (MDOC) employees. The U. S. Attorney's office was aware of at least two prior contacts Rice had with Mosley in which he had leveled conspiracy allegations against MDOC employees. In other instances, Rice had found the allegations by Mosley as being baseless. Mosley also provided a copy of a tape cassette that was supposed to reflect basis for his allegations, however, Rice with the assistance of FBI sound experts was unable to find any basis to support his allegations.

After Rice discussed the above facts with the U. S. Attorney's Office, they indicated they would recommend no further action with regard to Mosley's allegations.

MGH/lr
97-SMCI-10

DATE OF INTERVIEW: October 23, 1997	FILE NUMBER: 97-SMCI-10
INTERVIEWER: M. Gene Hill	PLACE OF INTERVIEW: Telephonically conducted

OFFICIAL USE ONLY
MDOC INTERNAL AUDIT DIVISION

This report is the property of the Mississippi Department of Corrections.
Neither it, nor its contents may be disseminated outside the agency to which it is loaned.

Britton Mosley, Sr.

Mississippi Department of Corrections

CONFIDENTIAL

REPORT OF INTERVIEW
Internal Audit Division

MALCOLM VIRGIL MCLENDON, Chief, Internal Audit Division (IAD), South Mississippi Correctional Institution (SMCI), Leakesville, MS, (601) 394-5600, extension 1032 was contacted regarding his knowledge of an alleged conspiracy against Britton Mosley, Correctional Officer II (CO II), SMCI.

McLendon is a white male, age 57, date of birth May 4, 1940, has Social Security Number and has been employed with MDOC since November 1, 1987.

McLendon alleges there has been no conspiracy against Mosley.

During the month of March 1997, Louis Kittrell, CO II, advised McLendon that Anthony Reed, Inmate #81964 and Will Reed, Inmate #81722, members of the Black Gangster Disciples, were volunteering to assist in supplying information on staff members dealing drugs.

The Reeds provided several names of staff members dealing drugs at SMCI. Listed among the names was Britton Mosley, CO II.

McLendon also provided this information to Jerry Dettman, Integrity Investigator, IAD, Central Office, Jackson, MS.

/lr
(97-SMCI-11.G)

DATE OF INTERVIEW: December 16, 1997	FILE NUMBER: 97-SMCI-11
INTERVIEWER: L. Smith	PLACE OF INTERVIEW: SMCI, Leakesville, MS

OFFICIAL USE ONLY
MDOC INTERNAL AUDIT DIVISION

This report is the property of the Mississippi Department of Corrections.
Neither it, nor its contents may be disseminated outside the agency to which it is loaned.

Page 10

Fabricating Evidence

Mississippi Department of Corrections

CONFIDENTIAL

REPORT OF INTERVIEW
Internal Audit Division

MARVIN RAY THOMAS, Inmate #79517, Unit #29, Mississippi State Penitentiary (MSP), Parchman, MS, was contacted regarding his knowledge of a conspiracy against Britton Mosley, Correctional Officer II (CO II), by South Mississippi Correctional Institution (SMCI), Leakesville, MS staff.

Thomas is a black male, age 22 years, date of birth January 6, 1975, has Social Security Number He is serving eight (8) years for sale of cocaine out of Scott County, MS.

In August 1997, Will Reed, Inmate at SMCI, told Thomas if he needed any help, go to Lewis Kittrell, CO II. Reed told Thomas, Kittrell could help him get out of prison. Thomas went to Kittrell and asked him if he could help him get out of prison.

Kittrell told him he had information that Britton Mosley, CO II, was bringing dope into the prison through the maintenance shop. Kittrell told Thomas if he could get Mosley to bring drugs into the prison he would help him. He would see that he did not get messed around like the Reed brothers, referring to a problem that Will and Andrew Reed had at SMCI. Thomas told Kittrell that he wanted to help catch a dirty officer. Kittrell told Thomas that he would notify Malcolm McLendon, Chief IAD, SMCI, that Thomas needed to see him urgently.

Later that day McLendon had Thomas brought to his office. He asked Thomas, "Do you think Mosley is a dirty officer and is he selling dope?" Thomas told McLendon, "No, I can't say he is." Thomas described Mosley as a role model type. McLendon told Thomas that since an incident occurred with Michael Miller, an Ex-CO I, he had heard a lot of talk about Mosley bringing dope to the convicts in the Maintenance Shop.

Thomas claims that McLendon was going to approve him for a working detail at the Maintenance Shop. He would give him $120.00. Thomas would give the money to Mosley to by one (1) ounce of dope (marijuana) and bring it into the prison. Thomas would pay Mosley $20.00. Thomas asked McLendon, "What if that does not work?" McLendon told him, he

DATE OF INTERVIEW: October 12, 1997	FILE NUMBER: 97-SMCI-11
INTERVIEWER: L. Smith	PLACE OF INTERVIEW: IAD MSP, Parchman, MS

OFFICIAL USE ONLY
MDOC INTERNAL AUDIT DIVISION

This report is the property of the Mississippi Department of Corrections.
Neither it, nor its contents may be disseminated outside the agency to which it is loaned.

Page 3

REPORT OF INTERVIEW – MARVIN RAY THOMAS
97-SMCI-11
Page 2

would get some dope and let Thomas take it to the Maintenance Shop. He would hide the dope inside the small office where the guards sit. Thomas was to let him know when the dope was hidden and McLendon and K-9 Officers would search the Maintenance area, finding the dope and blame it on Mosley. (Refer to page 2 of 4 in Transcript of Inmate Kittrell)

Three (3) days later Thomas was approved for work at the Maintenance Shop. It bothered Thomas that he had agreed to set-up Mosley. Approximately 1½ hours after Thomas started working at the Maintenance Shop, he told Mosley, "Man, they are really out to get you." Mosley did not ask who was out to get him but replied, "I know they are, but what do you know?" Thomas told Mosley that Kittrell and McLendon wanted Thomas to set-up a drug deal with him.

Three (3) or four (4) days later, Mosley asked Thomas if he would wear a tape recorder to McLendon's office. He told Mosley that was not a good idea, but he agreed to wear it at the Maintenance Shop and record a conversation with Kittrell. Thomas denied the suggestion that the tape recorder was his idea. He stated that Mosley knew he was not supposed to have a tape recorder for an inmate to record conversations, however, he told Thomas a Federal Judge knew what was going on.

Three (3) days after talking to Thomas about the recorder, Mosley brought the recorder to him at Maintenance. That day he recorded a conversation with Kittrell and returned the tape and recorder to Mosley.

When Thomas returned to his unit, Nathaniel Scott, Case Manager, and inmate Alvin Guice, approached him and told him, "We got to get you out of here." Guice told him, "I know about the tape." Thomas never acknowledged that he knew what they were talking about. The next morning at 03:00 hours, he was moved to Delta Correctional Facility (DCF), Greenwood, MS.

Thomas is temporarily housed at Mississippi State Penitentiary (MSP), Parchman, MS, for an eye surgery. He will then return to Greenwood.

Kittrell and McLendon told him they would help him get out of prison or get housed closer to home if he helped them set-up Mosley. He has not heard from them since.

In September 1997, Thomas disclosed that Mosley called Mary Thomas, his mother, phone number   Scott County, MS, and told her, Thomas had been moved from the Green County facility. Mosley told her, "Thomas had been used to set him up." Mary Thomas told him Mosley said he was a brave young man for helping him.

/lr
(97-SMCI-11.A)

Page 4

Fabricating Evidence

Mississippi Department of Corrections

CONFIDENTIAL

REPORT OF INTERVIEW
Internal Audit Division

JERRY DETTMAN, Integrity Investigator, IAD, Central Office, Jackson, MS, telephone 35(...)-5728, was contacted regarding his knowledge of Britton Mosley, Correctional Officer II (CO II) South Mississippi Correctional Institution (SMCI), Leakesville, MS, as a drug dealer.

Dettman acknowledged that he had received information from Malcolm V. McLendon, Chief, IAD, SMCI, regarding staff members trafficking drugs into SMCI. Among the names of staff members was the name of Britton Mosley.

In the month of December 1996 during an interview with Inmate Anthony Reed, #81964, Mosley's name was provided to Dettman as a staff member that delt drugs, but Reed admitted he had not received drugs from Mosley.

Inmate Marvin Thomas provided Mosley's name as a drug dealer, however, had no first hand experience with Mosley.

Also in the fall of 1996, a confidential informer from Greene County allowed he had hear(d) Mosley's name mentioned as a source of marijuana, but had no first hand knowledge of Mosley's alleged activity.

This is information was described by Dettman as raw intelligence, meaning he did not have anything to substantiate his information.

(97-SMCI-11 P)

DATE OF INTERVIEW: December 16, 1997	FILE NUMBER: 97-SMCI-11
INTERVIEWER: L.Smith	PLACE OF INTERVIEW: MDOC Central Office, Jackson, MS

OFFICIAL USE ONLY
MDOC INTERNAL AUDIT DIVISION

This report is the property of the Mississippi Department of Corrections

Mississippi Department of Corrections

CONFIDENTIAL

REPORT OF INTERVIEW
Internal Audit Division

NATHANIEL SCOTT, Case Manager, South Mississippi Correctional Institution (SMCI), Leakesville, MS, telephone (601) 394-5600, extension 1083, was contacted regarding his knowledge of a staff request that transferred Marvin Ray Thomas, Inmate #79517B from SMCI to the Delta Correctional Facility (DCF), Private Prison, Greenwood, MS, on August 12, 1997.

Scott is a black male, age 40, date of birth December 19, 1957, has Social Security Number and has been employed with Mississippi Department of Corrections (MDOC) since May 5, 1980.

Scott was provided with a Disciplinary Interview Advice of Rights form in which he read, and signed as understanding. Upon questioning Scott in regards of Thomas' transfer, Lee stated, Billy Ekesl provided a staff request for Thomas via computer. Thomas' date of request to be transferred will be in Ekesl computer. There could have possibly been ten (10) or twelve (12) inmates along with Thomas that were moved to Delta Correctional Facility (DCF), Greenwood, MS. Scott signed Thomas' request then took the form to the Unit Supervisor for his signature. (Staff request could have been done on the 10th, however the signatures are dated August 12, 1997.) After all signatures are gathered and classification committee meets, Florence Jones, Classification Director, will sign staff requests.

Scott has not assisted Thomas nor does he have knowledge of anyone assisting Thomas to leave SMCI. He has never had a conversation with Thomas regarding getting Thomas out of SMCI.

/lr
(97-SMCI-11.F)

DATE OF INTERVIEW: December 8, 1997	FILE NUMBER: 97-SMCI-11
INTERVIEWER: L. Smith and J. Dettman	PLACE OF INTERVIEW: SMCI, Leakesville, MS

OFFICIAL USE ONLY
MDOC INTERNAL AUDIT DIVISION

This report is the property of the Mississippi Department of Corrections.
Neither it, nor its contents may be disseminated outside the agency to which it is loaned.

Fabricating Evidence

Mississippi Department of Corrections

REPORT OF INVESTIGATION
Internal Audit Division
C O N F I D E N T I A L

CONFIDENTIAL

SUBJECT(S):	Lewis Kittrell Jr., Correctional Officer II (CO II), South Mississippi Correctional Institution (SMCI), Leakesville, MS, and Malcolm McLendon, Chief, Internal Audit Division (IAD), SMCI
VICTIM(S):	Britton Mosley, CO II, SMCI, Leakesville, MS

TYPE INVESTIGATION:	CASE STATUS:	FILE NUMBER: 97-SMCI-11
CRIMINAL ____	ACTIVE ____	DATE: December 17, 1997
ADMINISTRATIVE X	CLOSED ____	PAGE 1 OF ___ PAGES
APPLICANT ____	OTHER ____	

REPORTING OFFICER: L. P. Smith, Integrity Investigator, IAD

OFFENSE: Alleged Conspiracy and Possible Cover-up of Corrupt Activity by SMCI Staff Members.

SYNOPSIS:

This investigation was initiated as a result of a letter from Mark Henry, Chief Legal Counsel, of the Governor's Office providing documents and a cassette tape sent to him by Mosley. The documents contain allegations of corrupt activity and a possible cover-up by SMCI Officials.

Mosley was interviewed and claims that SMCI staff has twice attempted to set him up as a drug dealer to discredit him and his wife, Brenda Mosley, Correctional Officer, who has a federal lawsuit filed against Mississippi Department of Corrections (MDOC) alleging race discrimination for not receiving a telecommunications position at SMCI.

Mosley alleges Michael Miller, ex-MDOC, CO was utilized by staff in the first attempt to set him up as a drug dealer. Miller left a package at SMCI for Mosley that contained marijuana, that ultimately resulted in Miller's termination, however, Mosley believes that Miller suffered no consequences and was allowed to resign from SMCI.

CONFIDENTIAL

DISTRIBUTION:	SIGNATURE:		
1 - Commissioner			
1 - DCI, Grubbs			
1 - Superintendent SMCI, Turner	APPROVED (Name and Title)		DATE:
1- Legal Counsel, Goff	M. Dean Hill,		12/18/97
2 - IAD File	Director, Internal Audit		

OFFICIAL USE ONLY
MDOC INTERNAL AUDIT DIVISION

This report is the property of the Mississippi Department of Corrections
Neither it, nor its contents may be disseminated outside the agency to which it is loaned.

REPORT OF INVESTIGATION - 97-SMCI-11
Page 2

Mosley contends Inmate Marvin Thomas was utilized by SMCI staff in the second attempt to set him up as a drug dealer. Thomas told Mosley, Lewis Kittrell, CO II, and Malcolm McLendon, Chief, IAD, wanted him set up as a drug dealer.

Internal Audit Division intelligence files at SMCI and MDOC Central Office indicated that Inmates Will Reed, Anthony Reed and Marvin Thomas have provided Mosley's name to staff members as a drug dealer.

Mosley admitted he provided a recorder and a tape to Thomas for recording conversations with staff members and is aware that it is against MDOC policy. Thomas admitted using Mosley's recorder to record a conversation with Kittrell, however, he denies recording a conversation with McLendon

Interviews with Thomas and Kittrell confirm that Thomas originally approached Kittrell with information about Mosley. Thomas was told to contact Kittrell by Inmate Will Reed. Reed had provided information to Kittrell in the past. Thomas told Kittrell that he wanted to help catch a dirty officer and that Mosley was going to bring marijuana into the prison. Kittrell arranged for McLendon to talk with Thomas.

Thomas claims McLendon approved him for a work detail at the Maintenance shop where Mosley was assigned. McLendon was going to provide Thomas with money to give to Mosley to purchase marijuana and deliver it to SMCI or McLendon would give Thomas the marijuana to be hidden in the Maintenance area by Thomas. McLendon and K-9 officers would search the maintenance area, find the marijuana and blame it on Mosley.

Records indicate Terry Hill, Maintenance Supervisor, SMCI, requested Thomas be assigned to Maintenance through inmate classification.

McLendon disclosed he discussed with Thomas, providing buy money for Mosley to purchase marijuana. He also instructed Thomas not to bring the marijuana from the maintenance shop, but to leave the marijuana at the Maintenance shop and notify security.

Thomas contends on the same day he recorded Kittrell for Mosley he was transferred from SMCI to Delta Correctional Facility (DCF), Greenwood, MS. Thomas claims that Nathaniel Scott, Case Manager, approached him and advised him he was leaving SMCI. Scott denies ever having a conversation with Thomas about transferring to another facility. Florence Jones, Director of Classification, has no knowledge of Marvin Ray Thomas having assistance leaving SMCI. She claims he was chosen from a list of eligibles.

Denver Glazier, Personnel Officer, SMCI, indicates Mosley has not worked since July 25, 1997, when the alleged conspiracy began. On July 28, 1997, Mosley began notifying Watch Commanders that he was sick.

Mosley has provided his allegations and a copy of the taped cassette to support his allegations to Lent Rice, FBI, who was unable to find any basis to support his allegations.

Fabricating Evidence

REPORT OF INVESTIGATION – 97-SMCI-11
Page 4

DETAILS:

PREDICATION:

This investigation was initiated as a result of a letter from Mark Henry, Chief, Legal Counsel, of the Governor's Office providing documents and a cassette tape sent to him by Mosley. The documents contain allegations of corrupt activity and a possible cover-up by SMCI Officials.

INTERVIEWS:

NAME	PAGE NUMBER
Britton Mosley, Correctional Officer II, SMCI Date of Interview – November 19, 1997	1-2
Marvin Ray Thomas, Inmate #79517, MSP Date of Interview – October 12, 1997	3-4
Lent Rice, Special Agent, FBI Date of Interview – October 23, 1997	5
Nancy Nibett Pennock, Claims Supervisor, Sedgwich James of Mississippi, Inc. Date of Interview – November 4, 1997	6
Denver Glazier, Personnel Officer, SMCI Date of Interview – November 24, 1997	7
Nathaniel Scott, Case Manager, SMCI Date of Interview – December 8, 1997	8
Florence Marie Jones, Classification Director, SMCI Date of Interview – December 9, 1997	9
Malcolm Virgil McLendon, Chief, IAD, SMCI Date of Interview – December 16, 1997	10
Jerry Dettman, Integrity Investigator, IAD Date of Interview – December 16, 1997	11

REPORT OF INTERVIEWS:

Post — To Grubbs 12/18/97

STATE OF MISSISSIPPI
DEPARTMENT OF CORRECTIONS
M. GENE HILL
Director, Internal Audit Division

MS DEPARTMENT OF CORRECTIONS
CORRECTIVE ACTION/DISPOSITION REPORT

To be completed by the Office of Deputy Commissioner or Superintendent

(Complete form for each subject of Investigation)

Case #: 97-SMCI-11　　　　Facility: SMCI
Subject's Name: Malcolm McFerda　　#/Position: Chief, IAD, SMCI

Incident Narrative/Allegations: Alleged Conspiracy or Possible Cover-up of Corrupt Activity by SMCI Staff Members

DISPOSITION
____ Cause to believe alleged misconduct occurred.
____ No cause to believe alleged misconduct occurred.
____ Cause to believe other misconduct occurred.

Comments: (List below the allegation(s) by number that were substantiated by the report):

ACTION TAKEN
Allegations are: ____ Substantiated　　X Unsubstantiated

For all Cases:
____ Counseling　____ Reprimand　____ Suspension　____ RVR
____ Criminal　　____ Dismissal　　____ Resignation　____ Other　____ None
Comments:

M. Gene Hill　　　5/28/98
Deputy Commissioner/Superintendent/Designee　　Date

DISPOREP.FRM　Please return to IAD

Fabricating Evidence

Criminal Justice Professional of the Year
Steve Puckett, MDOC Commissioner

NOTICE!!
Golf Tournament
Steve Puckett
Michael Miller
Hal Walley
Greg Havard

Britton Mosley, Sr.

STATE OF MISSISSIPPI
DEPARTMENT OF CORRECTIONS
ROBERT L. JOHNSON
COMMISSIONER

April 28, 2000

Mr. Britton Mosley
P. O. Box 390
State Line, Mississippi 39362

Dear Mr. Mosley:

I am in receipt of your request for an investigation and meeting regarding your allegations against the administration at South Mississippi Correctional Institution.

It is my understanding that your allegations have already been investigated by Mississippi Department of Corrections (MDOC), Mississippi Highway Patrol and the Federal Bureau of Investigations.

I also learned that you have filed a lawsuit against MDOC that is pending in United States District Court. For these reasons, I am not willing to reopen an investigation into your allegations and I am unable to meet with you at this time.

Respectfully,

Robert L. Johnson

RLH/JAG/ejc

Fabricating Evidence

From: Capt. Britton Mosley

Date : 04 22-00

Re: Drug Setup and Conspiracy

To : Robert Johnson, Commissioner of The Mississippi Dept. of Corrections
723 North President St.
Jackson, Ms, 39202

Mr. Johnson,

Enclosed are various documents that you have requested, following your meeting with Morris Hill, Supervisor of Beat #2 in Greene County. These documents will reinforce the allegations of a conspiracy and cover up, involving several high ranking officials at South Mississippi Correctional Instsitution, in Leaksville. This overwhelming evidence will show the attempt of an apparent Drug Set'up and Cover'up. Had the conspirators been successful in their attempt, the effects would have caused my imprisonment. This has been a very traumatic experience for my family and I, as well as a great injustice. This letter is a formal appeal to the integrity of you and your Department. With due respect that this matter was inherited by you and your Department, upon your recent appointment to the position of Commissioner, we pray that this is an opportunity to resolve the issue in the best of best of manners for all parties concerned. Historically matters of ths magnitude have been resolvrd as a result of Mass Media attention to the racial malicious motives that prompted such attempts. We hope that the matter can be resolved internally to avoid such situations, as history has shown. If more information is needed in this matter please feel free to contact Lt.Nelson Tate,of the Mississippi Hwy. Patrol to obtain it. Thank you for your time, consideration, and cooperation in this matter.

Sincerely,

Britton Mosley, Sr.
Captain, Britton Mosley

CHAPTER THREE
County District Attorney Investigation

Selective prosecution based on race has always been the norm in Mississippi, even during the post Jim Crow era.

In August 1999, I met with District Attorney Jay Bradley and Investigator Bobby Johnson at the Greene County Courthouse. During that meeting, I presented information and evidence consisting of an audio tape and documents to support my allegations of my being set up for drug possession by high-ranking officials and coworkers at South Mississippi Correctional Institute (SMCI). Three months later in November, Jay Bradley lost her election and the District Attorney position went to Attorney Keith Miller. Jay Bradley remained the District Attorney until Attorney Keith Miller was sworn into office in January 2000.

In spring 2000, I met with District Attorney Keith Miller and his assistants (Ben Saucier and Wilton McNair) on the issues of conspiracy to plant drugs on me by SMCI officials and staff. During the meeting, I submitted evidence showing that former CO Michael Miller did not "introduce drugs onto SMCI property," as per indictment (Case No. 21-98-10,010(2)): Introduction of Drugs onto Mississippi Department of Corrections Property, Section 47-5-193, Miss. Code of 1972, but had conspired with high-ranking officials and staff to plant drugs on me that were already on the compound in the K-9 unit, and he should have been charged with Conspiracy State Statue: 97-1-1 instead. Because District Attorney Miller formerly represented Michael Miller in this case, his office couldn't present the case to the grand jury. However, he offered to provide a special prosecutor to present the case to the grand jury.

On March 20, 2002, L.A. Warren (now deceased), Chairman of Legal Redress Committee of the Mississippi State Conference of the National Association for the Advancement of Colored People (NAACP) sent a letter to District Attorney Keith Miller regarding their phone conversation where District Attorney Keith Miller informed L.A. Warren that Attorney Fred Dobbins (now deceased) was appointed by the court to serve as special prosecutor over the eleven affidavits that I had filed. Because of the NAACP's review of Attorney Dobbins appointment, the NAACP was concerned about potential conflicts of interest. Their investigation revealed that Attorney Dobbins:

- May have represented Joe Errington and Johnny Denmark in other cases,

- May have provided, under contract, legal counsel for inmates at SMCI,
- May have relatives working with SMCI including:
  - A daughter, Shelly Eubanks, Director of Legal Services for SMCI,
  - Brother, Ronnie Dobbins, and uncle of Shelly Eubanks, Maintenance Director for the correctional facility.
  - Also, Patricia Dobbins, wife of Ronnie Dobbins, who was appointed by Superintendent David Turner, one of the accused in the case filed by Britton Mosley, as American Correction Association manager for the correctional facility.

I met with Attorney Dobbins (now deceased) at his office in Leakesville, Mississippi. Dobbins informed me that he was unaware of being appointed special prosecutor. I found out later that the charges on CO Michael Miller were dismissed without prejudice on October 15, 1999.

Now former CO Michael Miller was politically well connected. It was alleged that some of his family members were former sheriffs, an attorney (i.e., District Attorney Keith Miller), and he was a golf friend of Steve Puckett's, former commissioner of MDOC. Historically in Mississippi, when White law enforcement officers committed criminal acts against a person of color, the results are similar—no justice. So, I was not surprised, but very disappointed. Selective prosecutions, by local district attorneys, that are politically and racially motivated within the criminal justice system has mainly targeted people of color that created great, racial disparity within the prison population

NATIONAL ASSOCIATION FOR THE ADVANCEMENT OF COLORED PEOPLE
MISSISSIPPI STATE CONFERENCE

March 20, 2002

EUGENE BRYANT, SR.
President

George Roberts
1st Vice President

Curley Clark
2nd Vice President

Melvin Hollins
3rd Vice President

Derrick Johnson
4th Vice President

Kelvin Buck
5th Vice President

Eddie Smith
6th Vice President

Janette Self
Secretary

Dorothy Isaac
Asst. Secretary

James Crowell
Treasurer

James Creer
Asst. Treasurer

Attorney Keith Miller
District Attorney
P.O. Box 1756
Pascagoula, MS. 39568

Dear Attorney Miller,

Per our telephone conversation, you informed us that Fred Dobbins was appointed by the court to serve as special prosecutor over the eleven affidavits filed by Britton Mosley. As a result of our review of Attorney Dobbins appointment, we are concerned about potential conflicts of interest. Our investigation reveals that Attorney Dobbins:

- May have represented Joe Errington and Johnny Denmark in other cases,
- May have provided, under contract, legal counsel for inmates at SMCI,
- May have relatives working with SMCI including:
  - A daughter Shelly Eubanks, Director of Legal Services for SMCI,
  - Brother Ronnie Dobbins and Uncle of Shelly Eubanks, Maintenance Director for the correctional facility.
  - Also, Patricia Dobbins, wife of Ronnie Dobbins, who was appointed by Superintendent David Turner, one of the accused in the case filed by Britton Mosley, as American Correction Association manager for the correctional facility.

The Mississippi State Conference of NAACP is concerned that there is a potential conflict of interest. Therefore, we request your immediate attention in this matter. Please provide written correspondence within ten (10) days. Should you have any questions regarding this request please do not hesitate to contact us.

Thanking you in advance,

L.A. Warren
Chairman of Legal Redress Committee

cc: Attorney Dennis Hayes, National General Council
Mr. Eugene Bryant, President of MS State Conference
Attorney Mike Moore, Attorney General of State of Mississippi
Mr. Britton Mosley

Fabricating Evidence

OFFICE OF THE DISTRICT ATTORNEY
NINETEENTH CIRCUIT COURT DISTRICT
JACKSON, GEORGE, GREENE COUNTIES

KEITH MILLER
DISTRICT ATTORNEY

May 21, 2002

Mr. L. A. Warren
MS State Conference NAACP
1072 West Lynch Street Ste 10
Jackson, MS 39203

RE: Arnell Hill

Dear Mr. Warren:

I was quite surprised to receive your letter dated May 16, 2002. I have spoken personally to Mr. James Crowell in my office concerning this matter. I thought I made my position clear but I am responding to you in writing because I do not want any misunderstanding.

The Grand Jury is comprised of up to 20 citizens of Jackson County. They hear and see all of the evidence available on every case presented. Once that evidence is presented, they vote on whether or not to return an indictment. The law requires at least 12 Grand Jurors to vote "yes" for an indictment to be returned. If there are not 12 votes for an indictment, the result is known as a "No-Bill" and the matter is dismissed.

In every Grand Jury session there are dozens of cases which the Grand Jury declines to indict resulting in one side or the other being disappointed and sometimes bitter. Disappointment and bitterness also exist when cases are indicted.

In order to maintain the dignity of the Grand Jury confidence must be place in their decisions. My policy is firmly entrenched and consistent with no exceptions: Once a matter is presented to the Grand Jury and they decline to return an indictment (No Bill); that matter is over unless there arises new credible evidence that was not presented to the Grand Jury for its deliberation.

To make an exception would require all "No Billed" cases be resubmitted. Obviously that cannot be an acceptable procedure. At this point I do not have any new credible evidence that would allow me to re-submit this matter to a new Grand Jury.

Your inquiries are always welcome. I hope this letter fully and finally explains my position on all cases presented to a Grand Jury in this District.

Sincerely,

KEITH MILLER
District Attorney

PASCAGOULA OFFICE	WEST JACKSON COUNTY OFFICE	GEORGE COUNTY OFFICE	GREENE COUNTY OFFICE
2ND FLOOR COURTHOUSE	6904 N. WASHINGTON AVENUE	COURTHOUSE	1ST FLOOR COURTHOUSE
P.O. BOX 1756	SUITE C	P.O. BOX 588	P.O. BOX 219
PASCAGOULA, MS 39568-1756	OCEAN SPRINGS, MS 39564	LUCEDALE, MS 39452	LEAKESVILLE, MS 39451
TELEPHONE: 228-769-3045	TELEPHONE: 228-872-4385	TELEPHONE: 601-947-6801	TELEPHONE: 601-394-6511

Britton Mosley, Sr.

INDICTMENT

ATTEMPT: Section 97-1-7, Miss. Code of 1972
INTRODUCTION OF DRUGS ONTO MISSISSIPPI DEPARTMENT OF CORRECTIONS PROPERTY
Section 47-5-193, Miss. Code of 1972

STATE OF MISSISSIPPI   CIRCUIT COURT, MAY 1998 TERM, RECALLED JUNE 9, 1998

COUNTY OF GREENE   Cause No. 21-98-10,010 (2)

    THE GRAND JURORS of the State of Mississippi, taken from the body of the good and lawful citizens of Greene County, duly elected, empaneled, sworn and charged to inquire in and for the said State, County and District, at the Term of Court aforesaid, in the name and by the authority of the State of Mississippi, upon their oaths present: That

MICHAEL CALVIN MILLER

in Greene County, Mississippi, on or about NOVEMBER 4, 1996, did willfully, unlawfully and feloniously, and without authorization of law, design and endeavor to attempt to commit the offense of Introduction of Drugs onto Mississippi Department of Corrections property, a felony denounced by Section 47-5-193, Miss. Code of 1972 (as amended), in that he intended to furnish a certain controlled substance, to-wit: Marijuana, to Mendell Walker, an offender of the Mississippi Department of Corrections at the South Mississippi Correctional Institute, Leakesville, Mississippi, and did then and there an overt act toward the commission thereof, to-wit: by delivering a package containing said controlled substance for delivery to the inmate, Mendell Walker; but he failed therein, in that the controlled substance was found when the package was inspected, contrary to the form of the statute in such cases made and provided, and against the peace and dignity of the State of Mississippi.

A TRUE BILL

_____   _____
DALE HARKEY, DISTRICT ATTORNEY   FOREMAN OF THE GRAND JURY

AFFIDAVIT

    Comes now CORBIT LEE SULLIVAN, Foreman of the Grand Jury, and makes oath that this indictment presented to this Court was concurred in by twelve (12) or more members of the Grand Jury and that at least fifteen (15) members of the Grand Jury were present during all deliberations.

_____
FOREMAN OF THE GRAND JURY

Sworn to and subscribed before me, this the 2nd day of July, 1998.

_____
CHARLOTTE FORTINBERRY
CIRCUIT CLERK

BY: _____
               DEPUTY CLERK

Fabricating Evidence

IN THE CIRCUIT COURT OF GREENE COUNTY, MISSISSIPPI

STATE OF MISSISSIPPI   PLAINTIFF

VERSUS   CAUSE NUMBER: 21-98-10,010(2)

MICHAEL CALVIN MILLER   DEFENDANT

FILED OCT 19 1999

ENTRY OF NOLLE PROSEQUI

COMES NOW, DAVID FUTCH, Assistant District Attorney in and for the Nineteenth Circuit Court District of Mississippi, and makes Entry of Nolle Prosequi as to the above referenced defendant.

RESPECTFULLY SUBMITTED, this the 14th day of October, 1999.

STATE OF MISSISSIPPI

BY: _____
DAVID C. FUTCH, ADA

NOLLE PROSEQUI

Upon application of the State of Mississippi, the Court hereby consents to Entry of Nolle Prosequi herein and this cause is dismissed without prejudice as to the above styled Defendant.

ORDERED, this the 15th day of Oct., 1999.
ENTERED, this the 15th day of Oct., 1999.

_____
KATHY K. JACKSON
CIRCUIT COURT JUDGE

CHAPTER 1

Conspiracy, Accessories and Attempts

Sec.
97-1-1. Conspiracy.
97-1-3. Accessories before the fact.
97-1-5. Accessories after the fact.
97-1-6. Directing or causing felony to be committed by person under age of seventeen years.
97-1-7. Attempt to commit offense; punishment.
97-1-9. Attempt to commit offense; no conviction if offense completed.

§ 97-1-1. Conspiracy.

If two (2) or more persons conspire either:

(a) To commit a crime; or

(b) Falsely and maliciously to indict another for a crime, or to procure to be complained of or arrested for a crime; or

(c) Falsely to institute or maintain an action or suit of any kind; or

(d) To cheat and defraud another out of property by any means which are in themselves criminal, or which, if executed, would amount to a cheat, or to obtain money or any other property or thing by false pretense; or

(e) To prevent another from exercising a lawful trade or calling, or doing any other lawful act, by force, threats, intimidation, or by interfering or threatening to interfere with tools, implements, or property belonging to or used by another, or with the use of employment thereof; or

(f) To commit any act injurious to the public health, to public morals, trade or commerce, or for the perversion or obstruction of justice, or of the due administration of the laws; or

(g) To overthrow or violate the laws of this state through force, violence, threats, intimidation, or otherwise; or

(h) To accomplish any unlawful purpose, or a lawful purpose by any unlawful means; such persons, and each of them, shall be guilty of a felony and upon conviction may be punished by a fine of not more than five thousand dollars ($5,000.00) or by imprisonment for not more than five (5) years, or by both.

Provided, that where the crime conspired to be committed is capital murder or murder as defined by law or is a violation of section 41-29-139(b)(1) or section 41-29-139(c)(2)(D), Mississippi Code of 1972, being provisions of the Uniform Controlled Substances Law, the offense shall be punishable by a fine of not more than five hundred thousand dollars ($500,000.00) or by imprisonment for not more than twenty (20) years, or by both.

§ 97-1-7. Attempt to commit offense; punishment.

Every person who shall design and endeavor to commit an offense, and shall do any overt act toward the commission thereof, but shall fail therein, or shall be prevented from committing the same, on conviction thereof, shall, where no provision is made by law for the punishment of such offense, be punished as follows: If the offense attempted to be committed be capital, such offense shall be punished by imprisonment in the penitentiary not exceeding ten years; if the offense attempted be punishable by imprisonment in the penitentiary, or by fine and imprisonment in the county jail, then the attempt to commit such offense shall be punished for a period or for an amount not greater than is prescribed for the actual commission of the offense so attempted.

SOURCES: Codes, Hutchinson's 1848, ch. 64, art. 12, Title 8 (3); 1857, ch. 64, art. 20; 1871, § 2809; 1880, § 2713; 1892, § 973; 1906, § 1049; Hemingway's 1917, § 777; 1930, § 793; 1942, § 2017.

Britton Mosley, Sr.

HB1262 (As Sent to Governor) - 1998 Regular S...

MISSISSIPPI LEGISLATURE

1998 Regular Session

To: Penitentiary

By: Representative McInnis

House Bill 1262

(As Sent to Governor)

AN ACT TO AMEND SECTION 47-5-193, MISSISSIPPI CODE OF 1972, TO DELETE PROHIBITIONS AGAINST FURNISHING ANY ALCOHOLIC BEVERAGE, CONTROLLED SUBSTANCE OR NARCOTIC DRUG TO ANY OFFENDER WITHIN THE CUSTODY OF THE DEPARTMENT OF CORRECTIONS, AND TO DELETE PROHIBITIONS AGAINST BRINGING THESE SUBSTANCES ONTO THE PROPERTY OF THE DEPARTMENT OF CORRECTIONS; TO PROVIDE THAT IT SHALL BE UNLAWFUL FOR ANY OFFICER OF ANY COUNTY SHERIFF'S DEPARTMENT OR ANY PRIVATE CORRECTIONAL FACILITY IN THIS STATE IN WHICH OFFENDERS ARE CONFINED TO FURNISH AN OFFENDER WITH ANY WEAPON OR CONTRABAND ITEM; TO AMEND SECTION 47-5-195, MISSISSIPPI CODE OF 1972, TO REVISE THE PENALTIES FOR PROVIDING OFFENDERS WITH ALCOHOL, DRUGS, WEAPONS AND OTHER CONTRABAND ITEMS; TO CREATE A NEW CODE SECTION TO BE CODIFIED AS SECTION 47-5-198, MISSISSIPPI CODE OF 1972, TO PROVIDE THAT IT SHALL BE UNLAWFUL TO SELL OR USE ANY CONTROLLED SUBSTANCE OR NARCOTIC DRUG IN ANY STATE CORRECTIONAL FACILITY, COUNTY JAIL, MUNICIPAL JAIL OR OTHER JAIL AND TO PRESCRIBE A CRIMINAL PENALTY FOR VIOLATION OF THIS LAW; TO AMEND SECTION 97-31-35, MISSISSIPPI CODE OF 1972, TO PRESCRIBE A PENALTY FOR ANY PERSON THAT SELLS OR BRINGS ANY ALCOHOLIC BEVERAGE WITHIN ANY STATE PENITENTIARY, COUNTY JAIL OR MUNICIPAL JAIL; AND FOR RELATED PURPOSES.

BE IT ENACTED BY THE LEGISLATURE OF THE STATE OF MISSISSIPPI:

SECTION 1. Section 47-5-193, Mississippi Code of 1972, is amended as follows:

47-5-193. It is unlawful for any officer or employee of the department, of any county sheriff's department, of any private correctional facility in this state in which offenders are confined or for any other person to furnish, attempt to furnish, or assist in furnishing to any offender confined in this state any * * * weapon, deadly weapon or contraband item. It is unlawful for any person to take, attempt to take, or assist in taking any * * * weapon, deadly weapon or contraband item on property belonging to the department which is occupied or used by offenders, except as authorized by law.

SECTION 2. Section 47-5-195, Mississippi Code of 1972, is amended as follows:

47-5-195. Any person who violates any provision of Section 47-5-193 or 47-5-194 shall be guilty of a felony and upon conviction shall be punished by confinement in the Penitentiary for not less than three (3) years nor more than fifteen (15) years, and may be fined not more than Twenty-five Thousand Dollars ($25,000.00), or both.

SECTION 3. The following shall be codified as Section

47-5-198, Mississippi Code of 1972:

47-5-198. (1) It is unlawful for any person to sell within, bring to, or be in possession of, in any correctional facility or convict camp within the state or any county, municipal or other jail within the state, except as authorized by law, any controlled substance or narcotic drug.

ftp://billstatus.ls.state.ms.us/1998/IIB/1200-1299/HB1262SG.htm   3/27/98

CHAPTER FOUR

The Office of the Attorney General Investigation

The attorney general of Mississippi is the chief legal officer of the state and serves as the state's lawyer. Only the attorney general can bring or defend a lawsuit on behalf of the state.

On August 19, 1997, former 5th District of Mississippi United States Representative Gene Taylor presented compelling evidence to the Office of the Attorney General. Representative Taylor's aide, District Representative Mrs. Jerry Martin (deceased), provided former Attorney General Mike Moore with the evidence (audio tape and documentation), which I had given her so the attorney general could investigate the criminal misconduct (conspiracy) of high-ranking officials at South Mississippi Correctional Facility (SMCI) in Leakesville, Mississippi.

My supervisors and coworkers conspired to plant drugs on me on two separate occasions. Inmates were used in these attempts with the promise of early release from prison for their deeds. All conspirators involved in this allegation were White males. The inmates were Black males. I am a Black male.

Other various documents and witnesses that reinforced the allegations of a conspiracy and cover-up were sent to former Attorney General Mike Moore. The Office of the Attorney General never conducted an official investigation into the allegations. The chief prosecutor of the state of Mississippi will not investigate or prosecute state law enforcement personnel operating under the color of law, but will deny and defend criminal misconduct in a civil lawsuit.

Former Assistant Attorney General Joe Goff and former Corrections Commissioner Chris Epps reviewed and approved all Standard Operation Procedures and/or other directives related to the implementation and enforcement of Mississippi Department of Corrections (MDOC) Policy Number 03.01 General Standard of Professional Conduct ACA Standards 3-4067 (Paragraph 20-23): "Employees shall report any unethical, corrupt, or criminal behaviors (if such employees have knowledge that such behaviors are occurring within the department) in such a manner as to ensure that appropriate corrective action is taken." The Office of the Attorney General looked the other way.

Fabricating Evidence

On May 28, 1998, and after seven years of loyal, upstanding employment, and two drug set-up attempts, I was forced to resign from my position as Correctional Officer-11. I resigned under "Constructive Discharge." I was harassed and feared for my safety and my life.

On June 9, 1998, I filed an Equal Employment Opportunity Commission Charge of Discrimination (retaliation) against the MDOC (EEOC No. 131981361). In a written response to the EEOC, Assistant Attorney General Joe Goff denied charges of discrimination and retaliation.

On October 1, 1998, the U.S. Department of Justice gave me notice of Right to Sue EEOC charge against the State of Mississippi Department of Corrections South Mississippi Correctional Institute (No. 131981361).

On April 12, 1999, MDOC Commissioner S.W. Puckett was given a Notice of Lawsuit that was filed in the United States District Court for the Southern District of Mississippi, docket number 2:98CV357-P-G.

On a personal note, former Attorney General Mike Moore and I were born in Twin Cities in Jackson County, Mississippi four years apart. Mike Moore was born in Pascagoula (1952) and I was born in Moss Point (1948) during the Jim Crow Era, so we lived in two different worlds. The wealthy neighborhood near the then segregated Pascagoula Beach and the Black neighborhood of Jackson Park where I lived were only a few miles apart. However, mutual friendship between their family maid/nanny, the late Pauline Lott, and family friend, the late Ralph (Kay) Hollister, caused our paths to cross many times. Pauline Lott and my sister, Mattie McMillian, were next-door neighbors and best friends. My sister worked as a maid/nanny for several wealthy White families in Mike Moore's neighborhood and she knew him and his family well.

While in high school in the late '60s, on the weekends I worked at the home of Ralph (Kay) Hollister, doing various odd jobs and sometimes babysitting the children. The Hollister children and Mike Moore were friends, and he often attended birthday parties at the Hollister home on weekends. He also attended the wedding of Mr. Hollister's daughter, where he and I interacted. So when former Attorney General Mike Moore started his political career by winning the district attorney for Jackson County, Mississippi, my family members and I worked hard to help get him elected. We all were proud of him. However, One of my biggest regrets in life today is that I voted for Mike Moore.

Governor Phil Bryant has appointed former Attorney General Mike Moore to be one of the five members of a task force to review prison contracts after the indictment of former Corrections Commissioner Christopher Epps.

Fabricating Evidence

GENE TAYLOR
5TH DISTRICT, Mississippi

COMMITTEE ON NATIONAL SECURITY

COMMITTEE ON TRANSPORTATION
AND INFRASTRUCTURE

Congress of the United States
House of Representatives
Washington, DC 20515-2405

2447 RAYBURN BUILDING
WASHINGTON, DC 20515-2405
(202) 225-5772

DISTRICT OFFICES:

2424 14TH ST.
GULFPORT, MS 39501
(601) 864-7670

701 MAIN ST.
SUITE 215
HATTIESBURG, MS 39401
(601) 582-3246

1215 B-GOVERNMENT ST.
OCEAN SPRINGS, MS 39564
(601) 872-7950

August 19, 1997

The Honorable Mike Moore
Attorney General
State of Mississippi
P.O. Box 220
Jackson, MS 39205

RE: BRITTON MOSLEY

State Line, MS 39362

Dear Mike:

Through this means, I am requesting your assistance regarding the above named constituent. Enclosed you will find a copy of the information I received from Mr. Mosley. Please look into this matter and see what can be done to assist him. I will appreciate your attention to this matter at your earliest possible convenience.

If you require any additional information, please contact my District Representative, Mrs. Jerry Martin, in the Hattiesburg Office located at 701 Main Street - Suite 215, Hattiesburg, MS 39401. Otherwise, I will await your reply regarding this matter.

Thanking you in advance for your support, I am

Sincerely yours,

GENE TAYLOR
Member of Congress

GT:jm

Enclosure

CHAPTER 1
Conspiracy, Accessories and Attempts

SEC.
97-1-1. Conspiracy.
97-1-3. Accessories before the fact.
97-1-5. Accessories after the fact.
97-1-6. Directing or causing felony to be committed by person under age of seventeen years.
97-1-7. Attempt to commit offense; punishment.
97-1-9. Attempt to commit offense; no conviction if offense completed.

§ 97-1-1. Conspiracy.

If two (2) or more persons conspire either:

(a) To commit a crime; or

(b) Falsely and maliciously to indict another for a crime, or to procure to be complained of or arrested for a crime; or

(c) Falsely to institute or maintain an action or suit of any kind; or

(d) To cheat and defraud another out of property by any means which are in themselves criminal, or which, if executed, would amount to a cheat, or to obtain money or any other property or thing by false pretense; or

(e) To prevent another from exercising a lawful trade or calling, or doing any other lawful act, by force, threats, intimidation, or by interfering or threatening to interfere with tools, implements, or property belonging to or used by another, or with the use of employment thereof; or

(f) To commit any act injurious to the public health, to public morals, trade or commerce, or for the perversion or obstruction of justice, or of the due administration of the laws; or

(g) To overthrow or violate the laws of this state through force, violence, threats, intimidation, or otherwise; or

(h) To accomplish any unlawful purpose, or a lawful purpose by any unlawful means; such persons, and each of them, shall be guilty of a felony and upon conviction may be punished by a fine of not more than five thousand dollars ($5,000.00) or by imprisonment for not more than five (5) years, or by both.

Provided, that where the crime conspired to be committed is capital murder or murder as defined by law or is a violation of section 41-29-139(b)(1) or section 41-29-139(c)(2)(D), Mississippi Code of 1972, being provisions of the Uniform Controlled Substances Law, the offense shall be punishable by a fine of not more than five hundred thousand dollars ($500,000.00) or by imprisonment for not more than twenty (20) years, or by both.

Fabricating Evidence

MISSISSIPPI DEPARTMENT OF CORRECTIONS POLICY NUMBER 03.01	
GENERAL STANDARDS OF PROFESSIONAL CONDUCT	ACA STANDARDS 3-4067
EFFECTIVE DATE 10-01-97	INITIAL DATE 12-01-82 PAGE 1 OF 2

1 POLICY:

2 It shall be the policy of the Mississippi Department of Corrections
3 (MDOC) that all employees shall conduct themselves, and perform their
4 duties, in a professional manner.

5 DEFINITIONS:

6 None.

7 PRECEPTS:

8 The MDOC Director of Personnel shall develop procedures to ensure that
9 a written code of ethics prohibits employees from using their official
10 position to secure privileges for themselves or others and from engaging
11 in activities that constitute a conflict of interest. This code is
12 available to all employees.

13 This code of ethics manual shall include but not be limited to the
14 following:

15   Employees shall protect the civil and legal rights of all
16   offenders.

17   Employees are expected to conduct themselves in a dignified, honest
18   and professional manner.

19   No employee shall use his official position to secure special
20   advantage for himself, any offender, or any other person(s).

21   No employee shall use his official position to promote any partisan
22   agenda.

23   Employees responsible for personnel actions shall not use their
24   position to hire, appoint, promote, or dismiss any person on the
25   basis of either person's personal or political interest.

26   Information pertaining to offenders and obtained under the color of
27   office shall be considered confidential and shall not be released
28   to anyone not authorized to receive it.

29   Any public statement shall be worded to indicate that the statement
30   is either a personal statement or an official statement made on
31   behalf of the Department.

32   No employee shall accept from or provide to any offender any item
33   not authorized by the MDOC nor shall any employee accept from or
34   provide to any offender any item in a manner not authorized by MDOC.

MISSISSIPPI DEPARTMENT OF CORRECTIONS POLICY NUMBER 03.01
GENERAL STANDARDS OF PROFESSIONAL CONDUCT   ACA STANDARDS 3-4067
EFFECTIVE DATE 10-01-97   INITIAL DATE 12-01-82   PAGE 2 OF 2

1
2   No employee shall accept from or provide to any offender, offender's family, agent, or other representative any gifts or favors.

3   Any employee who becomes aware of any offender with which he has had
4   any previous or existing relationship, whether a kinship
5   relationship (by blood or marriage, adoption, common law) or not;
6   the employee shall immediately report this in writing to his
7   Supervisor/Department Head AND the Superintendent/Community
8   Services Director. The Superintendent/Community Services Director
9   shall immediately report this information in writing to the
10   respective Deputy Commissioners who in turn shall report this
11   information to the Commissioner.

12   No employee shall establish close friendships or fraternize with
13   offenders. The development of any relationship with an offender
14   shall be reported immediately. This reporting shall follow the
15   chain of command listed above.

16   These reports shall include but not be limited to the following:

17   Employee name, social security number, and pin number
18   Employee current work assignment at the time of the report
19   Name of offender, offender number if known, and RELATIONSHIP

20   Employees shall report any unethical, corrupt, or criminal behaviors
21   (if such employees have knowledge that such behaviors are occurring
22   within the department) in such a manner as to ensure that
23   appropriate corrective action is taken.

24   **REPORTS REQUIRED**:

25   As required by this policy and through the chain of command.

ENFORCEMENT AUTHORITY
All SOP's and/or other directive documents related to the implementation and enforcement of this policy shall bear the signature of and be issued under the authority of the Commissioner and the Director of Personnel.
Reviewed and Approved for Issuance   General Counsel   9-3-97   Commissioner   9-4-97

Fabricating Evidence

CHARGE OF DISCRIMINATION

This form is affected by the Privacy Act of 1974; See Privacy Act Statement before completing this form.

AGENCY	CHARGE NUMBER
☐ FEPA	
☒ EEOC	131-98-1361

_____ and EEOC
State or local Agency, if any

NAME (Indicate Mr., Ms., Mrs.): Mr. Britton Mosley, Sr.

STREET ADDRESS | **CITY, STATE AND ZIP CODE**: State Line, MS 39362 | **HOME TELEPHONE** (Include Area Code): _____ | **DATE OF BIRTH**: 09/30/48

NAMED IS THE EMPLOYER, LABOR ORGANIZATION, EMPLOYMENT AGENCY APPRENTICESHIP COMMITTEE, STATE OR LOCAL GOVERNMENT AGENCY WHO DISCRIMINATED AGAINST ME (If more than one list below.)

NAME: South MS Correctional Facility | **NUMBER OF EMPLOYEES, MEMBERS**: Cat C (201-500) | **TELEPHONE** (Include Area Code): (601) 394-5600

STREET ADDRESS: P.O. Box 1419, Leakesville, MS 39451 | **COUNTY**: 041

CAUSE OF DISCRIMINATION BASED ON (Check appropriate box(es)):
☐ RACE ☐ COLOR ☐ SEX ☐ RELIGION ☐ NATIONAL ORIGIN
☒ RETALIATION ☐ AGE ☐ DISABILITY ☐ OTHER (Specify)

DATE DISCRIMINATION TOOK PLACE
EARLIEST: 05/28/98 LATEST: 05/28/98
☐ CONTINUING ACTION

THE PARTICULARS ARE (If additional space is needed, attach extra sheet(s)):

On 5-28-98, I was forced to resign from my position as COII. I had been employed since 9-13-91.

I was forced to quit because one of the employees heard the Superintendent tell a Captain that they needed to get rid of me because I could get them all in trouble.

I believe that I have been discriminated against in retaliation in violation of Title VII of the Civil Rights Act of 1964, as amended, inasmuch as:

My wife has filed an EEOC discrimination charge against the Respondent.

I was harassed and subjected to two drug set ups.

I feared for my safety and life.

I had detailed information about what went on inside the prison.

I had been subpoenaed by one the inmates to testify in a court case.

RECEIVED JUN 9 1998 EEOC/JAO

☐ I want this charge filed with both the EEOC and the State or local Agency, if any. I will advise the agencies if I change my address or telephone number and cooperate fully with them in the processing of my charge in accordance with their procedures.

I declare under penalty of perjury that the foregoing is true and correct.

Date 6/9/98   Britton Mosley, Sr.
Charging Party (Signature)

NOTARY - (When necessary for State and Local Requirements)

I swear or affirm that I have read the above charge and that it is true to the best of my knowledge, information and belief.

SIGNATURE OF COMPLAINANT

SUBSCRIBED AND SWORN TO BEFORE ME THIS DATE (Day, month, and year)

EEOC FORM 5 (Rev. 06/92)   CHARGING PARTY COPY

STATE OF MISSISSIPPI
DEPARTMENT OF CORRECTIONS
JOE GOFF
ASSISTANT ATTORNEY GENERAL

RECEIVED JUN 2 5 1998 EEOC / JAO

June 24, 1998

Ms. Geraldine Kelly
Equal Employment Opportunity Commission
Jackson Area Office
207 West Amite Street
Jackson, Mississippi 39201

Re: Charging Party – Britton Mosley
EEOC #131981361

Dear Ms. Kelly:

Enclosed please find MDOC's response to the above referenced EEOC claim. If you have any questions or comments please do not hesitate to contact me.

Sincerely,

Joe Goff
Assistant Attorney General

JAG/ejc

Enclosure

cc   Denver Glazier
     Personnel Officer IV

723 NORTH PRESIDENT STREET • JACKSON, MISSISSIPPI 39202-3097 • PH: (601) 359-5672

Fabricating Evidence

RESPONSE TO BRITTON MOSLEY
EEOC CHARGE #131981361

RECEIVED JUN 2 5 1998 EEOC / JAO

1. Give the correct name and address of the facility named in the charge.

   Mississippi Department of Corrections, South Mississippi Correctional Institution, P.O. Box 1419, Leakesville, MS. 39451

2. Submit a written position statement on each of the allegations of the charge, accompanied by documentary evidence and/or written statements, where appropriate. Also include any additional information and explanation you deem relevant to the charge.

   On 5/28/98, I was forced to resign from my position as COII.

   Untrue. The charging party voluntarily resigned effective 6/1/98, he was not forced to resign.

   I had been employed since 9/13/91.

   True.

   I was forced to quit because one of the employees heard the Superintendent tell a Captain that they needed to get rid of me because I could get them all in trouble.

   Untrue.

   I believe that I have been discriminated against in retaliation in violation of Title VII of the Civil Rights Act of 1964, as amended, inasmuch as:

   My wife has filed an EEOC discrimination charge against the Respondent.

   Untrue, the charging party has not been discriminated against or retaliated against. It is true the charging party's wife filed a discrimination charge against the Respondent.

   I was harassed and subjected to two drug set ups.

   Untrue.

   I feared for my safety and life.

   The respondent has no way of answering this question as this statement goes to the state of the charging party's mind.

RESPONSE TO BRITTON MOSLEY Page 2
EEOC CHARGE #131981361

I had detailed information about what went on inside the prison.

The respondent has no way of knowing whether this is a true or untrue statement.

I had been subpoenaed by one the inmates to testify in a court case.

The respondent has no way of knowing if this is true or not and even if it is true, the respondent fails to see how this is relevant to the charges levied in this matter.

3. Submit copies of all written rules, policies and procedures relating to the issue(s) raised in the charge. If such does not exist in written form, explain the rules, policies and procedures.

Issue: CONSTRUCTIVE DISCHARGE

The Mississippi Department of Corrections has no rules, policies or procedures regarding constructive discharge and has no such action called "constructive discharge" that can be applied to a employee action. The Department of Corrections follows the policies and procedures of the State Personnel Board as outlined in the Mississippi State Personnel Board Policy and Procedure Manual (Section 9.20.5, Dismissal) that states "The appointing authority may dismiss a permanent state service status employee only for good cause......".

1. Submit information regarding Charging Party's resignation as follows:
   a. date employment was terminated

   June 1, 1998

   b. a detailed statement of the occurrence which led to Charging Party's resignation, to include whether Charging Party was asked to take an early leave of absence, was asked to resign, or voluntarily resigned without any coercion, and

   The respondent has no knowledge of any "occurrence" that led to the charging party's resignation. The respondent never requested the charging party take an early leave of absence, or resign. The charging party voluntarily resigned without any coercion.

Fabricating Evidence

RESPONSE TO BRITTON MOSLEY Page 3
EEOC CHARGE #131981361

    c. what, if any, alternatives were available to charging party other than that which occurred.

        Charging party could have continued his employment with the Mississippi Department of Corrections.

2. Submit a list of all employees asked to resign during the relevant period, by name, and position. Submit the following information for each listed:
   a. date of hire
   b. position held
   c. disciplinary record
   d. the date of request to resign
   e. details of the specific reason(s) for request, and
   f. name, and position of person(s) who requested resignation.

        No individual(s) employed by the Mississippi Department of Corrections and working at the South Mississippi Correctional Institution were asked to resign during the relevant period.

Patrol participated in the cover-up and ignored the compelling evidence presented to them by me. My supervisors and fellow officers conspired to plant drugs on me on two different occasions. Inmates were also used in these attempts with the promise of early release from prison for their deeds. Inmate Marvin Thomas did not want to participate; he agreed instead to wear a "wire" on my behalf to prove wrongdoing by MDOC Staff

All conspirators in this allegation are white males and the inmates are black, and I am a black male. I provided Mr. Moore the taped conversation and transcript between Lt. Louis Kittrell and Inmate Marvin Thomas. Other various documents and witnesses that reinforced the allegations of a conspiracy and cover-up were sent to Attorney General Mike Moore.

Fabricating Evidence

Michael D. Cooke
Attorney At Law

106 Front Street . Post Office Box 625 . Iuka, Mississippi 38852
Tel: (601) 423-2000   Fax: (601) 423-2052

November 4, 1998

Equal Employment Opportunity Commission
Crossroads Building Complex
207 West Amite Street
Jackson, Mississippi 39201

Re: Britton Mosley, Sr.

Dear Madam/Sir:

Please file the enclosed Charge of Discrimination on behalf of the above referenced individual and **immediately issue a Right to Sue.**

This Charge is a supplement to a Charge which Mr. Mosley previously filed (Charge No. 131-98-1361) and in which the Department of Justice issued a Right to Sue on October 1, 1998. Mr. Mosley wishes to incorporate the charge of race discrimination in addition to his charge of retaliation. Upon receipt of the Right to Sue for this latest charge, we will initiate a federal lawsuit.

A self-addressed stamped envelope is enclosed for your use in returning a **copy of the enclosed Charge with a "filed" date stamped thereon** to this office. Please direct or at least copy all future correspondence concerning this claim to this office including a copy of the Right to Sue.

Sincerely yours,

Michael D. Cooke
Michael D. Cooke

MDC/dpd
Enclosure
cc: Mr. Britton Mosley

U.S. Department of Justice

Civil Rights Division

NOTICE OF RIGHT TO SUE
WITHIN 90 DAYS

CERTIFIED MAIL
Z 394 099 476

Washington, DC 20530
October 1, 1998

Mr. Britton Mosley, Sr.

State Line, MS 39362

Re: EEOC Charge Against State of Mississippi, Dept. of Corrections, South Mississippi Correctional Facility
No. 131981361

Dear Mr. Mosley:

Because you filed the above charge with the Equal Employment Opportunity Commission, and the Commission has determined that it will not be able to investigate and conciliate that charge within 180 days of the date the Commission assumed jurisdiction over the charge and the Department has determined that it will not file any lawsuit(s) based thereon within that time, and because you have specifically requested this Notice, you are hereby notified that you have the right to institute a civil action under Title VII of the Civil Rights Act of 1964, as amended, 42 U.S.C. 2000e, et seq., against the above-named respondent.

If you choose to commence a civil action, such suit must be filed in the appropriate Court within 90 days of your receipt of this Notice. If you cannot afford or are unable to retain an attorney to represent you, the Court may, at its discretion, assist you in obtaining an attorney. If you plan to ask the Court to help you find an attorney, you must make this request of the Court in the form and manner it requires. Your request to the Court should be made well before the end of the time period mentioned above. A request for representation does not relieve you of the obligation to file suit within this 90-day period.

The investigative file pertaining to your case is located in the EEOC Jackson Area Office, Jackson, MS.

This Notice should not be taken to mean that the Department of Justice has made a judgment as to whether or not your case is meritorious.

Sincerely,

Karen L. Ferguson
Civil Rights Analyst
Employment Litigation Section

cc: Jackson Area Office, EEOC
State of Mississippi, Dept. of Corrections, South

Fabricating Evidence

Racism tactic is cheap shot, tiring

Concerning the confirmation of U.S. District Judge Charles Pickering, Mississippians of all races and political stripes should feel demeaned and betrayed.

To push the political leaning of the 5th U.S. Circuit Court of Appeals to the left, groups such as People for the American Way and the National Abortion and Reproductive Rights Action League have resorted to the character assassin's bullet of choice, the charge of racism.

These leftist groups find a man from the South and let fly with allegations of complicity with the Klan and ties to various other dens of disgusting bigotry.

If the above were the only facts in this instance, it would be so unfortunately common as to not even be news. But in one of the more shocking and tragic happenings so far this year, the Mississippi NAACP has entered the fray, to its eternal shame and our state's great loss. Its press conference was a vivid display of how far that once-important organization has fallen, resorting now to attacking a man who has done so much for black Mississippians.

The true facts about Judge Pickering have been reprinted hundreds of times, so there's no need to use ink on them here.

The real issue is how you cannot be a conservative white man from the South and expect to enter public life without being branded a racist, however unfair the charge.

It's way past time for Mississippians to forgo these tactics and the politicians, like 2nd District U.S. Rep. Bennie Thompson, who practice them.

Matt Eichelber
Ox

U.S. District Judge Charles Pickering (left) and state Attorney General Mike Moore meet with President Bush last week.

Pickering's pro-life stance real issue

This concerns the nomination of U.S. District Judge Charles Pickering by President Bush to the 5th U.S. Circuit Court of Appeals in New Orleans.

He has been accused of being a racist, at least of being insensitive to civil rights.

I understand that Mississippi Attorney General Mike Moore endorses him and that Charles Evers, the brother of slain civil rights leader Medgar Evers, is very much in favor of the nomination. But you haven't heard the whole story — and this one statement is why so many are Judge Pickering.

He is pro-life.

If you agree with him, please contact our senators at 1-202 224-3121.

Mildred Smith
Quitman

GOP can dish it out, so now take it!

Now that the Democrats are in control of the Senate, when they oppose our president's choice for a federal judge, it is called a lynching.

But when the Republicans were in control, it was OK that they stonewalled President Clinton's judicial appointments.

It seems like a double standard to me. I think that if they can dish it out, they should be able to take it, without crying like a bunch of babies.

Johnny Smith

Thompson no better than Bilbo was

2nd District U.S. Rep. Bennie Thompson's use of lies and half- in the state's Capitol — right next to Sen. Bilbo's in the basement

Ralph Kinne Hollister

Born in Mobile, ALA. on May 8, 1927
Departed on Aug. 29, 2009 and resided in Pascagoula, MS.

Visitation: Tuesday, Sep. 1, 2009
Service: Tuesday, Sep. 1, 2009
Cemetery: Jackson County Memorial Park
Please click on the links above for locations, times, maps, and directions.

Ralph Kinne Hollister, Jr., "K", 82, of Pascagoula, MS, died August 29, 2009 in Ocean Springs, MS. He was born May 8, 1927 in Mobile, AL and was a lifelong resident of Pascagoula. He served in the Merchants Marine in World War II and in the Army in the Korean War. K was a member of the Board of Directors of Pascagoula – Moss Point Bank, and an advisory member of The Jackson County Board for Hancock Bank and was involved in many other community organizations throughout his life. He was a member of Sacred Heart Catholic Church in Pascagoula. K was known for his generosity, although most of his generosity was known by the recipient and him alone. A true gentleman, always putting others first, especially when it came to his family - who was the love and the center of his life. His greatest joy was being surrounded by his wife, children, and grandchildren laughing, joking, dancing, and celebrating life to the fullest in whatever way the spirit led.

He was preceded in death by his parents Ralph Kinne Hollister, Sr. and Hilda Marie Allen Hollister.

He is survived by his wife Claudia Horn Hollister of Pascagoula, MS; daughter and son-in-law Marie and Vincent Castigliola of Pascagoula, MS; son and daughter-in-law R. Huston and Lisa Hollister of Mobile, AL; daughter and son-in-law Claudia "Beedo" and Richard Latady of Fairhope, AL; daughter and son-in-law Caroline and Pat Driver of Pascagoula, MS; daughter and son-in-law Alison and Fred Osing of Ocean Springs, MS. He is also survived by his grandchildren; Elizabeth Latady Zubic and her husband Ethan Zubic, Anne Marie Castigliola, Richard Latady III, Caroline Castigliola, Mary Huston Latady, Vincent Castigliola III, Catherine Lee, Therese Castigliola, Michael Latady, Christman Lee, Huston "Hootie" Hollister, Joseph Driver, Lillian Osing,

Fabricating Evidence

OBITUARIES

LOTT

Pauline Walker Lott, 69, of Pascagoula, Miss., departed this life May 18, 2000, in her home following a lengthy illness. She was born July 15, 1930, in Simpson County, and had been a resident of the Jackson County area for the past 50 years. She was a member of the Greater Antioch Missionary Baptist Church in Pascagoula. She was preceded in death by her parents, Samuel and Lucy Walker; one brother, Mr. Samuel Dennis Walker; one aunt, Ms. Dora Gardner; special friends, Mr. Pete Odom and Mss Willie Mitchell.

She leaves to cherish her memory three sons, Mr. Bill (Denyce) Lott, Tully, N.Y., Mr. Melvin (Willie Rose) Lott, Houston, Texas, Mr. Pete (Barbara) Odom Jr. Pascagoula, Miss.; three daughters, Mrs. Paulette (Ron) Smith, Gautier, Miss., Mrs. Lela (Reginald) Stroud, Crestview Fla., Mrs. Helen (Robert) Hunter, Sanford, Fla.; one sister, Mrs. Martha Ann (M.A.) Miller, Mendenhall, Miss.; one cousin, Mr. Fred (Sarah) Gardner, Clinton Township, Mich., her devoted friends, Johnnie Mae Brister, Janice Sellers, Ms. Betty Collier, Ms. Mattie MacMillian, Mr. and Mrs. Hugh Moore, Mr. Charles Hardin, all of Pascagoula, Mrs. Alice Richardson, Mr. and Mrs. Fred Woods of Moss Point, Miss.; 18 grandchildren and 14 great grandchildren; a host of nieces, nephews and friends.

The family would like to take this opportunity to acknowledge Pauline's other children, Mr. Mike Moore, Mrs. Jane (Jack) Pickett, Mrs. Lisa Ash, Mr. Wilson Moore, and Mrs. Kelly Henning.

Memorial services will be held at the Greater Antioch Missionary Baptist Church in ᵔascagoula on May 29, 2000, at

Britton Mosley, Sr.

MOORE BOWS OUT OF POLITICAL SCENE

■ Won't seek re-election, won't run for governor

By EMILY WAGSTER PETTUS
Associated Press Writer

JACKSON — Democrat Mike Moore reshaped Mississippi's political landscape Tuesday by announcing he will neither run for governor nor seek a fifth term as attorney general.

His decision erases the possibility of a hotly contested Democratic gubernatorial primary with incumbent Ronnie Musgrove.

Moore, a dynamic politician who jokes about his own propensity to seek out news cameras, is nationally known as the first state attorney general to sue tobacco companies in the 1990s.

He acknowledged being ambivalent about his decision to step away from public office and said he is not ruling out future campaigns, including one for the U.S. Senate in a few years.

"I think public service is the highest calling," Moore, 50, said during a news conference in his office overlooking the Capitol. "I have not done this, I think, in a slow trot. I think I have done my public service in a sprint."

Moore said he would enter private law practice, probably in the Jackson area, and spend more time with his wife Tisho and their 16-year-old son, Kyle. He said he does not have any job offers.

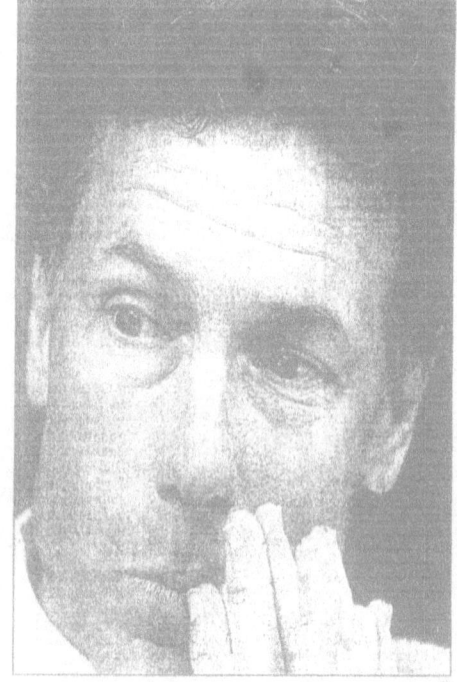

Mike Moore pauses to compose himself Tuesday at a press conference in his office in Jackson.

See MOORE, Page 8-A

Career Highlights

- 1979: Elected Jackson County district attorney at 27, the state's youngest ever. Prosecuted corrupt officials on the Gulf Coast, making statewide headlines.
- 1987: Elected Mississippi attorney general.
- 1989: Runs unsuccessfully for south Mississippi congressional seat after the death of Republican U.S. Rep. Larkin Smith.
- 1991: Wins second term.
- 1992-96: Persuades state lawmakers to create a statewide grand jury to issue drug indictments.
- 1994: Files the first lawsuit against Big Tobacco to recover tax money spent treating sick smokers.
- 1994: Named most outstanding attorney general in the nation.
- 1995: Wins third term.
- 1997: Key player in negotiations for a national tobacco settlement. He helped negotiate a separate $4.1 billion tobacco settlement for Mississippi.
- 1999: Won fourth term.

CHAPTER FIVE

Mississippi Highway Patrol (Criminal Investigation Bureau) Investigation

On September 20, 1999, Sergeant David Oubre (B-47) and Investigator Darrell Perkins from the Mississippi Department of Public Safety Criminal Investigation Bureau interviewed me at the Greene County Sheriff's office. During the interview, I explained to Sergeant Oubre and Investigator Perkins that CO Michael Miller, Captain Johnny Denmark and Lieutenant Victor Brewer conspired to plant marijuana at my desk. However, when the conspiracy was exposed, the Mississippi Department of Corrections fired CO Miller for the *introduction of drugs onto MDOC property* to cover-up the drug possession set-up attempts on me by CO Miller and coworkers at SMCI.

During the interview, Sergeant Oubre stated, "It is unknown if Miller knew there was marijuana in the package and it is unknown why Miller wanted specifically to deliver the package to you," even though my job assignment did not allow me to be inside the gated housing area of SMCI without proper authorization. Sergeant Oubre alleged an attempt to interview CO Miller by contacting his attorney, Keith Miller, in Pascagoula, Mississippi. However, Attorney Miller did not return Sergeant Oubre's call, the former district attorney that dropped the charges against Michael Miller.

Sergeant Oubre and Investigator Perkins interviewed MDOC Sergeant Daniel Paff. CO Miller left the package with the marijuana inside with Sergeant Paff to give to me. Sergeant Paff and I had a conversation as to why CO Miller, a person I didn't even know, would leave a package for me to deliver to an inmate who worked *for him* on a day-to-day work assignment. The reason the drug possession set-up did not work was that I was never alone with the package. CO Harold James assisted me with searching the package. Sergeant Oubre and Investigator Perkins never interviewed CO Harold James, a prime witness.

Also during that interview, I provided a tape-recorded conversation between CO Louis Kittrell and Inmate Marvin Thomas. The discussion on the tape was a plan to have me set up with drugs. The conversation on the tape was clear and compelling. After listen to the tape, Sergeant Oubre and Investigator Perkins alleged they were unable to ascertain what was being said on the tape and who the parties were. However, both parties were identified on the tape. Sergeant Oubre was

Fabricating Evidence

also given names of people of interest in both set-up attempts. Those people were never interviewed in the investigation report.

However, the people interviewed by Sergeant Oubre and Investigator Perkins were chosen by them and were not relevant and had no knowledge of what had transpired. This investigation was a deliberate attempt to minimize the seriousness of the events surrounding my allegations (cover-ups). It was the opinion of Sergeant Oubre and Investigator Perkins that MDOC personnel were not involved in a conspiracy to plant drugs on Britton Mosley, Sr.

This investigation, by the Mississippi Department of Public Safety, was requested by United States District Judge Charles W. Pickering, Sr. My attorney, Michael Cook, advised me that the investigative report was complete. However, Judge Pickering had not previously indicated that he was in receipt of the report. When I asked Attorney Cooke the reason for this, he did not know. As per Attorney Cook, commonly US district judges do not request a state agency to investigate a state agency. However, US District Judge Charles W. Pickering, Sr., made his own rules.

I personally went to Judge Pickering's office inside the Federal Building in Hattiesburg, Mississippi, and received a copy of the investigative report. The evidence produced by the investigation was massive and gave the appearance of a thorough investigation. However, when I reviewed the report, the people of interest I had submitted to Sergeant Oubre and Investigator Perkins *were not interviewed*. The people interviewed did not have any knowledge of the drug set up. The Mississippi Department of Public Safety Criminal Investigation Bureau had conducted a *compromised investigation*. My first emotion was disappointment, but I was not surprised. Historically, the Mississippi Highway Patrol has had political and racial agendas against people of color. The law enforcement personnel that attempted the set-ups were all White males, using Black inmates as perpetrators.

It was alleged that Sergeant Oubre and former Chief Investigator Malcolm McClendon worked together with the Mississippi Highway Patrol before McClendon became Chief Investigator at SMCI. The Mississippi Highway Patrol investigation suggested I contact L. M. Claiborne, Director of Mississippi Highway Patrol/Assistant Commissioner of Public Safety, and the first Black to hold this position. My complaint to Claiborne was that the investigation was a "cover-up." Claiborne told me to file a complaint with Lieutenant Nelson Tate at Mississippi Highway Patrol's main office.

The meeting with Lieutenant Nelson, a Black male, did not go well at all. During the meeting, I'd given Lieutenant Nelson the tape and evidence. However, when he heard the audiotaped conversation between CO Lewis Kittrell and Inmate Marvin Thomas conspiring to plant drugs on me, he stated, "That's those people's lives you are messing with." He had blamed me. At this point, the interview ended and I've never heard from Claiborne and Tate again.

Having Blacks in key positions in Mississippi doesn't really matter. My life didn't matter to Tate. In Mississippi, it's the same pie but a different crust.

During my youth, the all-White Mississippi Highway Patrol (state troopers) was the elite law enforcement agency in the state. The state troopers have the power to arrest for any crime committed in their presence statewide. The front license plates on their automobiles displayed the rebel flag. The MHP also maintains a Special Operations Group (SOG) that responds to civil disturbances, prison uprisings at MDOC. The opinion of the Mississippi Department of Public Safety Investigation was very disappointing, yet, not surprised knowing the history of this agency.

Highway Patrol guilty of racial discrimination

ABERDEEN, Miss. (AP) — A federal jury has ruled that State Trooper Dennis Erby was the victim of racial discrimination and awarded him $150,000 in damages.

The seven-member biracial jury on Wednesday sided with Erby and against the Mississippi Highway Patrol. The verdict followed a three-day trial.

Erby alleged that he was denied a promotion to troop commander in 1997 and 1998 because he is black. He said the patrol retaliated after he filing a complaint with the Equal Employment Opportunity Commission.

The jury found the patrol had not wrongly discriminated against Erby in 1997, but found race was a factor in the 1998 promotion denial.

The jury's damage award was based how much money the MHP should pay Erby to make up for the income and career opportunities that were lost due to the agency's actions.

Say you saw it in
THE MISSISSIPPI PRESS

Fabricating Evidence

November 29, 1999

Michael D. Cooke
Attorney at Law
106 Front Street
Post Office Box 625
Iuka, Mississippi 38852

Dear Mr. Cooke:

Enclosed are copies of the investigative reports submitted by M/Sgt. David Oubre, B-47.

Please be advised that the detailed account of the interview conducted with Sgt. Paff and myself were omitted. I feel it was a deliberate act to try and minimize the seriousness of the events surrounding my allegations. Please note that M/Sgt. Oubre and co-conspiritor Malcolm McLendeon worked together for years with the MHP before McLendon retired in 1987. Investigator McLendon informed Sgt. Oubre that CO Harold James assisted me with the search of the package on Nov. 4, 1996, but in the investigative report that McLendon submitted he stated that Sgt. Paff assisted me. Sgt. Oubre was given a list of names of people to interview; he only interviewed Sgt. Paff and myself.

Sincerely,

Britton Mosley, Sr.

Britton Mosley, Sr.

Britton Mosley, Sr.

MISSISSIPPI DEPARTMENT OF PUBLIC SAFETY
CRIMINAL INVESTIGATION BUREAU
POST OFFICE BOX 958
JACKSON, MISSISSIPPI 39205

PAGE: 01
CASE NO.: B-1215-99

On September 20, 1999, at 2:25 p.m., Investigator Darrell Perkins and I interviewed Britton Mosley at the Greene County Sheriff's Office. (See enclosed tape). In this interview, Mosley alleged that a correctional officer (CO) named Michael Miller attempted to have Mosley deliver a package containing marijuana to an inmate named Mandall Walker. As a result of Mosley searching the package, finding the marijuana, and notifying his superiors, Mosley was clear of any wrongdoing. However, Miller was fired from MDOC and indicted for introduction of drugs onto MDOC property by the Greene County Grand Jury, May term 1998. (Copy enclosed)

On the morning September 21, 1999, this investigator made an attempt to interview Michael Miller by contacting his attorney, Keith Miller, in Pascagoula, Mississippi. I left a message at this law office for Attorney Miller to return my call. The call has not been returned and I do not anticipate Attorney Miller allowing me to talk to his client.

On September 22, 1999, at 9:55 a.m., Investigator Darrell Perkins and I interviewed CO Sgt. Daniel Paff at the MDOC facility in Leakesville (see enclosed tape). Mosley stated that Sgt. Paff was the CO that Miller left the package with for Mosley to deliver. The CO that assisted Britton Mosley with the search of the package on November 4, 1996, was Harold James. I was informed by MDOC Chief Investigator Malcolm McClendon that James had left MDOC employment on April 28, 1998.

During the September 20, 1999, interview with Mosley, he provided a tape that he alleged was a conversation between CO Louis Kittrell and inmate Marvin Thomas. Mosley said the discussion on the tape was a plan to have Mosley set up with drugs. After listening to the tape, Investigator Perkins and I were unable to ascertain what was being said and who the parties were. It was in July 1997 when Britton Mosley claimed he placed a tape recorder on inmate Marvin Thomas to record Louis Kittrell. Shortly after this incident on July 25, 1997, Mosley started major medical leave until his resignation on June 1, 1998.

It is unknown if CO Michael Miller knew there was marijuana in the package and it is unknown why Miller wanted Mosley specifically to deliver the package. Mosley was not charged by MDOC because he did the proper procedure by searching the package with a witness present and notifying his supervisor.

Britton Mosley has signed affidavits on eleven employees at the MDOC facility in Leakesville for conspiracy to set him up with drugs. (Copies enclosed) Mosley presented his case to the Greene County Grand Jury on September 22, 1999. Enclosed is a letter from the U.S. Justice Department which states that the FBI investigation revealed no criminal civil rights violation and this case would not be prosecuted.

It is the opinion of this investigator that MDOC personnel were not involved in a conspiracy to plant drugs on Britton Mosley.

David Oubre B-47
REPORTING OFFICER, BADGE NUMBER
M/Sgt. David Oubre, B-47

This document contains neither recommendations nor conclusions of the CIB. It is the property of the CIB and is loaned to your agency. This document nor its contents are to be distributed outside this agency.

Fabricating Evidence

Michael D. Cooke
Attorney At Law

106 Front Street . Post Office Box 625 . Iuka, Mississippi 38852
Tel: (662) 423-2000   Fax: (662) 423-2052

November 5, 1999

Honorable Charles W. Pickering, Sr.
United States District Judge
701 North Main St., Suite 228
Hattiesburg, MS 39401

RE: *Mosley v. MDOC*
      US District Court No. 2:98CV357PG

Dear Judge Pickering:

I talked with Joe Goff on Tuesday, November 2, 1999 concerning the investigation into the above matter which you requested. My understanding was that the Mississippi Department of Public Safety would be back in touch with me after a report was completed, but I have never heard from anyone.

I have purposefully held off beginning discovery until I could see a copy of any investigative report. I now understand that you have a copy of a report in your file.

I respectfully request a copy of the investigative report be provided to me and to counsel opposite. I certainly need to review that before I can determine what discovery will be necessary on behalf of the Plaintiff.

Thank you for your attention to this correspondence.

Respectfully yours,

Michael D. Cooke

MDC/dpd
Enclosure
cc: Mr. Britton Mosley

Michael D. Cooke
Attorney At Law

106 Front Street . Post Office Box 625 . Iuka, Mississippi 38852
Tel: (662) 423-2000   Fax: (662) 423-2052

November 5, 1999

Mr. Britton Mosley
Post Office Box 390
State Line, Mississippi 39362

Re: Mosley v. MDOC

Dear Britt:

I talked with Joe Goff on Tuesday, November 2, 1999. He advised me that the investigative report is complete. However, Judge Pickering had not previously indicated that he was in receipt of the report. The reason for this, I do not know.

As you can see, I have requested a copy of the report from Judge Pickering. Once I receive same, I will provide you with a copy of same. Hopefully we can then start the discovery process within the next few weeks.

Sincerely yours,

Michael D. Cooke

MDC/dpd
Enclosure

Fabricating Evidence

Michael D. Cooke
Attorney At Law

106 Front Street . Post Office Box 625 . Iuka, Mississippi 38852
Tel: (662) 423-2000   Fax: (662) 423-2052

December 20, 1999

Mr. Britt Mosley
Post Office Box 390
State Line, Mississippi 39362

Re: *Mosley v. MDOC*

Dear Britt:

I am writing due to repeated calls you have made to the office regarding the investigatory papers which you obtained and provided to me. I know you are concerned about your case, as I am.

I simply have not had the time over the past few weeks to review those documents. I will try to review them soon, but it could be another month. If that doesn't please you and you feel I am not able to get to it in time, you are certainly welcome to employ someone else. I am not trying to disregard your case, I just simply have had a lot of deadlines and I can't get to the review of the documents.

I would ask you to not call as much as you have been. All that does is delay Deb and puts more work on her. I know that is not your intention, but when Deb can't get things out, it puts more work back on me and then I am delayed.

If there are specific items you think need to be in the report that are missing, please write me and tell me what those are. I will note those when I go through the report. Don't get too detailed. Think of the big issues and not every little issue. I don't think I can go to the Judge with 10 items that aren't in there, but I certainly can go to him with two or three or four.

Sincerely yours,

Michael D. Cooke

MDC/dpd

Michael D. Cooke
Attorney At Law

106 Front Street . Post Office Box 625 . Iuka, Mississippi 38852
Tel: (662) 423-2000   Fax: (662) 423-2052

February 10, 2000

Mr. Britton Mosley
P.O. Box 390
State Line, MS 39362

Re: Mosley v. MDOC

Dear Mr. Mosley:

I have read and re-reviewed the Mississippi Department of Public Safety report that you sent to me the first of December. After review of the report, realizing that you say that there are some major items not contained in the report, I am very concerned about our chances of success in this case.

First, let me say that Judge Pickering is going to take the position after reading this report that this is a lot of smoke and no fire.

Secondly, I am concerned about how we are going to prove these allegations. Not a single person that was interviewed has indicated that there was any conspiracy to set up anyone with drugs at the MDOC Correctional Facility in Greene County.

Upon receipt of this letter please contact me by telephone so that we may discuss this. We are at a juncture in this lawsuit that I need to be taking depositions. However, I have some serious reservations about expending large sums of money on depositions and other discovery when I don't see any way to prevail in this matter. I am sorry to be so candid with you in this letter, but I think you need to know my feelings without them being sugar coated.

I shall await your call.

Sincerely yours,

Michael D. Cooke

MDC/bmz

Britton Mosley, Sr.

MISSISSIPPI DEPARTMENT OF PUBLIC SAFETY
CRIMINAL INVESTIGATIVE DIVISION
P. O. BOX 958
JACKSON, MISSISSIPPI 39205

CASE NO. __B-1184-99__

OFFENSE __GENERAL INVEST.__ COUNTY __GREENE__ LOCATION _____
DATE OF REPORT _____ INVEST. NAME AND BADGE _____
OFFICERS I.D. NO. _____ REQ. AGENCY _____
DATE AND TIME OF CRIME _____ OTHER OFFICERS NAME(S) _____

VICTIM'S NAME (LAST, FIRST, MIDDLE) _____ NO ___ OF ___
RACE ___ SEX ___ HEIGHT ___ WEIGHT ___ HAIR ___ EYES ___ DATE OF BIRTH ___
VICTIM'S ADDRESS _____ CITY _____ STATE ___ ZIP ___
FIRM NAME _____ TYPE OF FIRM _____ ADDRESS _____
DESCRIBE WEAPON, INSTRUMENT, EQUIPMENT, DEVICE OR FORCE USED _____

SUSPECT VEHICLE USED: COLOR ___ YEAR ___ MAKE ___ MODEL ___
LICENSE # ___ VIN # ___ OTHER IDENTIFIERS ___
ESTIMATED LOSS VALUE IN DOLLARS ___ VALUE OF PROPERTY RECOVERED ___
PHOTOS TAKEN ___ BY WHOM ___
PRINTS LIFTED ___ BY WHOM ___

PERSONAL HISTORY INFORMATION SHEET ARRESTEE ___ SUSPECT ___ JUVENILE ___ NO ___ OF ___
NAME __GARY LEE FREEMAN__ AKA'S __GARY__
ADDRESS _____ CITY __MCLAIN__ STATE __MS__ ZIP __39456__
DATE OF BIRTH __09-08-49__ PLACE OF BIRTH—CITY __LEAF__ STATE __MS__ SSN ___
TELEPHONE _____ RACE __W__ SEX __M__ HEIGHT ___ WEIGHT ___ HAIR ___ EYES ___
GLASSES ___ IF YES, EXPLAIN _____
SPOUSE _____ ADDRESS _____ NO. OF CHILDREN ___
CAUTION ___ IF YES, EXPLAIN _____
ARRESTEE ARMED ___ IF YES, TYPE OF WEAPON(S) _____
SERIAL # _____ NCIC CHECK ___ HIT ___
BUILD ___ HANDEDNESS ___ SHOE SIZE ___ SKIN TONE ___
OCCUPATION __CORRECTIONAL OFFICER II__ EMPLOYER NAME __MS. DEPARTMENT OF CORRECTIONS__
ADDRESS __HWY. 63__ CITY __LEAKESVILLE__ STATE __MS__ ZIP __39451__
TELEPHONE _____ LENGTH OF EMPLOYMENT __5 YEARS__ EDUCATION YEARS ___
OTHER SSN OR DOB USED _____ D.L.# _____ STATE __MS__
S/MIT _____

This document contains neither recommendations nor conclusions of the CIB. It is the property of the CIB and is loaned to your agency. This document nor its contents are to be distributed outside this agency.
ID-74 (1-89)

Fabricating Evidence

MISSISSIPPI DEPARTMENT OF PUBLIC SAFETY
CRIMINAL INVESTIGATION BUREAU
JACKSON, MISSISSIPPI 39205

SUPPLEMENTAL

PAGE 01

CASE NO. B-1184-99

ON MONDAY SEPTEMBER 20, 1999 AT APPROXIMATELY 0915 HOURS MASTER SERGEANT JIMMY HERZOG AND THIS WRITER ARRIVED AT THE MISSISSIPPI DEPARTMENT OF CORRECTIONS LOCATED ON HIGHWAY 63 IN LEAKESVILLE,MS. UPON ARRIVAL HERZOG AND THIS WRITER SPOKE BRIEFLY WITH CHIEF INVESTIGATOR MALCOLM MCCLENDON. MCCLENDON THEN ASSISTED HERZOG AND THIS WRITER IN LOCATING NECOL MCCANN. MCCANN WAS ADVISED BY THIS WRITER OF AN INVESTIGATION INTO ALLEGED"DRUG SET UPS" AT THE MISSISSIPPI DEPARTMENT OF CORRECTIONS IN GREENE COUNTY. MCCANN SUBMITTED TO AN INTERVIEW WHICH WAS TAPED. SEE TAPE DATED 09-20-99 INTERVIEW WITH NECOL MCCANN. SHORTLY AFTER MCCANN'S INTERVIEW WAS COMPLETED HERZOG AND THIS WRITER MET WITH GARY FREEMAN. FREEMAN WAS ADVISED BY THIS WRITER OF AN INVESTIGATION INTO ALLEGED "DRUG SET UPS" AT THE MISSISSIPPI DEPARTMENT OF CORRECTIONS IN GREENE COUNTY. FREEMAN SUBMITTED TO AN INTERVIEW WHICH WAS TAPED. SEE TAPE DATED 09-20-99 INTERVIEW WITH GARY FREEMAN. INVESTIGATION CONTINUES.

REPORTING OFFICER, BADGE

This document contains neither recommendations nor conclusions of the CIB. It is the property of the CIB and is loaned to your agency. This document nor its contents are to be distributed outside this agency

Britton Mosley, Sr.

MISSISSIPPI DEPARTMENT OF PUBLIC SAFETY
CRIMINAL INVESTIGATIVE DIVISION
P. O. BOX 958
JACKSON, MISSISSIPPI 39205

CASE NO._____ B-1184-99

OFFENSE GENERAL INVEST. COUNTY GREENE LOCATION_____
DATE OF REPORT_____ INVEST. NAME AND BADGE_____
OFFICERS I.D. NO._____ REQ. AGENCY_____
DATE AND TIME OF CRIME_____ OTHER OFFICERS NAME(S)_____

VICTIM'S NAME (LAST, FIRST, MIDDLE)_____ NO.___ OF___
RACE___ SEX___ HEIGHT___ WEIGHT___ HAIR___ EYES___ DATE OF BIRTH___
VICTIM'S ADDRESS_____ CITY_____ STATE___ ZIP___
FIRM NAME_____ TYPE OF FIRM_____ ADDRESS_____
DESCRIBE WEAPON, INSTRUMENT, EQUIPMENT, DEVICE OR FORCE USED_____

SUSPECT VEHICLE USED: COLOR_____ YEAR_____ MAKE_____ MODEL_____
LICENSE #_____ VIN #_____ OTHER IDENTIFIERS_____
ESTIMATED LOSS VALUE IN DOLLARS_____ VALUE OF PROPERTY RECOVERED_____
PHOTOS TAKEN ___ BY WHOM_____
PRINTS LIFTED ___ BY WHOM_____

PERSONAL HISTORY INFORMATION SHEET ARRESTEE___ SUSPECT___ JUVENILE___ NO.___ OF___
NAME DON ERICK LEWIS AKA'S_____
ADDRESS:_____ CITY WAYNESBORO STATE MS ZIP 39367
DATE OF BIRTH 02-26-59 PLACE OF BIRTH—CITY WAYNESBORO STATE MS SSN_____
TELEPHONE_____ RACE M SEX F HEIGHT 601 WEIGHT 212 HAIR BLK EYES BRO
GLASSES ___ IF YES, EXPLAIN_____
SPOUSE_____ ADDRESS_____ NO. OF CHILDREN___
CAUTION ___ IF YES, EXPLAIN_____
ARRESTEE ARMED ___ IF YES, TYPE OF WEAPON(S)_____
SERIAL #_____ NCIC CHECK ___ HIT ___
BUILD_____ HANDEDNESS_____ SHOE SIZE_____ SKIN TONE_____
OCCUPATION CORRECTIONAL ADMIN. II EMPLOYER NAME MS.DEPARTMENT OF CORRECTIONS
ADDRESS HIGHWAY 63 CITY LEAKESVILLE STATE MS ZIP___
TELEPHONE_____ LENGTH OF EMPLOYMENT_____ EDUCATION YEARS___
OTHER SSN OR DOB USED_____ D.L.#_____ STATE MS
S/MIT_____

This document contains neither recommendations nor conclusions of the CIB. It is the property of the CIB and is loaned to your agency. This document nor its contents are to be distributed outside this agency.
ID-74 (1-89)

Fabricating Evidence

MISSISSIPPI DEPARTMENT OF PUBLIC SAFETY
CRIMINAL INVESTIGATION BUREAU
JACKSON, MISSISSIPPI 39205

SUPPLEMENTAL

PAGE 01

CASE NO. B-1184-99

ON FRIDAY SEPTEMBER 17, 1999 AT APRROXIMATELY 0900 HOURS THIS WRITER ARRIVED AT THE WAYNE COUNTY SHERIFF'S DEPARTMENT LOCATED IN WAYNESBORO, MISSISSIPPI AND MET WITH DON LEWIS. LEWIS WAS ADVISED OF AN INVESTIGATION INTO ALLEGED "DRUG SET UPS" AT THE MISSISSIPPI DEPARTMENT OF CORRECTIONS. LEWIS WAS ASKED TO BE INTERVIEWED IN REFERENCE TO THESE ALLEGATIONS. LEWIS SUBMITTED TO AN INTERVIEW. SEE TAPE DATED 09-17-99. INTERVIEW WITH DON LEWIS. INVESTIGATION CONTINUES.

[signed] Jim Stone B17
REPORTING OFFICER, BADGE

This document contains neither recommendations nor conclusions of the CIB It is the property of the CIB and is loaned to your agency.
This document nor its contents are to be distributed outside this agency.
ID-74
(19-87)

Britton Mosley, Sr.

MISSISSIPPI DEPARTMENT OF PUBLIC SAFETY
CRIMINAL INVESTIGATIVE DIVISION
P. O. BOX 958
JACKSON, MISSISSIPPI 39205

CASE NO. _____ B-1184-99
OFFENSE GENERAL INVEST.   COUNTY GREENE _____ LOCATION: _____
DATE OF REPORT _____ INVEST. NAME AND BADGE _____
OFFICERS I.D. NO. _____ REQ. AGENCY _____
DATE AND TIME OF CRIME _____ OTHER OFFICERS NAME(S) _____

VICTIM'S NAME (LAST, FIRST, MIDDLE) _____ NO ___ OF ___
RACE ___ SEX ___ HEIGHT ___ WEIGHT ___ HAIR ___ EYES ___ DATE OF BIRTH ___
VICTIM'S ADDRESS _____ CITY _____ STATE ___ ZIP ___
FIRM NAME _____ TYPE OF FIRM _____ ADDRESS _____
DESCRIBE WEAPON, INSTRUMENT, EQUIPMENT, DEVICE OR FORCE USED _____

SUSPECT VEHICLE USED: COLOR _____ YEAR _____ MAKE _____ MODEL _____
LICENSE # _____ VIN # _____ OTHER IDENTIFIERS _____
ESTIMATED LOSS VALUE IN DOLLARS _____ VALUE OF PROPERTY RECOVERED _____
PHOTOS TAKEN ___ BY WHOM _____
PRINTS LIFTED ___ BY WHOM _____

PERSONAL HISTORY INFORMATION SHEET ARRESTEE ___ SUSPECT ___ JUVENILE ___ NO. ___ OF ___
NAME JOHN MELTON FANCHER _____ AKA'S _____
ADDRESS _____ CITY COLUMBIA _____ STATE MS ZIP 39429
DATE OF BIRTH 12-11-49 PLACE OF BIRTH—CITY GREENWOOD _____ STATE MS SSN _____
TELEPHONE _____ RACE W SEX M HEIGHT _____ WEIGHT _____ HAIR ___ EYES ___
GLASSES ___ IF YES, EXPLAIN _____
SPOUSE _____ ADDRESS _____ NO. OF CHILDREN ___
CAUTION ___ IF YES, EXPLAIN _____
ARRESTEE ARMED ___ IF YES, TYPE OF WEAPON(S) _____
SERIAL # _____ NCIC CHECK ___ HIT ___
BUILD _____ HANDEDNESS _____ SHOE SIZE _____ SKIN TONE _____
OCCUPATION _____ EMPLOYER NAME _____
ADDRESS _____ CITY _____ STATE ___ ZIP ___
TELEPHONE _____ LENGTH OF EMPLOYMENT _____ EDUCATION YEARS ___
OTHER SSN OR DOB USED _____ D.L # _____ STATE MS
S/MIT _____

This document contains neither recommendations nor conclusions of the CIB. It is the property of the CIB and is loaned to your agency. This document nor its contents are to be distributed outside this agency.
ID-74 (1 -89)

Fabricating Evidence

MISSISSIPPI DEPARTMENT OF PUBLIC SAFETY
CRIMINAL INVESTIGATION BUREAU
JACKSON, MISSISSIPPI 39205

SUPPLEMENTAL

PAGE _____01_____

CASE NO. _____B-1184-99_____

ON THURSDAY SEPTEMBER 16, 1999 MASTER SERGEANT DAVID OUBRE AND THIS WRITER ARRIVED AT THE MARION AND WALTHALL REGIONAL CORRECTIONAL FACILITY AT APPROXIMATELY 0956 HOURS TO INTERVIEW JAMES MELTON FANCHER. FANCHER WAS ADVISED OF AN INVESTIGATION INTO ALLEDGED "DRUG SET UPS" AT THE MISSISSIPPI DEPARTMENT OF CORRECTIONS LOCATED IN LEAKESVILLE,MS. FANCHER WAS ASKED IF HE WOULD SUBMIT TO AN INTERVIEW REGARDING THIS MATTER. FANCHER SUBMITTED TO A TAPED INTERVIEW. SEE TAPE DATED 09-16-99 INTERVIEW WITH JIMMY FANCHER. INVESTIGATION CONTINUES.

_____Jim Stone B17_____
REPORTING OFFICER, BADGE

This document contains neither recommendations nor conclusions of the CIB. It is the property of the CIB and is loaned to your agency. This document nor its contents are to be distributed outside this agency

Britton Mosley, Sr.

MISSISSIPPI DEPARTMENT OF PUBLIC SAFETY
CRIMINAL INVESTIGATIVE DIVISION
P. O. BOX 958
JACKSON, MISSISSIPPI 39205

CASE NO. _____ B-1184-99 _____

OFFENSE <u>GENERAL INVEST.</u> COUNTY <u>GREENE</u> LOCATION <u>GREENE CO. CORRECTIONAL FACILITY</u>
DATE OF REPORT <u>09-15-99</u> INVEST. NAME AND BADGE <u>LT. JIM STONE B17</u>
OFFICERS I.D. NO. <u>470</u> REQ. AGENCY <u>MS. HIGHWAY PATROL</u>
DATE AND TIME OF CRIME <u>JULY98/JANUARY 99</u> OTHER OFFICERS NAME(S) <u>M/SGT DAVID OUBRE B47</u>
<u>M/SGT DARRELL PERKINS B37</u>
VICTIM'S NAME (LAST, FIRST, MIDDLE)_____ NO ___ OF ___
RACE ___ SEX ___ HEIGHT ___ WEIGHT ___ HAIR ___ EYES ___ DATE OF BIRTH ___
VICTIM'S ADDRESS _____ CITY _____ STATE ___ ZIP ___
FIRM NAME _____ TYPE OF FIRM _____ ADDRESS _____
DESCRIBE WEAPON, INSTRUMENT, EQUIPMENT, DEVICE OR FORCE USED _____

SUSPECT VEHICLE USED: COLOR ___ YEAR ___ MAKE ___ MODEL ___
LICENSE # ___ VIN # ___ OTHER IDENTIFIERS ___
ESTIMATED LOSS VALUE IN DOLLARS ___ VALUE OF PROPERTY RECOVERED ___
PHOTOS TAKEN ___ BY WHOM ___
PRINTS LIFTED ___ BY WHOM ___
PERSONAL HISTORY INFORMATION SHEET ARRESTEE ___ SUSPECT ___ JUVENILE ___ NO. ___ OF ___
NAME <u>TERESA GRAHAM UPSHAW</u> AKA'S <u>TERESA GRAHAM</u>
ADDRESS _____ CITY <u>STATE LINE</u> STATE <u>MS</u> ZIP <u>39362</u>
DATE OF BIRTH <u>09-11-59</u> PLACE OF BIRTH—CITY <u>HATTIESBURG</u> STATE <u>MS</u> SSN ___
TELEPHONE ___ RACE <u>W</u> SEX <u>F</u> HEIGHT <u>503</u> WEIGHT <u>105</u> HAIR <u>BRO</u> EYES <u>BRO</u>
GLASSES <u>Y</u> IF YES, EXPLAIN <u>READING</u>
SPOUSE <u>JOHN CLARK</u> ADDRESS <u>SAME AS ABOVE</u> NO. OF CHILDREN <u>02</u>
CAUTION ___ IF YES, EXPLAIN ___
ARRESTEE ARMED ___ IF YES, TYPE OF WEAPON(S) ___
SERIAL # ___ NCIC CHECK ___ HIT ___
BUILD ___ HANDEDNESS ___ SHOE SIZE ___ SKIN TONE ___
OCCUPATION ___ EMPLOYER NAME ___
ADDRESS ___ CITY ___ STATE ___ ZIP ___
TELEPHONE ___ LENGTH OF EMPLOYMENT ___ EDUCATION YEARS ___
OTHER SSN OR DOB USED ___ D.L.# ___ STATE <u>MS</u>
MIT ___

This document contains neither recommendations nor conclusions of the CIB. It is the property of the CIB and is loaned to your agency. This document nor its contents are to be distributed outside this agency.
-74 (1-89)

Fabricating Evidence

MISSISSIPPI DEPARTMENT OF PUBLIC SAFETY
CRIMINAL INVESTIGATIVE DIVISION
P. O. BOX 958
JACKSON, MISSISSIPPI 39205

UBJECT VEHICLE: COLOR_____ YEAR _____ MAKE_____ MODEL_____
ICENSE #_____ VIN #_____ OTHER IDENTIFIERS _____
EH. DISP. _____
RRESTING OFFICER _____ BADGE AND I.D.# _____ AGENCY _____
RREST DATE _____ ARREST TIME _____ LOCATION _____
UG SHOTS TAKEN ____ BY WHOM _____
NGERPRINTS TAKEN ____ BY WHOM _____
BI NO. _____ MSP NO. _____
HARGE NO. 1 _____ CHARGE NO. 2 _____
HARGE NO. 3 _____ CHARGE NO. 4 _____
ESCRIPTION OF EVIDENCE: _____

ESCRIPTION OF PROPERTY STOLEN: _____

SE STATUS: INVESTIGATION CONTINUES.

NOPSIS:
TERESA GRAHAM UPSHAW FILED A COMPLAINT IN THE UNITED STATES DISTRICT COURT FOR THE
OUTHERN DISTRICT OF MISSISSIPPI HATTIESBURG DIVISON. TERESA INDICATED IN HER COMPLAINT SHE
LIEVED THAT DRUGS WOULD BE PLANTED UPON HER AS A RESULT OF HER FILING A COMPLAINT WITH THE
UAL EMPLOYMENT OPPORTUNITY COMMISSION WHILE EMPLOYED WITH THE MISSISSIPPI DEPARTMENT OF
RRECTIONS IN GREENE COUNTY.

Jim Stone 817 470
OFFICERS SIGNATURE, BADGE, AND I.D. NO.

DIST JES_____ DATE TYPED 09-21-99

Britton Mosley, Sr.

MISSISSIPPI DEPARTMENT OF PUBLIC SAFETY
CRIMINAL INVESTIGATION BUREAU
JACKSON, MISSISSIPPI 39205

SUPPLEMENTAL

PAGE 01

CASE NO. B-1184-99

ON WEDNESDAY SEPTEMBER 15, 1999 MASTER SERGEANT DAVID OUBRE AND THIS WRITER ARRIVED IN WAYNESBORO, MISSISSIPPI AND INTERVIEWED TERESA GRAHAM UPSHAW. TERESA WAS INTERVIEWED REGARDING THE COMPLAINT FILED IN THE UNITED STATES DISTRICT COURT FOR THE SOUTHERN DISTRICT OF MISSISSIPPI HATTIESBURG DIVISION. IN TERESA'S COMPLAINT, UNDER ROMAN NUMERAL VI. TERESA BELIEVED AFTER SHE HAD FILED HER EQUAL EMPLOYMENT OPPORTUNITY COMMISSION COMPLAINT, THIS CAUSED HER TO BELIEVE THAT DRUGS WOULD BE PLANTED UPON HER. DURING THE INTERVIEW WITH TERESA, SHE ADMITTED, THAT SHE HAS NO PERSONAL KNOWLEDGE OF ANYONE ATTEMPTING TO SET HER UP WITH DRUGS NOR HAS SHE SEEN ANYONE PLANT DRUGS ON AN EMPLOYEE. TERESA STATED THAT SHE BECAME CONCERNED ABOUT BEING SET UP AFTER HER CONVERSATIONS WITH CAPTAIN JIMMY FANCHER AND CORRECTIONAL OFFICER LOYD JAMES ODOM. TERESA STATED AFTER HER CONVERSATION WITH FANCHER AND ODOM SHE DID NOT FILE A COMPLAINT WITH THE ADMINISTRATION OR INVESTIGATORS REGARDING HER CONCERNS, ABOUT BEING SET UP. TERESA STATED AFTER HER CONVERSATION WITH FANCHER AND ODOM SHE CONTINUED TO WORK FOR THE MISSISSIPPI DEPARTMENT OF CORRECTIONS UNTIL JANUARY 01,1999.

THIS INVESTIGATION HAS REVEALED THERE IS INSIGNIFICANT EVIDENCE TO CONTINUE WITH A CRIMINAL INVESTIGATION INTO THE ALLEGED "DRUG SET UPS" AT THE MISSISSIPPI DEPARTMENT OF CORRECTIONS IN GREENE COUNTY. HOWEVER, IT IS THE OPINION OF THIS WRITER, THE MISSISSIPPI DEPARTMENT OF CORRECTIONS IN GREENE COUNTY SHOULD CONSIDER PLACING INDIVIDUAL LOCK BOXES, TO BE LOCATED, AT THE ENTRY POINT(S) TO THE COMPOUND WHERE EMPLOYEES ARE REQUIRED TO LEAVE THEIR KEYS UPON REPORTING TO WORK. THESE LOCK BOXES WOULD ENSURE THE SECURITY OF THE EMPLOYEES KEYS AND REMOVE THE OPPORTUNITY FOR THE KEYS TO BE TAKEN WITHOUT THE EMPLOYEES AUTHORIZATION.

REPORTING OFFICER, BADGE

This document contains neither recommendations nor conclusions of the CIB. It is the property of the CIB and is loaned to your agency. This document nor its contents are to be distributed outside this agency.

ID-74
(12-87)

Fabricating Evidence

MISSISSIPPI DEPARTMENT OF PUBLIC SAFETY
CRIMINAL INVESTIGATIVE DIVISION
P. O. BOX 958
JACKSON, MISSISSIPPI 39205

CASE NO. _____ B-1184-99 _____
OFFENSE GENERAL INVEST. COUNTY GREENE LOCATION _____
DATE OF REPORT _____ INVEST. NAME AND BADGE _____
OFFICERS I.D. NO. _____ REQ. AGENCY _____
DATE AND TIME OF CRIME _____ OTHER OFFICERS NAME(S) _____

VICTIM'S NAME (LAST, FIRST, MIDDLE) _____ NO ___ OF ___
RACE ___ SEX ___ HEIGHT ___ WEIGHT ___ HAIR ___ EYES ___ DATE OF BIRTH ___
VICTIM'S ADDRESS _____ CITY _____ STATE ___ ZIP ___
FIRM NAME _____ TYPE OF FIRM _____ ADDRESS _____
DESCRIBE WEAPON, INSTRUMENT, EQUIPMENT, DEVICE OR FORCE USED _____

SUSPECT VEHICLE USED: COLOR _____ YEAR _____ MAKE _____ MODEL _____
LICENSE # _____ VIN # _____ OTHER IDENTIFIERS _____
ESTIMATED LOSS VALUE IN DOLLARS _____ VALUE OF PROPERTY RECOVERED _____
PHOTOS TAKEN ___ BY WHOM _____
PRINTS LIFTED ___ BY WHOM _____
PERSONAL HISTORY INFORMATION SHEET ARRESTEE ___ SUSPECT ___ JUVENILE ___ NO. ___ OF ___
NAME NECOL MCCANN AKA'S NIKKI
ADDRESS _____ CITY LEAKESVILLE STATE MS ZIP 39451
DATE OF BIRTH 10-30-71 PLACE OF BIRTH—CITY LEAKESVILLE STATE MS SSN _____
TELEPHONE _____ RACE B SEX F HEIGHT ___ WEIGHT ___ HAIR ___ EYES ___
GLASSES ___ IF YES, EXPLAIN _____
SPOUSE _____ ADDRESS _____ NO. OF CHILDREN ___
CAUTION ___ IF YES, EXPLAIN _____
ARRESTEE ARMED ___ IF YES, TYPE OF WEAPON(S) _____
SERIAL # _____ NCIC CHECK ___ HIT ___
BUILD _____ HANDEDNESS _____ SHOE SIZE _____ SKIN TONE _____
OCCUPATION CORRECTIONAL OFFICER II EMPLOYER NAME MS. DEPARTMENT OF CORRECTIONS
ADDRESS HWY. 63 CITY LEAKESVILLE STATE MS ZIP 39451
TELEPHONE _____ LENGTH OF EMPLOYMENT 4 1/2 YEARS EDUCATION YEARS _____
OTHER SSN OR DOB USED _____ D.L # _____ STATE MS
S/MIT _____

This document contains neither recommendations nor conclusions of the CIB. It is the property of the CIB and is loaned to your agency. This document nor its contents are to be distributed outside this agency.
ID-74 (1-89)

MISSISSIPPI DEPARTMENT OF PUBLIC SAFETY
CRIMINAL INVESTIGATION BUREAU
JACKSON, MISSISSIPPI 39205

SUPPLEMENTAL

PAGE 01

CASE NO. B-1184-99

ON MONDAY SEPTEMBER 20, 1999 AT APPROXIMATELY 0915 HOURS MASTER SERGEANT JIMMY HERZOG AND THIS WRITER ARRIVED AT THE MISSISSIPPI DEPARTMENT OF CORRECTIONS LOCATED ON HIGHWAY 63 IN LEAKESVILLE,MS. UPON ARRIVAL HERZOG AND THIS WRITER SPOKE BRIEFLY WITH CHIEF INVESTIGATOR MALCOLM MCCLENDON. MCCLENDON THEN ASSISTED HERZOG AND THIS WRITER IN LOCATING NECOL MCCANN. MCCANN WAS ADVISED BY THIS WRITER OF AN INVESTIGATION INTO ALLEGED"DRUG SET UPS" AT THE MISSISSIPPI DEPARTMENT OF CORRECTIONS IN GREENE COUNTY. MCCANN SUBMITTED TO AN INTERVIEW WHICH WAS TAPED. SEE TAPE DATED 09-20-99 INTERVIEW WITH NECOL MCCANN. SHORTLY AFTER MCCANN'S INTERVIEW WAS COMPLETED HERZOG AND THIS WRITER MET WITH GARY FREEMAN. FREEMAN WAS ADVISED BY THIS WRITER OF AN INVESTIGATION INTO ALLEGED "DRUG SET UPS" AT THE MISSISSIPPI DEPARTMENT OF CORRECTIONS IN GREENE COUNTY. FREEMAN SUBMITTED TO AN INTERVIEW WHICH WAS TAPED. SEE TAPE DATED 09-20-99 INTERVIEW WITH GARY FREEMAN. INVESTIGATION CONTINUES.

REPORTING OFFICER, BADGE

This document contains neither recommendations nor conclusions of the CIB. It is the property of the CIB and is loaned to your agency. This document nor its contents are to be distributed outside this agency.

CHAPTER SIX

Congressional Inquiry

On August 19, 1997, I requested assistance from United States Congressmen Gene Taylor for a congressional inquiry to the Offices of the Attorney General in Washington, DC and Mississippi. During the meeting with Congressman Taylor and District Representative Jerry Martin (deceased), compelling evidence (audio tape and documents) was given to her. District Representative Martin also gave my file and the evidence to US District Judge Charles W. Pickering, Sr., whose office was across the hall from Congressman Taylor's office. Evidence was also sent to former US Attorney General Janet Reno and former Mississippi Attorney General Mike Moore. Former Attorney General Janet Reno was responsive to Congressman Taylor's request. However, former Mississippi Attorney General Mike Moore never responded to the congressman's request. Attorney General Moore was the attorney for the Mississippi Department of Corrections and defended the agency in civil and criminal

misconduct by MDOC staff members. So, his lack of response was not surprising.

Although SMCI had spread rumors that I had brought drugs into the facility, I am the one who requested the inquiry, not SMCI.

On a personal note, I'd like to extend my sincere gratitude toward Congressman Taylor and District Representative Jerry Martin (now deceased) for working tirelessly on my behalf to ensure all compelling evidence was properly compiled and hand delivered by Mrs. Martin to the office of Judge W. Pickering.

This whole process and trying to prove my case has been trying, to say the least, and has taken its toll on me, but I am appreciative that Congressman Taylor and District Representative Martin believed in me, believed in my claim, and worked with me.

TO: Congressman Gene Taylor

From: COII Britton and Brenda Mosley

Date: August 18, 1997

RE: Your assistant is needed as our Congressman.

Congressman Taylor, enclosed you will find vital documentation in a conspiracy to set-up COII Britton Mosley with drugs by MDOC Staff. We contacted the US Justice Department on July 28 in Jackson, MS. We talked with US attorney Carlton Reeves and Jack Lacey. We have not been talked to by FBI agents to this date. We are in serious need of your help. We would like for you to please get this information to the Justice Department and the Attorney General of Mississippi as well as, the US attorney General.

Britton Mosley
Brenda Mosley

TO: THE UNITED STATES JUSTICE DEPARTMENT
CIVIL RIGHTS DIVISION

FROM: CO-II BRITTON MOSLEY, SMCI, MDOC

DATE: ~~JULY~~ August 15, 1996

RE: TWO ATTEMPTED DOPE SET-UP CONSPIRACIES BY MDOC STAFF

THIS FACTUAL SUMMERY IS AN INFORMATIVE OF CONSPIRACIES PLANNED BY MDOC STAFF TO SET-UP CORRECTIONAL OFFICER II BRITTON MOSLEY. BOTH ATTEMPTED AND PLANNED SET-UPS OF DOPE BY MDOC STAFF ARE IN RELALLIATION FOR MY WIFE, CORRECTIONAL OFFICER II BRENDA MOSLEY, FILING CHARGES WITH THE EEOC AND SUING IN FEDERAL COURT FOR DISCRIMINATION AND RETALIATION.

THE FIRST ATTEMPT *(SEE ATTACHMENT A; INCIDENT REPORT)* WAS ON NOVEMBER 4, 1996. MY WIFE WAS OUT ON MEDICAL LEAVE FOR STRESS AND DEPRESSION WHEN SHE FILED RETALIATION CHARGES ON MDOC WITH THE EEOC. SHE HAD ALREADY RECEIVED HER RIGHT-TO-SUE FROM HER INITIAL CHARGES OF DISCRIMINATION FROM THE EEOC. RECORDS WITH THE EEOC WILL SHOW THAT WHEN THE FIRST ATTEMPT TO SET ME UP WITH DOPE USING OFFICER MICHAEL MILLER, HER SECOND CHARGES WAS ON FILE TO BE ANSWERED BY MDOC. THE ONLY THING THAT HAS BEEN DONE TO OFFICER MILLER, TO THIS DATE, IS THAT HE WAS ALLOWED TO RESIGN. I FILED A COMPLAINT WITH THE MDOC AND THE JUSTICE DEPARTMENT.

THE SECOND ATTEMPTED PLANNED CONSPIRACY OF DOPE SET-UP IS ALSO IN RETALIATION OF FURTHER CHARGES OF DISCRIMINATION FILED WITH THE EEOC BY MY WIFE. THESE CHARGES OF DISCRIMINATION AND RETALIATION ARE PENDING AN ANSWER FROM MDOC AND THE PREVIOUS TWO COUNTS ARE ON FILE IN FEDERAL COURT.

IN MID-JULY 1997, INMATE MARVIN THOMAS, 79517, APPROACHED ME AND INFORMED ME THAT HE WAS ASSIGNED TO WORK AT THE MAINTENANCE DEPARTMENT, WHERE I'M ASSIGNED, TO SET ME UP WITH DOPE. THAT MR. MCLENDON, CHIEF INVESTIGATOR, MR. . DAVID TURNER, SUPERINTENDENT, AND OFFICER LOUIS KITTRELL WANTED HIM TO SET ME UP WITH

DOPE. HE TOLD ME THAT HE WAS UNABLE TO CARRY OUT THE
PLANS BECAUSE HE KNEW I WAS A CLEAN OFFICER, EVEN THOU,
THEY PROMISED HIM THAT THEY WOULD GET HIM OUT OF
PRISON. I KNEW THAT IF IT HAD NOT BEEN THIS TIME, THAT IT
WOULD BE ATTEMPTED AGAIN. I HAD TRIED ALL AVENUES ON
THE FIRST ATTEMPT AND NOTHING WAS DONE . I KNEW I HAD TO
DO SOMETHING ON MY OWN. I ASKED INMATE THOMAS IF HE
WOULD WEAR A TAPE RECORDER AND RECORD THEIR
CONVERSATION WHEN OFFICER KITTRELL CAME BACK TO THE
MAINTENANCE COMPLEX. INMATE THOMAS AGREED. I HAD TO
GET PROOF THAT THESE THINGS WERE DELIBERATE ATTEMPTS
OF DRUG SET-UPS BY MDOC STAFF AND THAT I WAS NOT A DIRTY
OFFICER.

ON JULY 25, 1997, INMATE THOMAS APPROACHED ME AT MY
ASSIGNED DUTY POST AND INFORMED ME THAT OFFICER
KITTRELL WAS BEHIND THE MAINTENANCE COMPLEX ON WORK
DETAIL. OFFICER KITTRELL WAS WITH OFFICER DANNY
WOODARD AND 25-35 COMMON LABOR INMATES. INMATE
THOMAS THEN TOOK THE TAPE RECORDER, PUT IT UNDER HIS
SHIRT INSIDE A BACK BRACE HE WAS WEARING, EXITED OUT
THE BACK OF THE BUILDING AND CALLED TO OFFICER KITTRELL.
*(SEE ATTACHMENT B; TRANSCRIBED INFORMATION AND
CONVERSATION SHEET AND SEE ATTACHMENT C; TAPE OF THE
RECORDED CONVERSTATION)*. AT THIS TIME, I CALLED OFFICER
NECOLE PEARSON WHO WAS WORKING TOWER 4 THAT OVER
LOOKS THE BACK OF THE MAINTENANCE COMPLEX, AND ASKED
HER TO WRITE A REPORT OF WHAT SHE SAW GOING ON IN THE
BACK OF BUILDING AT THE FENCE. *(SEE ATTACHMENT D; HAND
WRITTEN REPORT)*.

IN SUMMERY, IF EITHER ONE OF THESE ATTEMPTS HAD BEEN
FINALIZED AS PLANNED, I WOULD HAVE BEEN IMMEDIATELY
FIRED, INDITED FOR DRUG DISTRIBUTION ON STATE PROPERTY
AND SENT TO PRISON. THIS WOULD HAVE DESTROYED MY
CREDIBILITY, PUT MY FAMILY TO SHAME AND QUESTIONED MY
WIFE CREDIBILITY WITH HER CHARGES AND SUIT. THEY WOULD
HAVE MOST LIKELY BEEN ABLE TO USE THIS A BARGAINING TOOL
FOR HER TO DROP CHARGES. THIS IS A SERIOUS CRIMINAL
VIOLATION OF MY CIVIL RIGHTS. PLEASE NOTE THAT ALL
PARTICIPANTS ARE WHITE, I'M A BLACK MAN. RECORDS WILL
SHOW THAT BEFORE THIS AND UP TO NOW, I HAVE AN
UNBLEMISHED WORK RECORD. I HAVE HAD TO LEAVE MY JOB
UNDER MAJOR MEDICAL FOR STRESS AND DEPRESSION. I WAS
TRAINED TO MAINTAIN SECURITY OF THE INMATE PRISON
POPULATION, BUT NOT TRAINED TO MAINTAIN SECURITY OF THE

CORRUPTION OF MDOC STAFF. AT LEASE NOT TO THE POINT OF SITTING UP STAFF MEMBERS AND COMMITING CRIMINAL ACTS.

MDOC, DOES IT MEAN THE MISSISSIPPI DEPARTMENT OF CORRECTION OR *THE MISSISSIPPI DEPARTMENT OF CORRUPTION?* USING AN INMATE, ESPECIALLY A CONVICTED DRUG FELON, TO COMMIT A CRIME IN PRISON IS NOT REHABILITATING OR CORRECTING THIS OFFENDER, BUT FURTHER CORRUPTING HIM. THIS IS ALSO PUTTING CORRUPTION WITHIN THE MDOC STAFF.

Fabricating Evidence

DATE: 8/18/97

TO: Honorable Gene Taylor
U.S. House of Representatives
2447 Rayburn Building
Washington, D. C. 20515

FROM: **Britton Mosley** (Name)

P.O. Box 390 (Address)

State Line, MS **39362**
(City)   (Zip Code)

Tel. No.(s). _____ _____
             (Home)   (Work)

SUBJECT: Public Law 93-579 -- The "Privacy Act of 1974"

    I, the undersigned, hereby waive any and all rights and requirements of The Privacy Act of 1974 as they pertain to me, and hereby grant authority to Congressman Gene Taylor, and/or his Congressional staff, to request and obtain any and all information pertaining to my file(s).

    On the reverse side of this form is a complete written description of my problem concerning _____.
(Department or agency involved in case)

    The following case/file numbers are provided:

Social Security _____ V.A. _____

Civil Service _____ Other _____

Britton Mosley
Signature of Constitutient
Date: 8/18/97

Britton Mosley, Sr.

GENE TAYLOR
5TH DISTRICT, MISSISSIPPI

COMMITTEE ON NATIONAL SECURITY

COMMITTEE ON TRANSPORTATION
AND INFRASTRUCTURE

Congress of the United States
House of Representatives
Washington, DC 20515-2405

2447 RAYBURN ...
WASHINGTON, DC 20515-2405
(202) 225-5772

DISTRICT OFFICES:
2424 14TH ST.
GULFPORT, MS 39501
(601) 864-7670

701 MAIN ST.
SUITE 215
HATTIESBURG, MS 39401
(601) 582-3246

1215 B-GOVERNMENT ST.
OCEAN SPRINGS, MS 39564
(601) 872-7950

August 19, 1997

The Honorable Janet Reno
Attorney General
U.S. Department of Justice
Tenth Street and Constitution Avenue, NW
Washington, DC 20530

RE: BRITTON MOSLEY
P.O. Box 390
State Line, MS 39362

Dear Janet:

Through this means, I am requesting your assistance regarding the above named constituent. Enclosed you will find a copy of the information I received from Mr. Mosley. Please look into this matter and see what can be done to assist him. I will appreciate your attention to this matter at your earliest possible convenience.

If you require any additional information, please contact my District Representative, Mrs. Jerry Martin, in the Hattiesburg Office located at 701 Main Street - Suite 215, Hattiesburg, MS 39401. Otherwise, I will await your reply regarding this matter.

Thanking you in advance for your support, I am

Sincerely yours,

GENE TAYLOR
Member of Congress

GT:jm

Enclosure

Fabricating Evidence

GENE TAYLOR
5TH DISTRICT, MISSISSIPPI

COMMITTEE ON NATIONAL SECURITY

COMMITTEE ON TRANSPORTATION
AND INFRASTRUCTURE

Congress of the United States
House of Representatives
Washington, DC 20515-2405

2447 RAYBURN BUILDING
WASHINGTON, DC 20515-240
(202) 225-5771

DISTRICT OFFICES:
2424 14TH ST
GULFPORT, MS 39501
(601) 864-7670

701 MAIN ST
SUITE 215
HATTIESBURG, MS 39401
(601) 582-3246

1216 B GOVERNMENT ST
OCEAN SPRINGS, MS 39564
(601) 872-7950

August 19, 1997

The Honorable Mike Moore
Attorney General
State of Mississippi
P.O. Box 220
Jackson, MS 39205

RE: BRITTON MOSLEY
P.O. Box 390
State Line, MS 39362

Dear Mike:

    Through this means, I am requesting your assistance regarding the above named constituent. Enclosed you will find a copy of the information I received from Mr. Mosley. Please look into this matter and see what can be done to assist him. I will appreciate your attention to this matter at your earliest possible convenience.

    If you require any additional information, please contact my District Representative, Mrs. Jerry Martin, in the Hattiesburg Office located at 701 Main Street - Suite 215, Hattiesburg, MS 39401. Otherwise, I will await your reply regarding this matter.

    Thanking you in advance for your support, I am

Sincerely yours,

GENE TAYLOR
Member of Congress

GT:jm

Enclosure

Britton Mosley, Sr.

GENE TAYLOR
5TH DISTRICT, MISSISSIPPI

COMMITTEE ON NATIONAL SECURITY

COMMITTEE ON TRANSPORTATION
AND INFRASTRUCTURE

Congress of the United States
House of Representatives
Washington, DC 20515-2405

2311 RAYBURN BUILDING
WASHINGTON, DC 20515-2
(202) 225-5772

DISTRICT OFFICES:
2424 14TH ST.
GULFPORT, MS 39501
(228) 864-7670

701 MAIN ST.
SUITE 215
HATTIESBURG, MS 39401
(601) 582-3246

1216 B-GOVERNMENT ST.
OCEAN SPRINGS, MS 39564
(228) 872-7950

August 17, 1999

Britt Mosley
P.O. Box 390
State Line, Mississippi 39362

Dear Britt:

    I have copied your file and have given it to Judge Pickering. They felt that the tape was not of good quality so they plan to enhance the quality through your attorney.

    Meanwhile, if you have any questions or further information that would be helpful, please contact my District Representative, Mrs. Jerry Martin, in the Hattiesburg District Office located at 701 Main Street, Suite 215, Hattiesburg, MS 39401 or call 1-800-273-4363 (582-3246).

                                    Sincerely yours,

                                      GENE TAYLOR
                                      Member of Congress

GT:jm

Fabricating Evidence

GENE TAYLOR
5TH DISTRICT, MISSISSIPPI

COMMITTEE ON NATIONAL SECURITY

COMMITTEE ON TRANSPORTATION
AND INFRASTRUCTURE

Congress of the United States
House of Representatives
Washington, DC 20515-2405

2447 RAYBURN BUILDING
WASHINGTON, DC 20515-2406
(202) 225-5772

DISTRICT OFFICES:
2424 14TH ST.
GULFPORT, MS 39501
(601) 864-7670

701 MAIN ST.
SUITE 215
HATTIESBURG, MS 39401
(601) 582-3246

1215 B-GOVERNMENT ST.
OCEAN SPRINGS, MS 39564
(601) 872-7950

August 19, 1997

Britton Mosley
P.O. Box 390
State Line, Mississippi 39362

Dear Britton:

    I have made a congressional inquiry to the Attorney General's Office in Washington, DC and Mississippi. I will continue to monitor the situation with great interest. Enclosed you will find a copy of the correspondence that was sent on your behalf.

    Meanwhile, if you have any questions or further information that would be helpful, please contact my District Representative, Mrs. Jerry Martin, in my Hattiesburg District Office located at 701 Main Street, Suite 215, Hattiesburg, MS 39401 or call 1-800-273-4363 (582-3246).

Sincerely yours,

GENE TAYLOR
Member of Congress

GT:jm

Enclosures (2)

Britton Mosley, Sr.

GENE TAYLOR
5TH DISTRICT, MISSISSIPPI

COMMITTEE ON NATIONAL SECURITY
COMMITTEE ON TRANSPORTATION
AND INFRASTRUCTURE

Congress of the United States
House of Representatives
Washington, DC 20515-2405

2311 RAYBURN BUILDING
WASHINGTON, DC 20515-2405
(202) 225-5772

DISTRICT OFFICES:
2424 14TH ST.
GULFPORT, MS 39501
(228) 864-7670

701 MAIN ST.
SUITE 215
HATTIESBURG, MS 39401
(601) 582-3246

1215 B-GOVERNMENT ST.
OCEAN SPRINGS, MS 39564
(228) 872-7950

July 25, 2000

Britton Mosley
P.O. Box 390
State Line, MS 39362

Dear Britton:

    I have made a congressional inquiry to the U.S. Department of Justice and will continue to monitor this situation with great interest. Enclosed you will find a copy of the correspondence that was sent. As soon as I receive a reply, I will contact you.

    Meanwhile, if you have any questions or further information that would be helpful, please contact my District Representative, Mrs. Jerry Martin, in the Hattiesburg Office located at 701 Main Street – Suite 215, Hattiesburg, MS 39401 or call 1-800-273-4363 (582-3246).

                                         Sincerely yours,

                                           GENE TAYLOR
                                           Member of Congress

GT:jm

Enclosure

Fabricating Evidence

U.S. Department of Justice

Civil Rights Division

Office of the Assistant Attorney General   Washington, D.C. 20035

MAR 30 1998

The Honorable Gene Taylor
Member, U.S. House of Representatives
701 Main Street, Suite 215
Hattiesburg, MS 39401

Dear Congressman Taylor:

    This is a response to your letter dated August 19, 1997, in which you forwarded a complaint from your constituent, Britton Mosley. Mr. Mosley alleges that the Mississippi Department of Corrections conspired to plant drugs on him in retaliation for filing an EEOC discrimination charge. We apologize for the delay of this response.

    The Federal Bureau of Investigation has been requested to conduct an investigation into this matter. You can be assured that if the evidence shows that there was a prosecutable violation of federal criminal civil rights statutes, appropriate action will be taken.

    Thank you for bringing this matter to our attention.

Sincerely,

Bill Lann Lee
Acting Assistant Attorney General
Civil Rights Division

Britton Mosley, Sr.

P.O. Box 390
State Line, MS 39362

The Honorable Bill Lann Lee
Assistant Attorney of Justice
U.S. Department of Justice
Tenth Street and Constitution Avenue, NW
Washington, DC 20530

Re: File Number: 144-41-3177/2000-0369 (4234)

    Unidentified members of the Mississippi Department of Corrections-Subjects;

    Britton Mosley- Victims Civil Rights

Dear Mr. Lee:

    Through this means, I am requesting your assistance regarding civil rights violation (18 U.S.C. 241) and cover-up by officials of the Mississippi Department of Corrections. Enclosed, please find the Civil Right Divisions documents I received from the Freedom of Information Privacy Act Branch. Also enclosed are documents and evidence that were given to assistant U.S. Attorney General Jack Lacey, FBI Special Agent Lenton Rice, and FBI Special Agent Randall Neidecker.

    This detailed information was omitted from the documents I received from the Freedom of Information Privacy act Branch. Also evidence was provided by Congressman Gene Taylor's office and presented to Federal Judge Charles Pickering to substantiate the allegations of conspiracy and cover-up. Judge Pickering ordered the Mississippi Highway Patrol to investigate the allegations of conspiracy. On September 20, 1999 Master Sergeant David Oubre, B47 and Investigation Darrell Perkins interviewed me at the Greene County Sheriff's Office. All of the detailed information and evidence was given to Sergeant Oubre and Investigator Perkins. Enclosed please find Sergeant Oubre's investigation report. Sergeant Oubre omitted interviews with Mississippi Department of Corrections Officials and inmate.

    Please note it is alleged that the FBI Special Agent Lenton Rice and Mississippi Highway Patrol Sergeant David Oubre and co-conspirator MDOC Chief Investigator Malcolm McClendon worked for several years together with the Mississippi Highway Patrol before retired. Mr. Lee, my family, and I have been living in fear for the last 3 ½ years. Please help us exercise our XIV Amendment Right (nor deny any person within its jurisdiction the equal protection of the laws). Dear Sir please re-open my case file 144-41-314 base on the information and evidence that is provided to you by this writer. Additional information can be provided at your request.

Thanking you in advance for your support.

Sincerely Yours,

Britton Mosley, Sr.

Britton Mosley Sr.
Correction Captain
Marion/Wathall Correctional Facility

Fabricating Evidence

U. S. Department of Justice

Civil Rights Division

Office of the Assistant Attorney General   Washington, D.C. 20530

SEP 5 2000

The Honorable Gene Taylor
Member, U.S. House of Representatives
701 Main Street
Suite 215
Hattiesburg, Mississippi 39401

Dear Congressman Taylor:

    This is in response to your letter, dated July 25, 2000, forwarding correspondence from your constituent, Britton Mosely, Sr. Mr. Mosley requested that we re-evaluate evidence pertaining to his allegations that members of the Mississippi Department of Corrections conspired to violate his civil rights. We apologize for the delay in responding.

    As you know, the Criminal Section of the Civil Rights Division is responsible for enforcing specific federal criminal civil rights statutes. Indeed, those statutes require that we prove beyond a reasonable doubt a willful deprivation of a federally protected right.

    In response to Mr. Mosely's request, we have carefully reviewed the additional material he provided in support of his claim. However, it is our determination that the totality of the evidence does not present a prosecutable violation of federal criminal civil rights statutes. Therefore, we are unable to authorize additional investigation of this matter.

    We regret that we cannot be of further assistance to your constituent. Please do not hesitate to contact the Department if we can be of assistance in other matters.

Sincerely,

Bill Lann Lee
Assistant Attorney General
Civil Rights Division

U.S. Department of Justice
Civil Rights Division
Washington, D.C. 20530

Britton Mosley, Sr.
P.O. Box 390
State Line, MS 39362
601-848-7447

March 5, 2000

Mr. John M. Mott:

Under the Freedom of Information Act, please send me the investigative report DJ 144-41-3144, submitted by the Federal Bureau of Investigation. All reports containing information on Federal Civil Rights violations allegedly committed by officials of the Mississippi Department of Corrections.

Thank you,

Britton Mosley, Sr.

Britton Mosley, Sr.

Fabricating Evidence

To: U.S. Department of Justice;
        Co-Director of the Office of Information and Privacy

From: Britton Mosley, Sr.

Date: October 5, 2000

Re: Freedom of Information Appeal: FOIPA No. 925633

To whom it may concern,
    This letter is a letter of appeal to request any additional information from previous requests. I am requesting any additional information that has recently been sent to the U.S. Justice Department's Bill Lann Lee, Assistant Attorney General of the Civil Rights Division; NDH:SC 144-41-3144. Please send me a copy's of the interview that was conducted by FBI Agents Lent Rice and Randall Neidecker with the individuals on the attached copy of alleged conspirators and witnesses and other information that has been included. Thank you for your prompt consideration and attention to this matter.

                                  Sincerely,

                                  Britton Mosley, Sr.

U.S. Department of Justice

Office of Information and Privacy

Telephone: (202) 514-3642   Washington, D.C. 20530

Sep - 3 2002

Mr. Britton Mosley, Sr.
Post Office Box 390
State Line, MS 39362

Re: Appeal No. 01-0215
FBI No. 925633
RLH:ADW:BVE

Dear Mr. Mosley:

You appealed from the action of the Headquarters Office of the Federal Bureau of Investigation on documents referred to it by the Civil Rights Division pursuant to your request for access to records concerning you.

After carefully considering your appeal, I have decided to affirm the FBI's action on your request.

These records are exempt from the access provision of the Privacy Act of 1974 pursuant to 5 U.S.C. § 552a(j)(2). See 28 C.F.R. § 16.96 (2001). Because these records are not available to you under the Privacy Act, your request has been reviewed under the Freedom of Information Act in order to afford you the greatest possible access to the records you requested.

The FBI properly withheld certain information that is protected from disclosure pursuant to:

5 U.S.C. § 552(b)(2), which concerns matters that are related solely to internal agency practices; and

5 U.S.C. § 552(b)(7)(C), which concerns records or information compiled for law enforcement purposes, the release of which could reasonably be expected to constitute an unwarranted invasion of the personal privacy of third parties (including, in this instance, persons of investigative interest to the FBI and the names of FBI Special Agents and employees).

I have determined that this information is not appropriate for discretionary release.

Fabricating Evidence

Mississippi Department of Corrections

CONFIDENTIAL

REPORT OF INTERVIEW
Internal Audit Division

LENT RICE, Special Agent, FBI, formerly assigned to the Pascagoula Office of the FBI and now assigned to the Oxford Office, telephone (601) 234-1713, contacted Internal Audit Division (IAD) on October 23, 1997, relating to Britton Mosley, Correctional Officer, South Mississippi Correctional Institution (SMCI), Leakesville, MS.

Rice was recently contacted by the U. S. Attorney's Office, Biloxi, MS, as a result of a letter Mosley wrote to U. S. Attorney General Janet Reno, alleging a conspiracy against him by Mississippi Department of Corrections (MDOC) employees. The U. S. Attorney's office was aware of at least two prior contacts Rice had with Mosley in which he had leveled conspiracy allegations against MDOC employees. In other instances, Rice had found the allegations by Mosley as being baseless. Mosley also provided a copy of a tape cassette that was supposed to reflect basis for his allegations, however, Rice with the assistance of FBI sound experts was unable to find any basis to support his allegations.

After Rice discussed the above facts with the U.S. Attorney's Office, they indicated they would recommend no further action with regard to Mosley's allegations.

MGH/lr
97-SMCI-10

DATE OF INTERVIEW: October 23, 1997	FILE NUMBER: 97-SMCI-10
INTERVIEWER: M. Gene Hill	PLACE OF INTERVIEW: Telephonically conducted

OFFICIAL USE ONLY
MDOC INTERNAL AUDIT DIVISION

This report is the property of the Mississippi Department of Corrections.
Neither it, nor its contents may be disseminated outside the agency to which it is loaned.

Britton Mosley, Sr.

U. S. Department of Justice

Civil Rights Division

Office of the Assistant Attorney General *Washington, D.C. 20530*

SEP 5 2000

The Honorable Gene Taylor
Member, U.S. House of Representatives
701 Main Street
Suite 215
Hattiesburg, Mississippi 39401

Dear Congressman Taylor:

    This is in response to your letter, dated July 25, 2000, forwarding correspondence from your constituent, Britton Mosely, Sr. Mr. Mosley requested that we re-evaluate evidence pertaining to his allegations that members of the Mississippi Department of Corrections conspired to violate his civil rights. We apologize for the delay in responding.

    As you know, the Criminal Section of the Civil Rights Division is responsible for enforcing specific federal criminal civil rights statutes. Indeed, those statutes require that we prove beyond a reasonable doubt a willful deprivation of a federally protected right.

    In response to Mr. Mosely's request, we have carefully reviewed the additional material he provided in support of his claim. However, it is our determination that the totality of the evidence does not present a prosecutable violation of federal criminal civil rights statutes. Therefore, we are unable to authorize additional investigation of this matter.

    We regret that we cannot be of further assistance to your constituent. Please do not hesitate to contact the Department if we can be of assistance in other matters.

Sincerely,

Bill Lann Lee
Assistant Attorney General
Civil Rights Division

Fabricating Evidence

P.O. Box 390
State Line, MS 39362

The Honorable Bill Lann Lee
Assistant Attorney of Justice
U.S. Department of Justice
Tenth Street and Constitution Avenue, NW
Washington, DC 20530

Re: File Number: 144-41-3177/2000-0369 (4234)

Unidentified members of the Mississippi Department of Corrections-Subjects;

Britton Mosley- Victims Civil Rights

Dear Mr. Lee:

Through this means, I am requesting your assistance regarding civil rights violation (18 U.S.C. 241) and cover-up by officials of the Mississippi Department of Corrections. Enclosed, please find the Civil Right Divisions documents I received from the Freedom of Information Privacy Act Branch. Also enclosed are documents and evidence that were given to assistant U.S. Attorney General Jack Lacey, FBI Special Agent Lenton Rice, and FBI Special Agent Randall Neidecker.

This detailed information was omitted from the documents I received from the Freedom of Information Privacy act Branch. Also evidence was provided by Congressman Gene Taylor's office and presented to Federal Judge Charles Pickering to substantiate the allegations of conspiracy and cover-up. Judge Pickering ordered the Mississippi Highway Patrol to investigate the allegations of conspiracy. On September 20, 1999 Master Sergeant David Oubre, B47 and Investigation Darrell Perkins interviewed me at the Greene County Sheriff's Office. All of the detailed information and evidence was given to Sergeant Oubre and Investigator Perkins. Enclosed please find Sergeant Oubre's investigation report. Sergeant Oubre omitted interviews with Mississippi Department of Corrections Officials and inmate.

Please note it is alleged that the FBI Special Agent Lenton Rice and Mississippi Highway Patrol Sergeant David Oubre and co-conspirator MDOC Chief Investigator Malcolm McClendon worked for several years together with the Mississippi Highway Patrol before retired. Mr. Lee, my family, and I have been living in fear for the last 3 ½ years. Please help us exercise our XIV Amendment Right (nor deny any person within its jurisdiction the equal protection of the laws). Dear Sir please re-open my case file 144-41-314 base on the information and evidence that is provided to you by this writer. Additional information can be provided at your request.

Thanking you in advance for your support.

Sincerely Yours,

Britton Mosley Sr.
Correction Captain
Marion/Wathall Correctional Facility

CHAPTER SEVEN
The U.S. Department of Justice Investigation

The state of Mississippi has two United States Attorney Generals, each assigned a judicial district—Northern District and Southern District. There are two divisions inside each district—Civil Division and Criminal Division. The attorneys in the Criminal Division handle the investigation and prosecution of all types of federal crimes, including public corruption cases.

On July 28, 1997, Southern District Assistant US Attorney General Carlton Reeves interviewed me in his federal building office in Jackson, Mississippi. During the interview, we discussed public corruption and conspiracy to plant drugs on me by staff members at South Mississippi Correctional Institute (SMCI). Being interviewed by someone who looks like me was encouraging and for a brief moment, I felt as though I would receive justice. However, soon after the meeting, Assistant Attorney General Reeves informed me that Assistant US Attorney General Jack Lacey (now deceased) would be conducting the investigation.

The coworkers that had conspired against me were White males; therefore I didn't trust this investigation. Assistant US Attorney General Reeves tried to reassure me that Jack Lacey would conduct a fair investigation by explaining Lacey's track record on civil rights. After meeting with Jack Lacey, I still didn't trust him.

On a fall day in 1997, FBI Special Agent Lent Rice was assigned to the investigation to conduct a so-called interview with me on a parking lot outside the main gate of SMCI. The interview was so informal that Special Agent Rice took notes on a legal pad while standing in the parking lot. Ten minutes into the interview, I leveled conspiracy allegations against MDOC employees. However, when I named SMCI's Chief Internal Audit Investigator Malcolm McClendon, Agent Rice became upset and stated, "Malcolm would never do a thing like that," and abruptly ended the interview. It was alleged that Special Agent Rice and MDOC Investigator McClendon retired from the Mississippi Highway Patrol before working with the FBI and MDOC.

After meeting with Agent Rice, I telephoned FBI Regional Director Julius Gonzales, and filed a complaint about how Agent Rice had conducted the investigation. Director Gonzales then assigned FBI Special Agent Randall Neidecker to the investigation.

On April 7, 1998, Special Agent Neidecker interviewed me at my home. John Fancher, Joe Dewitt and Paul McClendon were in attendance. Special Agent Neidecker told me he was investigating criminal civil rights violation by staff members of the MDOC. During the interview, Special Agent Neidecker was given a list of coconspirators, an audio tape, and other compelling evidence and information. Special Agent Neidecker informed me that he would get back with me. After several weeks had passed without hearing from Special Agent Neidecker, I telephoned Assistant US Attorney General Jack Lacey. During the conversation, I made allegations that Special Agent Rice compromised the investigation by being friends with MDOC Investigator Malcolm McClendon. Attorney General Lacey vigorously defended Special Agent Rice and then informed me that because I had spoken with Vivian Austin, a reporter with *The Sun Herald*, the agency would be pulling out of the case. I told Attorney General Lacy that he was violating my First Amendment right, guaranteeing me freedom of the press. Special Agent Rice and Attorney General Lacy never told me that I could not speak with the press.

The US Department of Justice Civil Rights Division in Mississippi is comprised of, in most cases, retired and former Mississippi law enforcement officers. The evidence and results of the investigations were sent to the US Department of Justice in

Washington, DC to review and determine criminal prosecution if any laws were broken. The US Department of Justice's policy allows former and retired Mississippi law enforcement officers who are now FBI agents to conduct civil rights violation investigations in Mississippi when both parties are White males is questionable, to say the least. Historically, there's a pattern in Mississippi that White law enforcement officers are known to violate the civil rights of Black men.

After FBI Special Agent Randall Neidecker's investigation was completed, it was sent to the US Department of Justice in Washington, DC for review. On March 5, 2000, under the Freedom of Information Act, I requested the Department of Justice (DOJ) to send me FBI Agent Neidecker's Investigative Report DJ 144-41-3144; a report containing information on federal civil rights violations allegedly committed by officials of the MDOC.

When I received the investigator's report, the title was "Unidentified Members of the Mississippi Department of Corrections—Britton Mosley, Victim." Agent Neidecker interviewed me on April 7, 1998, and completed the investigation by May 12, 1998, thirty-five days later. During my interview with Agent Neidecker, the names of the twenty people who were involved or had knowledge of facts of the two failed drug set up attempts were not listed in his investigative report. Agent

Neidecker was also given an audio tape conversation between Inmate Marvin Thomas and Lieutenant Louis Kittrell that detailed the drug set-up conspiracy, which was not mentioned in the report.

In the report, Agent Neidecker only interviewed four witnesses and three of those names were blacked out. However, Agent Neidecker conducted an investigation on me by checking the National Crime Information Center records and the Interstate Identification Index of which both investigation checks returned as "negative." I thought this was simply amazing; I requested the DOJ investigation, but it appeared that I was the one being investigated. I violated no laws, yet I was the one violated.

On October 23, 1998, the US Department of Justice closed the file on the case. This was the day that I lost trust in the entire justice system of the United States of America.

On October 5, 2000, I sent a letter of appeal, requesting a report and any additional information that wasn't "blacked out" or altered. The US Department of Justice denied my appeal on September 3, 2002, almost two years later. The FBI determined that this information was not appropriate for discretionary release, which was very disappointing news. I telephoned the Department of Justice Attorney Jacqueline Spratt and pointed out the lack of "investigation" in Agent Neidecker's investigative report. She stated, "The federal criminal civil rights violation cannot be proved." Once again, I contacted Congressman Gene Taylor's office, and gave District Representative Mrs. Jerry Martin (now deceased) information that showed that justice had not been served well in my case. This congressional inquiry was sent to Bill Lann Lee, Assistant Attorney General of the Civil Rights Division. Assistant Attorney Lee responded, "The totality of the evidence does not present a prosecutable violation of federal criminal rights statues." This was disappointing news for me and it is my belief that politics and racism was the determining factor in this case because the people involved were White males with the MDOC.

On March 8, 2009, after years of struggling with the fact that justice and equality wasn't going to happen for me, I was encouraged when the first African American Attorney General, Eric Holder, was speaking at historic Brown Chapel AME Church as part of the Bridge Crossing Jubilee in Selma, Alabama. Attorney General Holden was introduced at the pulpit by Peggy Wallace Kennedy, the daughter of the late former Alabama Governor George C. Wallace. It was Governor Wallace who once stood in the door at the University of Alabama to block Attorney General Holder's sister-in-law, Vivian Malone Jones from entering. I was outside the church that day listening to his speech and the high point of the speech for me was when he talked about nobody being above the law. Attorney General

Holder's speech didn't completely change my mindset about the DOJ, but I had to do a lot of soul searching to give justice another chance.

However, after reading an article in the *Washington Post*, titled "Civil Rights Office Returns to Old Role," I was motivated. The article discussed how Attorney General Eric Holder pledged to make the Civil Rights Division his department "crown jewel" by returning its focus to protecting minorities against discrimination. What becomes of these cases, and others like them, will help determine the meaning of justice in the Obama administration. After reading this article, I contacted Holder's New Focus Civil Rights Division of the Justice department. I explained my case and requested the division to reopen my case. On October 8, 2009, I mailed copies of my documents to the US Department of Justice Civil Rights Division. Working with me on my case was DOJ Attorney Catherine L. Pugh, and although I never met her in person, my case was discussed with her via phone and fax. This communication went on for several weeks and after two failed appointments to meet in person at my home, I lost contact with her. Since Attorney Pugh didn't return my calls, I contacted the Special Litigation Department and requested to speak with her. I was informed that she no longer worked for the Department of Justice and they didn't know anything about my case. Needless to say, the call was yet *another* blow, as I felt

I was beginning to make some kind of leeway toward justice. I still haven't recovered from the "monumental damage" that news did to me that day. The Department of Justice hires thousands of people of all races and political agendas, so I find it impossible for Attorney General Holder to manage all these political and racial agendas.

High-ranking officials have "plausible deniability" to deny any awareness of my case to insulate them and shift blame to others. This is another day in the life of an African-American man's failed plea for justice to a department named justice. One would think that Resident Justice Department personnel in Mississippi should at least have the appearance of justice.

Sec. 241. Conspiracy against rights

If two or more persons conspire to injure, oppress, threaten, or intimidate any person in any State, Territory, Commonwealth, Possession, or District in the free exercise or enjoyment of any right or privilege secured to him by the Constitution or laws of the United States, or because of his having so exercised the same; or

If two or more persons go in disguise on the highway, or on the premises of another, with intent to prevent or hinder his free exercise or enjoyment of any right or privilege so secured -

They shall be fined under this title or imprisoned not more than ten years, or both; and if death results from the acts committed in violation of this section or if such acts include kidnapping or an attempt to kidnap, aggravated sexual abuse or an attempt to commit aggravated sexual abuse, or an attempt to kill, they shall be fined under this title or imprisoned for any term of years or for life, or both, or may be sentenced to death.

Fabricating Evidence

Michael D. Cooke
Attorney At Law

106 Front Street . Post Office Box 625 . Iuka, Mississippi 38852
Tel: (662) 423-2000   Fax: (662) 423-2052

May 1, 2000

Mr. Britton Mosley
Post Office box 390
State Line, MS 39362

Re: Mosley v. MDOC

Dear Britt:

I talked with FBI Agent, Randy Neddecker, on Friday, April 28, 2000, after we had been trying to call each other for about three weeks. He basically told me that he could not help me in any manner.

He was very nice on the phone. He said that he had conducted his investigation and sent it to the Justice Department in Washington and they did not find that there was enough to bring a civil rights conspiracy. He said that I would not be able to get any information from them as they would not release their information and he doubted that I could get it, even with a court order.

Based upon my conversation with him, I do not think the FBI is going to be of any help.

Sincerely yours,

Michael D. Cooke

MDC/dpd
Enclosure

IN THE UNITED STATES DISTRICT COURT
FOR THE SOUTHERN DISTRICT OF MISSISSIPPI
HATTIESBURG DIVISION

BRITTON MOSLEY   PLAINTIFF

v.   NO. 2:98CV357-P-G

MISSISSIPPI DEPARTMENT OF CORRECTIONS   DEFENDANT

PLAINTIFF'S PRE-DISCOVERY DISCLOSURE OF CORE INFORMATION

Pursuant to the amendments to the Civil Justice Reform Act, the Plaintiff provides herewith the name and, if known, the address and telephone number of each individual likely to have discoverable information relevant to the claim of the Plaintiff, along with a short summary of the anticipated discoverable knowledge of each individual; however, these summaries do not purport to encompass the extent of each person's knowledge, but only what the Plaintiff now believes to be the extent of their knowledge. Information that is incomplete or unavailable at the time of this filing will be supplemented as same becomes available.

In addition to the Plaintiff, the following persons may have discoverable knowledge:

     Brenda Mosley (Plaintiff's wife) - is aware of the circumstances that lead to the Plaintiff's constructive termination from the MDOC.

Paul McLendon (address unknown*) - Sgt. McLendon is aware of a conversation between two MDOC officers relative to "getting rid of the Plaintiff." Upon information and belief, Sgt. McLendon gave a statement of these facts to FBI Special Agent Randall L. Nedecker.

David Turner (address unknown*) - upon information and belief, Supt. Turner was involved in a second attempted set-up of the Plaintiff.

Joe Errington (address unknown*) - Capt. Errington was one of the Plaintiff's superiors. Upon information and belief, Capt. Errington was involved in a second attempted set-up of the Plaintiff.

Joe Beard (address unknown*) - Mr. Beard is aware of a vendetta that Joe Errington had against the Plaintiff. Upon information and belief, Joe Beard gave a statement to the FBI relevant to the his knowledge of these facts.

Michael Miller (address unknown*) - on November 4, 1996, CO Miller participated in an attempt to frame the Plaintiff when he left a package with Sgt. Daniel Paff at the maintenance complex with instructions to give the package to the Plaintiff with instructions that it be given to an inmate. It was later discovered that the packaged contained two ounces of marijuana and other items.

Daniel Paff (address unknown*) - Sgt. Paff delivered the package left by Michael Miller with instructions that it be given to the Plaintiff to be given to inmate Mandell Walker. Sgt. Paff suggested to the Plaintiff that he search the contents of the package.

Johnny Denmark (address unknown*) - upon information and belief, Capt. Denmark[1] has knowledge of, and upon information and belief, had a part in the attempted set-up of the Plaintiff.

Larry Smith (address unknown*) - Internal Audit Investigator who investigated the incidents regarding the attempted set-up of the Plaintiff. Mr. Smith is aware of the circumstances of the attempted framing of the Plaintiff and, upon information belief, is aware of the participants in that attempted set-up.

Victor Brewer (address unknown*) - Lt. Brewer[2] has knowledge of, and upon information and belief, had a part in the attempted set-up of the Plaintiff. Lt. Brewer directed the Plaintiff to not write an incident report about the findings of the package delivered on November 4, 1996.

Malcolm McClendon (address unknown*) - Investigator McClendon[3] was called to the Central Security Office to investigate the marijuana findings of the package delivered on November 4, 1996. Upon information and belief, Investigator McClendon had prior knowledge of and a part in the attempted drug set-up of the Plaintiff.

Louis Kittrell (address unknown*) - CO Kittrell, upon information and belief has knowledge of and/or a part in the attempted set-up of the Plaintiff.

Terry Burgess (address unknown*) - Lt. Burgess, upon information belief, has knowledge of and/or a part in the attempted set-up of the Plaintiff. Lt. Burgess was another of Plaintiff's superiors.

---

[1] Johnnie Demark subsequently promoted to Deputy Warden

[2] Victor Brewer subsequently promoted to Captain.

[3] Malcolm McClendon subsequently promoted to Chief Investigator.

John Graham (address unknown*) - Sgt. Graham, upon information belief, has knowledge of and/or a part in the attempted set-up of the Plaintiff.

Danny Woodard (address unknown*) - CO II Woodard[4], upon information belief, has knowledge of and/or a part in the attempted set-up of the Plaintiff.

Jerry Dettman (address unknown*) - Internal Audit Investigator, upon information belief, has knowledge of and/or a part in the attempted set-up of the Plaintiff. Mr. Dettman also participated in the investigation of the incident concerning the attempted set-up.

Harold James (address unknown) - CO II James[5] was present when the marijuana was discovered and present when Investigator McClendon investigated the incident.

Nicole Pearson (address unknown*) - upon information and belief CO II Pearson has knowledge of the attempted set-up of the Plaintiff.

Randall L. Nedecker, Special Agent, FBI - Agent Nedecker investigated incidents related to the Plaintiff's being set-up while employed at the MDOC facility in ____.

Linton Rice, FBI Special Agent - the Plaintiff gave Agent Rice a statement regarding the incidence which are the subject of this lawsuit.

Mandell Walker, Inmate #78206, SMCI-I, Leaksville, MS - Mr. Walker has knowledge of the attempted set up of the Plaintiff.

---

[4]Danny Woodard was subsequently promoted to Sergeant .

[5]Harold James subsequently resigned from the MDOC.

Marvin Thomas, Inmate #79517, Greenwood, MS - Mr. Thomas has knowledge of the attempted set up of the Plaintiff.

Nicole Pearson, US Department of Justice, Washington, DC - Ms. Pearson has knowledge of the Department of Justice's investigation into the incidents at the SMCI in Leaksville.

Jacqueline Spratt, US Department of Justice, Washington, DC - Ms. Spratt has knowledge of the Department of Justice's investigation into the incidents at the SMCI in Leaksville.

Julius Gonzales, Regional Director, FBI - has knowledge of the Plaintiff's averments and the FBI's subsequent investigation.

*employed with the SMCI

Plaintiff's physicians who have seen him in connection with stress, trauma and emotional harm:

Alexis Polles, MD

Terry L. Jordan, MD

R.L. Douglas, PhD, PA

Tracey Yost, MSLPC

Steve Morris, MD

Fabricating Evidence

Charles Hornfort, MALCP
(address unknown at present time)

II.

A copy of, or a description by category and location of, all documents, data compilations, and tangible things in the possession, custody, or control of the party that are relevant to the claims asserted are as follows:

1. Personnel file of the Plaintiff in the possession of the Defendant.

2. Personnel policies/manuals of the Defendant in the possession of the Defendant.

3. Internal operating procedures policies and/or procedures in the possession of the Defendant.

4. EEOC investigative file to Charge Nos. 131-99-0192 and 131-98-1361 in the possession of the Equal Employment Opportunity Commission, Jackson, Mississippi.

5. Internal Audit Investigative Reports and/or recorded/transcribed statements concerning any incident which is the subject of this lawsuit, all in the possession of the Defendant.

6. FBI Investigative Reports and/or recorded/transcribed statements concerning any incident which is the subject of this lawsuit, all in the possession of the FBI.

7. US Department of Justice Reports and/or recorded/transcribed statements concerning any incident which is the subject of this lawsuit, all in the possession of the US Department of Justice.

8. Mississippi Attorney General Reports and/or recorded/transcribed statements concerning any incident which is the subject of this lawsuit, all in the possession of the Mississippi AG's office.

9. Medical records of the Plaintiff which have not yet been obtained by the undersigned, but which will be provided to counsel opposite upon receipt of same.

III.

A computation of any category of damages claimed by the Plaintiff is as follows:

1. Arbitrary and unreasonable discriminatory treatment by the Defendant against the Plaintiff.

2. Compensatory damages due to the willful, wanton, outrageous, malicious, unlawful, and improper actions of the Defendant in violating the Plaintiff's rights.

3. Mental and emotional anguish and stress.

4. Damage to Plaintiff's reputation.

5. Lost wages.

6. Other lost benefits, including medical, hospital and dental insurance, life insurance, vacation pay, and/or retirement plan.

Documents and/or other evidentiary material on which said computation is based, including materials bearing on the nature and extent of injuries suffered, will be accumulated through discovery and will be made available for inspection and copying at the office of Attorney Michael D. Cooke, 106 Front Street, Iuka, Mississippi 38852 as same becomes available.

RESPECTFULLY SUBMITTED,

/s/ Michael D. Cooke

**MICHAEL D. COOKE, MSB #6503
ATTORNEY FOR PLAINTIFF**
Post Office Box 625
Iuka, MS 38852
(601)423-2000

282B-JN-25342
RLN:rln
1

TABLE OF CONTENTS

PAGE NO.

- I. PREDICATION...................................2
- II. VICTIM INTERVIEW..............................4
- III. WITNESS INTERVIEWS
  1) ▒▒▒▒▒▒▒▒▒▒▒▒▒▒▒▒▒▒....................6
  2) ▒▒▒▒▒▒▒▒▒▒▒▒▒▒▒▒▒▒....................8
  3) ▒▒▒▒▒▒▒▒▒▒▒▒▒▒▒▒▒▒....................9
  4) JOE BEARD..................................10
- IV. CRIMINAL HISTORY CHECKS.......................11
- V. FBI INDICES CHECK.............................12
- VI. NOTIFICATION LIST.............................13

b7C

3
153RLN03, INS

Fabricating Evidence

FD-204 (Rev. 12-1-95)

UNITED STATES DEPARTMENT OF JUSTICE
Federal Bureau of Investigation

Copy to: 1-USDOJ, CRD, Criminal Sect., Washington D.C.
DOJ# 144 41 3144
1-United States Attorney, Jackson, Ms.
Report of: SA ▓▓▓▓▓▓▓▓▓ Office: Jackson
Date: May 12, 1998

Case ID #: 282B-JN-25342

Title: UNIDENTIFIED MEMBERS OF THE
MISSISSIPPI DEPARTMENT OF CORRECTIONS;
BRITTON MOSLEY - VICTIM

Character: CIVIL RIGHTS - COLOR OF LAW

Synopsis: Status of case.

-P-

DETAILS:

Lead remains outstanding to interview ▓▓▓▓▓▓▓▓▓▓▓▓▓▓

144-41-3144

DEPARTMENT OF JUSTICE
MAY 18 1998
RECORD
P.A.O.

CRT · CRIMINAL SECTION

This document contains neither recommendations nor conclusions of the FBI. It is the property of the FBI and is loaned to your agency; it and its contents are not to be distributed outside your agency.

Britton Mosley, Sr.

FD-302 (Rev. 10-6-95)

- 1 -

FEDERAL BUREAU OF INVESTIGATION

Date of transcription   4/22/98

BRITTON MOSLEY, black male, date of birth September 30, 1948, Social Security Number _____, P.O. Box 390, State Line, Mississippi 39362, telephone number (601)848-7447, was interviewed at his residence. After being advised of the identity of the interviewing agent and the nature of the interview, MOSLEY provided the following information:

MOSLEY stated he is employed as a Correctional Officer at the SOUTH MISSISSIPPI CORRECTIONAL INSTITUTE (SMCI), Leakesville, Mississippi. MOSLEY said that on November 4, 1996, at approximately 7:15 A.M. in the Maintenance Support building at SMCI, he was approached by another SMCI Correctional Officer, MICHAEL MILLER and inmate MANTEL WALKER about allowing a package to enter the SMCI compound containing shower shoes and personal hygiene items. MOSLEY told Officer MILLER that he would have to get it cleared from the SMCI Watch Commander.

MOSLEY advised that when he returned to the SMCI maintenance building at approximately 3:20 P.M. Correctional Officer DANIEL PAFF informed him that Officer MILLER had left a package with him for MOSLEY to give to inmate WALKER. PAFF suggested that MOSLEY search the package. MOSLEY stated that he searched the package and discovered what appeared to be marijuana in a clear plastic bag inside a can of baby powder. MOSLEY said he then notified SMCI Captain JOHNNIE DENMARK, Lieutenant VICTOR BREWER, and SMCI Chief Investigator MALCOLM MCLENDON of his discovery.

MOSLEY feels this was an attempt by Officer MILLER to plant dope on him in order to have him fired.

MOSLEY advised that on July 25, 1997, he was told by SMCI inmate MARVIN THOMAS that SMCI Correctional Officer LEWIS KITTRELL had asked THOMAS to plant dope on MOSLEY.

MOSLEY stated that nine or ten other SMCI Correctional Officers are conspiring against him to have him fired from SMCI. MOSLEY stated he has had to see a psychiatrist since August 18, 1997, and has been unable to return to work for several months

Investigation on 4/7/98 at State Line, Ms.

File # 282B-JN-25342 _____ Date dictated 4/7/98

by SA _____
RLN:rln

112RLN01.302

This document contains neither recommendations nor conclusions of the FBI. It is the property of the FBI and is loaned to your agency; it and its contents are not to be distributed outside your agency.

282B-JN-25342

▓▓▓▓▓▓▓ Mississippi Department of Corrections (MDOC) Internal Audit Division (IAD), South Mississippi Correctional Institute (SMCI), advised that a full investigation into this matter was ordered by ▓▓▓▓▓ Director of MDOC IAD, ▓▓▓▓▓▓▓▓▓▓▓▓▓▓▓▓▓▓ advised all other SMCI staff members were cleared.

b7C

- P -

DETAILS:

Investigation predicated on a letter received from FBIHQ Civil Rights Unit on March 27, 1998.

This report is being forwarded to the U.S. Attorney, Southern District of Mississippi for a prosecutive opinion.

Britton Mosley, Sr.

(Rev. 12-1-95)

UNITED STATES DEPARTMENT OF JUSTICE
Federal Bureau of Investigation

Copy to: 1-USDOJ, CRD, Criminal Sect., Washington D.C. 20035
DOJ file # 144 41 3144
1-United States Attorney, Jackson, Mississippi
Report of: SA [redacted] Office: Jackson
Date: June 1, 1998

Case ID #: 282B-JN-25342

Title: UNIDENTIFIED MEMBERS OF THE
MISSISSIPPI DEPARTMENT OF CORRECTIONS;
BRITTON MOSLEY - VICTIM

Character: CIVIL RIGHTS - COLOR OF LAW

Synopsis:

On March 27, 1998, Jackson Division received a letter from FBIHQ Civil Rights Unit which listed Britton Mosley, a correctional officer at the South Mississippi Correctional Institute (SMCI), Leakesville, Mississippi, as a complainant who believes that unknown members of SMCI are conspiring to plant drugs on him in retaliation for his wife, Brenda Mosley filing EEO discrimination charges against employees of SMCI.

Mosley stated that on November 4, 1996, SMCI correctional officer Michael Miller left a package at SMCI for Mosley to deliver to an inmate. Upon inspection of the package by Mosley, he discovered marijuana hidden in a can of baby powder. Mosley believed this was an attempt by officer Miller to have him fired.

Mosley advised that on July 25, 1997, he was told by an inmate of SMCI, Marvin Thomas, that correctional officer Lewis Kittrell was planning to plant dope on him.

Mosley stated that nine or ten other SMCI officers are conspiring against him to have him fired from SMCI. Mosley advised he has had to see a psychiatrist since August 18, 1997, and has been unable to return to work for several months due to stress.

DEPARTMENT OF JUSTICE
RECORD
JUN 9 1998

This document contains neither recommendations nor conclusions of the FBI. It is the property of the FBI and is loaned to your agency; it and its contents are not to be distributed outside your agency.

282B-JN-25342
RLN:rln
1

The following investigation was conducted by SA [redacted] b7C
at Gulfport, Mississippi, on May 20, 1998:

A check of NCIC records and the Interstate Identification Index were negative for BRITTON MOSLEY, black male, date of birth September 30, 1948, Social Security Number

282B-JN-25342
RLN:rln
1

b7C

The following investigation was conducted by SA [redacted] on June 2, 1998, at Gulfport, Mississippi:

A review of the FBI indices revealed that BRITTON MOSLEY, black male, date of birth September 30, 1948, Social Security Number [redacted] was the main subject of case file JN 282-0, opened November 5, 1993.

12
153RLN01.INS

Fabricating Evidence

```
282B-JN-25342

              LIST OF PERSONS TO BE NOTIFIED:

   1) BRITTON MOSLEY, P.O. BOX 390, STATE LINE, MISSISSIPPI
390362.
                                                              b7C
   2)                      MISSISSIPPI DEPARTMENT OF CORRECTIONS,
SOUTH MISSISSIPPI CORRECTIONAL INSTITUTE, LEAKESVILLE,
MISSISSIPPI 39451.
```

FD-201 (Rev. 12-1-95)

UNITED STATES DEPARTMENT OF JUSTICE
Federal Bureau of Investigation

Copy to: 1-USDOJ, CRD, Criminal Sect, Washington D.C.
DOJ File# 144 41 3144
1-United States Attorney, Jackson, Ms.

Report of: SA ███████████   Office: Jackson
Date: April 22, 1998

Case ID #: 282B-JN-25342

Title: UNIDENTIFIED MEMBERS OF THE
MISSISSIPPI DEPARTMENT OF CORRECTIONS;
BRITTON MOSLEY - VICTIM;

Character: CIVIL RIGHTS - COLOR OF LAW

Synopsis: On March 27, 1998, Jackson Division received a complaint from Britton Mosley, a Correctional Officer at South Mississippi Correctional Institute (SMCI), Leakesville, Mississippi, that unknown members of SMCI were conspiring to plant drugs on him in retaliation for his wife, Brenda Mosley filing EEO discrimination charges against employees of SMCI.

Mosley stated that on November 4, 1996, SMCI Correctional Officer Michael Miller left a package at SMCI for Mosley to deliver to an inmate. Upon inspection of the package by Mosley, he discovered marijuana hidden in a can of baby powder. Mosley believed this was an attempt by Officer Miller to plant Dope on him.

Mosley advised that on July 25, 1997, he was told by an inmate of SMCI, Marvin Walker, that Correctional Officer Lewis Kittrell was planning to plant dope on him.

Mosley states that nine or ten other SMCI Officers are conspiring against him to have him fired from SMCI.

Mosley advised he has had to see a psychiatrist since August 18, 1997, and has been unable to return to work for several months due to stress.

███████████ Mississippi Department of Corrections (MDOC) Internal Audit Division (IAD)

This document contains neither recommendations nor conclusions of the FBI. It is the property of the FBI and is loaned to your agency; it and its contents are not to be distributed outside your agency.

Fabricating Evidence

FD-204 (Rev. 12-1-95)

UNITED STATES DEPARTMENT OF JUSTICE
Federal Bureau of Investigation

Copy to: 1 - USDOJ, CRD, Criminal Sect., Washington D.C. 20035
DOJ file # 144 41 3144
Report of: 1 - United States Attorney, Jackson, Mississippi
SA [redacted]
Office: Jackson
Date: June 19, 1998

Case ID #: 282B-JN-25342

Title: UNIDENTIFIED MEMBERS OF THE
MISSISSIPPI DEPARTMENT OF CORRECTIONS;
BRITTON MOSLEY - VICTIM

Character: CIVIL RIGHTS - COLOR OF LAW

Synopsis:
On March 27, 1998, Jackson Division received a letter from FBIHQ Civil Rights Unit which listed Britton Mosley, a correctional officer at the South Mississippi Correctional Institute (SMCI), Leakesville, Mississippi, as a complainant who believes that unknown members of SMCI are conspiring to plant drugs on him in retaliation for his wife, Brenda Mosley filing EEO discrimination charges against employees of SMCI.

Mosley stated that on November 4, 1996, SMCI correctional officer Michael Miller left a package at SMCI for Mosley to deliver to an inmate. Upon inspection of the package by Mosley, he discovered marijuana hidden in a can of baby powder. Mosley believed this was an attempt by officer Miller to have him fired.

Mosley advised that nine of ten other SMCI officers are conspiring against him to have him fired from SMCI. Mosley advised he has had to see a psychiatrist since August 18, 1997, and has been unable to return to work for several months due to stress.

DEPARTMENT OF JUSTICE
JUN 2 0 1998
R.A.O.

170RLN02.204

CRT - CRIMINAL SECTION

Britton Mosley, Sr.

FD-201 (Rev. 12-1-95)

UNITED STATES DEPARTMENT OF JUSTICE
Federal Bureau of Investigation

Copy to: 1-USDOJ, CRD, Criminal Sect, Washington D.C.
DOJ File# 144 41 3144
1-United States Attorney, Jackson, Ms.

Report of: SA ~~[redacted]~~ Office: Jackson
Date: April 22, 1998

Case ID #: 282B-JN-25342

Title: UNIDENTIFIED MEMBERS OF THE
MISSISSIPPI DEPARTMENT OF CORRECTIONS;
BRITTON MOSLEY - VICTIM;

Character: CIVIL RIGHTS - COLOR OF LAW

Synopsis: On March 27, 1998, Jackson Division received a complaint from Britton Mosley, a Correctional Officer at South Mississippi Correctional Institute (SMCI), Leakesville, Mississippi, that unknown members of SMCI were conspiring to plant drugs on him in retaliation for his wife, Brenda Mosley filing EEO discrimination charges against employees of SMCI.

Mosley stated that on November 4, 1996, SMCI Correctional Officer Michael Miller left a package at SMCI for Mosley to deliver to an inmate. Upon inspection of the package by Mosley, he discovered marijuana hidden in a can of baby powder. Mosley believed this was an attempt by Officer Miller to plant Dope on him.

Mosley advised that on July 25, 1997, he was told by an inmate of SMCI, Marvin Walker, that Correctional Officer Lewis Kittrell was planning to plant dope on him.

Mosley states that nine or ten other SMCI Officers are conspiring against him to have him fired from SMCI.

Mosley advised he has had to see a psychiatrist since August 18, 1997, and has been unable to return to work for several months due to stress.

~~[redacted]~~ Mississippi Department of Corrections (MDOC) Internal Audit Division (IAD),

282B-JN-25342

███████████ Mississippi Department of Corrections (MDOC) Internal Audit Division (IAD), South Mississippi Correctional Institute (SMCI), advised that a full investigation into this matter was ordered by ███████ Director of MDOC IAD. ████████████████████ advised all other SMCI staff members were cleared.

b7C

- P -

DETAILS:

　　Investigation predicated on a letter received from FBIHQ Civil Rights Unit on March 27, 1998.

　　This report is being forwarded to the U.S. Attorney, Southern District of Mississippi for a prosecutive opinion.

Britton Mosley, Sr.

FD-302 (Rev. 10-6-95)

- 1 -

FEDERAL BUREAU OF INVESTIGATION

Date of transcription 6/2/98

JOE BEARD, white male, date of birth January 5, 1959, Social Security Number _____ a Chancery Court Judge in the city of Leakesville, Mississippi, telephone number (601)394-5900 was advised of the identity of the interviewing Agent and the nature of the interview. BEARD provided the following information:

BEARD advised he was presiding over a land dispute hearing four or five years ago between BRITTON MOSLEY and JOE GLENN ERRINGTON, a correctional officer at SOUTH MISSISSIPPI CORRECTIONAL INSTITUTE (SMCI), Leakesville, Mississippi. BEARD stated he ruled in favor of MOSLEY

b7C

Investigation on	5/13/98	at Leakesville, Ms. (telephonically)
File #	282B-JN-25342	Date dictated 5/13/98
by	SA _____ RLN:rln	

This document contains neither recommendations nor conclusions of the FBI. It is the property of the FBI and is loaned to your agency; it and its contents are not to be distributed outside your agency.

282B-JN-25342

South Mississippi Correctional Institute (SMCI), advised a full investigation into this matter was ordered by ███████ Director of MDOC IAD. ████████████████████ advised all other SMCI staff members were cleared of any wrong doing.

- P -

DETAILS:

Investigation predicated on a letter received from FBIHQ ████████ Unit on March 27, 1998.

The only remaining investigation is to interview inmate Marvin Thomas, Parchman State Penitentiary as to any information he may have of correctional officers at SMCI conspiring against Mosley.

August 12, 1998

REFERENCE: Telephone conversation between DOJ Attorney
Jacqueine Spratt and SA ▬▬▬▬▬▬ on 7/28/98.
FBI file # 282B-JN-25342.

b7c

Dear Ms. Spratt,
    Here is the tape that Britton Mosley had South Mississippi Correctional Institute inmate Marvin Thomas make of his conversation with correctional officer Louis Kittrell.

    Mr. Mosley has informed me he no longer works at the South Mississippi Correctional Institute, Leakesville, Mississippi.

    Please let me know if I can be of any further help.

                              SA ▬▬▬▬▬▬
                              Gulfport, Mississippi

b2

Fabricating Evidence

```
JLS:kr
U.S. Department of Justice                    Notice to Close File

File Number:        Case Title:               Date:
144-41-3144         Unidentified Members Of The   October 23, 1998
                    Mississippi Department Of
                    Corrections - Subjects;
                    Britton Mosley - Victims
                    CIVIL RIGHTS
```

YOU ARE ADVISED THAT THE ABOVE FILE HAS BEEN CLOSED AS OF THIS DATE.

Remarks/Special Information:
Federal criminal civil rights violation cannot be proven because insufficient evidence that subject conspired to implicate victim in the delivery of drugs to a prison. The tape recording of an inmate speaking with the subject does not provide sufficient corroboration of the victim's allegation.

To:

    Files Unit   Civil Rights Division

Signature: Division:

Jacqueline L. Spratt
Jacqueline L. Spratt   Civil Rights Division

FORM OBD-25-A
MAR. 81

Britton Mosley, Sr.

Mr. Britton Mosley

State Line, MS 39362
      (phone #)

FAX TRANSMITTAL FORM

To:	From:
CATHERINE L. PUGH Special Litigation Civil Rights Division Department of Justice 950 Pennsylvania Avenue, NW - PHB Washington, D.C. 20530 (202) 305-4074 (direct line) (202) 532-5013 (BB) (202) 514-4883 (fax)	Mr. Britton Mosley Date Sent: July 2, 2010 Number of pages: 17

Message:

Ms Pugh,
Here is the info that we discussed.

Fabricating Evidence

Mississippi Department of Corrections

CONFIDENTIAL

REPORT OF INTERVIEW
Internal Audit Division

LENT RICE, Special Agent, FBI, formerly assigned to the Pascagoula Office of the FBI and now assigned to the Oxford Office, telephone (601) 234-1713, contacted Internal Audit Division (IAD) on October 23, 1997, relating to Britton Mosley, Correctional Officer, South Mississippi Correctional Institution (SMCI), Leakesville, MS.

Rice was recently contacted by the U. S. Attorney's Office, Biloxi, MS, as a result of a letter Mosley wrote to U. S. Attorney General Janet Reno, alleging a conspiracy against him by Mississippi Department of Corrections (MDOC) employees. The U. S. Attorney's office was aware of at least two prior contacts Rice had with Mosley in which he had leveled conspiracy allegations against MDOC employees. In other instances, Rice had found the allegations by Mosley as being baseless. Mosley also provided a copy of a tape cassette that was supposed to reflect basis for his allegations, however, Rice with the assistance of FBI sound experts was unable to find any basis to support his allegations.

After Rice discussed the above facts with the U.S. Attorney's Office, they indicated they would recommend no further action with regard to Mosley's allegations.

MGH/lr
97-SMCI-10

DATE OF INTERVIEW: October 23, 1997	FILE NUMBER: 97-SMCI-10
INTERVIEWER: M. Gene Hill	PLACE OF INTERVIEW: Telephonically conducted

OFFICIAL USE ONLY
MDOC INTERNAL AUDIT DIVISION

This report is the property of the Mississippi Department of Corrections.
Neither it, nor its contents may be disseminated outside the agency to which it is loaned.

CHAPTER EIGHT

Britton Mosley, Sr.

vs.

Mississippi Department of Corrections

On January 16 and 17, 2000, my long awaited EEOC discrimination civil lawsuit against Mississippi Department of Corrections (MDOC) took place in US District Court in Hattiesburg, Mississippi.

In civil cases, the standard of proof is the *preponderance of the evidence*, whereas in criminal matters the standard is *beyond a reasonable doubt*. I thought Mississippi had become a place where justice and due process were the order of the day, but quite the contrary.

During my court proceeding, the jury was not allowed to see or hear any of the evidence. In this chapter, the evidence will show how the outcome of my court case was *predetermined outside of the courtroom*. My attorney, Michael Cooke, Assistant Attorney General Joe Goff and MDOC Attorney Leonard Vincent conspired and suppressed all the compelling evidence from the jurors. The only evidence and exhibits the jurors were allowed to see were:

- P-1 – Pertinent portions of my personnel file.
- P-4 – Plaintiff's earning record.
- P-5 – Incident reported dated November 5, 1996.
- P-6 – My medical records.

Documents and audio taped evidence showing conspiracy and a drug set-up were withheld from the jurors, which was the sole basis of the case. I was not allowed to plead my case and present the compelling evidence. US District Judge Charles W. Pickering, Sr. was the presiding judge in my case and on August 17, 1999, Congressman Gene Taylor's District Representative Mrs. Jerry Martin (deceased) hand-carried all overwhelmingly compelling evidence to Judge Pickering. During the court proceeding, Judge Pickering gave unfair advantages to MDOC personnel. They were allowed to wear law enforcement uniforms into the courtroom and on the witness stand, which possibly could have persuaded the jurors. The audio tape recording, proving Lieutenant Louis Kittrell conspiring with Inmate Thomas to set me up with drug possession was not allowed to be entered into evidence. Lieutenant Kittrell was allowed to testify before the jurors. However, when my witness, Inmate Marvin Thomas testified, Judge Pickering excused the jurors from the courtroom, so Inmate Thomas's testimony was never heard by the jurors, only Lieutenant Kittrell's testimony was heard. My attorney, Michael Cooke, Assistant Attorney General Joe Goff, MDOC's Attorney Leonard Vincent and Judge Pickering knew that Lieutenant Kittrell's sworn testimony was false. The legal term is "subordination of perjury."

In November 2000, MDOC's Attorney Leonard Vincent went to the office of former Warden Jimmy Fancher (and my boss) at SMCI to discuss Warden Fancher's testimony in my case. Attorney Vincent asked Fancher if he could testify to the fact that *it was racially motivated*. Fancher replied, "No, I couldn't." Vincent replied, "Well they tried to fuck him, but it is not racially motivated." When Warden Fancher testified on my behalf, Judge Pickering, once again, excused the jurors from the courtroom. Warden Fancher later stated that this was a first for him and he had been to lots of courtroom proceedings.

Malcolm McClendon, chief investigator at SMCI, took the witness stand. The jury was present for his testimony. McClendon repeatedly gave false statements about the two failed drug set-up attempts at SMCI. Being the chief investigator, McClendon could steer the criminal investigation any way he wanted it to go and he was allowed to do just that. McClendon falsely alleged that I was dealing drugs at SMCI. If I were dealing drugs, why would I request an FBI investigation? His allegations didn't make sense. My attorney, Michael Cooke, conducted a poor cross-examination of McClendon, and did not cross-examine Lieutenant Kittrell at all. Attorney Cook never took any depositions from MDOC staff or any of my witnesses, jut his handwritten statements. Attorney Cook was the only attorney I could find in Mississippi that would take on MDOC. Their legal team was allowed to make allegations that I was dealing drugs, lazy and was just trying to win money in a lawsuit. Most of the jurors were White, so this was an easy sell in Mississippi. This case was designed for me to lose. All my suspicions of Attorney Michael Cooke, Assistant Attorney General Joe Goff, MDOC's Attorney Leonard Vincent and Judge Charles Pickering came full circle during the court proceeding, so when the jury verdict was returned in favor of MDOC, it didn't surprise me at all. This is how state-sanctioned racism works in Mississippi.

Jerry Mitchell, investigative report for *The Clarion-Ledger*, posted a story on Facebook about corruption in Mississippi, which topped the nation in corruption, according to an index developed from a study of federal convictions of public officials between 1976 and 2008. That study by researchers at the University of Hong Kong and Indiana University concluded corruption is costing Mississippi's taxpayers (and taxpayers in the other nine corrupt states) an average of $1,308 per person per year. The report found states with higher levels of corruption are likely to favor construction salaries, borrowing corrections and police protection.

In Mississippi race is always a factor during court proceedings. The US District Court for the Southern Division of Mississippi Hattiesburg Division personnel list in my court case shows this fact. It shows the who's who in law enforcement in Mississippi during my court date. Being traumatized by a rigged court proceeding has left me sad and angry with this diseased court system. Americans expect and deserve a level playing field when seeking justice in our country.

Fabricating Evidence

Notice of Lawsuit and Request for Waiver of Service of Summons

TO: S.W. Puckett, Commissioner, MDOC

A lawsuit has been commenced against you (or the entity on whose behalf you are addressed). A copy of the complaint is attached to this notice. It has been filed in the **United States District Court for the Southern District of Mississippi** and has been assigned docket number 2:98CV357-P-G

This is not a formal summons or notification from the court, but rather my request that you sign and return the enclosed waiver of service in order to save the cost of serving you with a judicial summons and an additional copy of the complaint. The cost of service will be avoided if I receive a signed copy of the waiver within **30 days** (or **60 days** if located in a foreign country) after the date designated below as the date on which this Notice and Request is sent. I enclose a stamped and addressed envelope (or other means of cost-free return) for your use. An extra copy of the waiver is also attached for your records.

If you comply with this request and return the signed waiver, it will be filed with the court and no summons will be served on you. The action will then proceed as if you had been served on the date the waiver is filed, except that you will not be obligated to answer the complaint before **60 days** from the date designated below as the date on which this notice is sent (or before **90 days** from that date if your address is not in any judicial district of the United States).

If you do not return the signed waiver within the time indicated, I will take appropriate steps to effect formal service in a manner authorized by the Federal Rules of Civil Procedure and will then, to the extent authorized by those Rules, ask the court to require you (or the party on whose behalf you are addressed) to pay the full costs of such service. In that connection, please read the statement concerning the duty of parties to waive the service of the summons, which is set forth on the reverse side (or at the foot) of the waiver form.

I affirm that this request is being sent to you on behalf of the plaintiff, this 12th day of April, 19 99.

[signature: Michael D. Cooke]

Michael D. Cooke, Attorney at Law
Post Office Box 625
Iuka, MS 38852
(601)423-2000
MSB #6503

Britton Mosley, Sr.

Waiver of Service of Summons

TO: Michael D. Cooke, Esq.

I acknowledge receipt of your request that I waive service of a summons in the action of **Britton Mosley v. Mississippi Department of Corrections** which is case number **2:98CV357-P-G**, in the United States District Court for the Southern District of Mississippi. I have also received a copy of the complaint in the action, two copies of this instrument, and a means by which I can return the signed waiver to you without cost to me.

I agree to save the costs of service of a summons and an additional copy of the complaint in this lawsuit by not requiring that I (or the entity on whose behalf I am acting) be served with judicial process in the manner proved by Rule 4.

I (or the entity on whose behalf I am acting) will retain all defenses or objections to the lawsuit or to the jurisdiction or venue of the court except for objections based on a defect in the summons or in the service of a summons.

I understand that a judgment may be entered against me (or the party on whose behalf I am acting) if an answer or motion under Rule 12 is not served upon you within **60 days** after April 12, 1999 (or within **90 days** after that date if the request was sent outside the United States).

_____   _____
Date   Signature

                                                _____
                                                Printed/typed name
                                                [as_____]
                                                [of_____]

Duty to Avoid Unnecessary Costs of Service of Summons

Rule 4 of the Federal Rules of Civil Procedure requires certain parties to cooperate in saving unnecessary costs of service of the summons and complaint. A Defendant located in the United States who, after being notified of an action and asked by a plaintiff located in the United States to waive service of a summons, fails to do so will be required to bear the costs of such waiver.

It is not good cause for a failure to waive service that a party believes that the complaint is unfounded, or that the action has been brought in an improper place or in a court that lacks jurisdiction over the subject matter of the action or over its person or property. A party who waives service of a summons retains all defenses and objections (except any relating to the summons or service of summons), and may later object to the jurisdiction of the court or to the place where the action has been brought.

A defendant who waives service must within the time specified on the waiver form serve on the plaintiff's attorney a response to the complaint and must also file a signed copy of the response with the court. If the answer or motion is not served within this time, a default judgment may be taken against that defendant. By waiving service, a defendant is allowed more time to answer than if the summons has been actually served when the request for waiver of service was received.

Fabricating Evidence

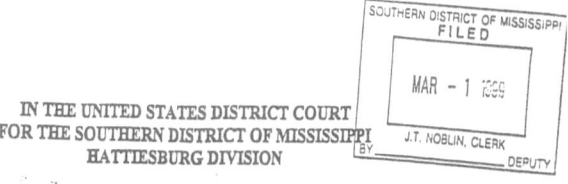

IN THE UNITED STATES DISTRICT COURT
FOR THE SOUTHERN DISTRICT OF MISSISSIPPI
HATTIESBURG DIVISION

BRITTON MOSLEY   PLAINTIFF

V.   NO. 2:98CV357-P-G

MISSISSIPPI DEPARTMENT OF CORRECTIONS   DEFENDANT

JURY TRIAL DEMANDED

AMENDED COMPLAINT

COMES NOW the Plaintiff, Britton Mosley, and files this his Amended Complaint, suing the Defendant, the Mississippi Department of Corrections, for compensatory and punitive damages, and for this cause of action would most respectfully show unto this Court the following facts, to wit:

PARTIES

1. The Plaintiff, Britton Mosley, is an adult resident citizen of State Line, Green County, Mississippi.

2. The Defendant, Mississippi Department of Corrections (MDOC), is a state entity suable, despite the Eleventh Amendment of the United States Constitution by virtue of Title VII of the Civil Rights Act of 1964. The MDOC may be served with process by service upon its Commissioner, S.W. Puckett, 723 North President Street, Jackson, MS 39202.

JURISDICTION AND VENUE

3. This action is brought pursuant to Title VII of the Civil Rights Act of 1964 as amended by the Civil Rights Act of 1991, cited as 42 USC §2000, et.seq., and the 14th Amendment to the United States Constitution. Jurisdiction is founded upon 28 USC §1331 and 28 USC §1343, and the previously mentioned statutory provisions. Plaintiff further invokes the pendent jurisdiction of this Court to hear and decide claims arising under State law.

FACTUAL SITUATIONS

4. The Plaintiff, Britton Mosley, is a black male. He became employed with the Mississippi Department of Corrections in Leaksville, Mississippi in September of 1991. In addition, the Plaintiff's wife, Brenda Mosley, a black female, was likewise employed with the Mississippi Department of Corrections in Leaksville. In 1996, the Plaintiff's wife filed a Charge of Discrimination with the Equal Employment Opportunity Commission for failure to promote on the basis of race. In September of 1996, the Plaintiff's wife was transferred to a position at great personal risk to her. The Plaintiff's wife ultimately initiated a federal lawsuit on the basis of race discrimination for the failure to promote and on the basis of retaliation for transfer in retribution for filing the Charge of Discrimination. Sometime prior to the trial date of May 11, 1998, Mrs. Mosley settled her lawsuit and she was given the position for which she had applied, but had been denied.

5. In November of 1996, certain individuals employed by the Defendant, many of whom were the Plaintiff's superiors, conspired and attempted to set up the Plaintiff herein, Britton Mosley, by placing a package of marijuana in his possession. Then in July of 1997, certain individuals employed by the Defendant, many of whom where the Plaintiff's superiors, again conspired and attempted to set up the Plaintiff with drugs. Had these attempts been successful, the Plaintiff would have been fired, indicted on drug charges and possibly sent to prison.

6. In early 1998 the Plaintiff learned that certain individuals employed by the Defendant and who were the Plaintiff's superiors made threats "to get rid" of him. It was at this point in time that the Plaintiff resigned from his position with the MDOC, effective June 1, 1998, due to the hostile work environment and the stress and anxiety that he was caused to suffer at the hands of his employer.

7. All of the individuals who perpetrated the above referenced acts upon the Plaintiff were of the white race.

8. The Plaintiff contends that his resignation, due to the hostile work environment, amounts to constructive termination in violation of Title VII of the Civil Rights Act of 1967. Further, the Plaintiff contends that the Defendant retaliated against him for his wife's charges of discrimination and further for his testimony given on behalf of an inmate.

9. Throughout the Plaintiff's employment with the Defendant, he had an exemplary record.

10. The Plaintiff filed an EEOC Charge of Discrimination claiming retaliation, being Charge No. 131-98-1361, and the United States Department of Justice issued a Notice of Right to Sue letter on October 1, 1998. The Plaintiff filed a supplement Charge of Discrimination with the EEOC on November 6, 1998 alleging race discrimination, being Charge No. 131-99-0192, and the EEOC issued a Dismissal and Notice of Rights on November 17, 1998. By virtue of the EEOC and Department of Justice's dismissal and the issuance of the Notice of Rights letter, all administrative prerequisites have been met prior to the filing of this litigation.

CAUSES OF ACTION

11. The Defendant violated numerous federal and state laws in the unlawful termination of the Plaintiff. The Defendant has severely affected the Plaintiff's substantial interest in his ability to pursue his vocation. The Defendant's constructive termination of the Plaintiff was arbitrary, unreasonably, discriminatory and retaliatory, all in violation of Title VII of the Civil Rights Act of 1967, and the

14th Amendment to the United States Constitution. The Defendant exhibited ill will, malice, improper motive, and indifference to the Plaintiff's civil rights.

DAMAGES

12. The Plaintiff, as a result of the actions of the Defendant, has suffered lost wages, mental anxiety and stress, and other damages which he will show at a trial of this cause of action.

13. The Plaintiff has suffered compensatory damages as a result of the actions of the Defendant. He is entitled to back pay, front pay and/or reinstatement.

PRAYER FOR RELIEF

WHEREFORE, the Plaintiff, Britton Mosley, respectfully prays for the following relief against the Defendant:

    A.   Compensatory damages in an amount to be determined by this Court.

    B.   Punitive damages in an amount to be determined by this Court.

    C.   Back pay in an amount to be determined by this Court.

    C.   Front pay in an amount to be determined by this Court.

    D.   Reasonable attorney's fees and all costs of this court.

    E.   Such other general and special relief as appears reasonable and just in this cause.

RESPECTFULLY SUBMITTED,

(signature)

MICHAEL D. COOKE, MSB #6503
ATTORNEY FOR PLAINTIFF
Post Office Box 625
Iuka, MS 38852
(601)423-2000

Fabricating Evidence

IN THE UNITED STATES DISTRICT COURT
FOR THE SOUTHERN DISTRICT OF MISSISSIPPI
HATTIESBURG DIVISION

BRITTON MOSLEY   PLAINTIFF

VS.   2:98CV357-PG

MISSISSIPPI DEPARTMENT OF CORRECTIONS   DEFENDANT

ANSWER

COMES NOW, the Defendant, Mississippi Department of Corrections, in the above styled and numbered civil action, by and through counsel, and states the following in response to Plaintiff's complaint herein:

PARTIES

1. The Defendant admits the allegations in subsection (1) entitled "Parties".

2. The Defendant admits the allegations in subsection (2) entitled "Parties", except that Steve Puckett is no longer employed by the MDOC and therefore, process may not be had upon him through the MDOC, nor upon MDOC through him.

JURISDICTION AND VENUE

3. The Defendant admits the allegations of subsection (3) entitled "Jurisdiction and Venue", except to deny proper service of process, and that this Court has jurisdiction.

FACTUAL SITUATIONS

4. The Defendant admits that the Plaintiff is a Black male who became employed by the Defendant in 1991, and that his wife had filed an EEOC complaint, and is employed by the MDOC. The Defendant denies all other allegations in subsection (4) entitled "Factual Situations".

5. The Defendant denies the allegations in subsection (5) entitled "Factual Situations".

6. The Defendant admits that the Plaintiff left his employment with the Defendant, but denies all other allegations set forth in subsection (6) entitled "Factual Situations".

7. The Defendant denies the allegations in subsection (7) entitled "Factual Situations".

8. The Defendant denies the allegations in subsection (8) entitled "Factual Situations", and all subparts.

9. The Defendant denies the allegations in subsection (9) entitled "Factual Situations".

10. The Defendant can neither admit nor deny the allegations in subsection (10) entitled "Factual Situations", and therefore under the rules must deny.

CAUSES OF ACTION

11. The Defendant denies the allegations in subsection (11) entitled "Causes of Action", and all subparts.

DAMAGES

12. The Defendant denies the allegations in subsection (12) entitled "Damages".

13. The Defendant denies the allegation in subsection (13) entitled "Damages".

PRAY FOR RELIEF

The Defendant denies the Plaintiff is entitled to any relief prayed for in the complaint, or any subparts, and further that the Plaintiff is entitled to no relief whatsoever, and moves this Honorable Court to dismiss this complaint with prejudice, at Plaintiff's costs, and grant what other relief is deemed necessary and proper under the circumstances.

AFFIRMATIVE DEFENSES

AND NOW, having fully answered the allegations of the complaint herein, the Defendant offers the following defenses:

FIRST DEFENSE

The Plaintiff's complaint fails to state a charge against the Defendant upon which relief may be granted.

SECOND DEFENSE

The Court lacks jurisdiction over the parties in this cause.

THIRD DEFENSE

The Defendant is entitled to and hereby affirmatively pleads its federal law qualified immunity to suit and liability in this cause, including relief from discovery procedures,

FOURTH DEFENSE

The Defendant is entitled to and hereby affirmatively pleads its state law qualified immunity defenses to suit and liability in this cause, including relief from discovery procedures.

FIFTH DEFENSE

The Defendant is entitled to and hereby affirmatively pleads its sovereign immunity defenses to suit and liability in this cause pursuant to and inclusive of the provisions of Section 11-46-1, *et seq.*, Miss. Code of 1972, as annotated and amended.

Respectfully submitted,

MIKE MOORE, ATTORNEY GENERAL
STATE OF MISSISSIPPI

JOE GOFF
ASSISTANT ATTORNEY GENERAL

BY: _____
LEONARD C. VINCENT
GENERAL COUNSEL

CERTIFICATE OF SERVICE

I, Leonard C. Vincent, attorney for the Mississippi Department of Corrections and one of the attorneys for the Defendants, do hereby certify that I have, this date, mailed via United States Postage prepaid, a true and correct copy of Defendant's Answer to:

Michael D. Cooke, Esq.
Post Office Box 625
Iuka MS 38852

This, the 29th day of April, 1999.

[signature]

LEONARD C. VINCENT
GENERAL COUNSEL
Post Office Box 38
Parchman, Mississippi 38738
(601) 745-6611, Ext. 2307
MSB# 6615

Michael D. Cooke
Attorney At Law

106 Front Street . Post Office Box 625 . Iuka, Mississippi 38852
Tel: (662) 423-2000   Fax: (662) 423-2052

December 22, 2000

P-1
P-4
P-5

Honorable Charles W. Pickering, Sr.
United States District Judge
701 North Main St., Suite 228
Hattiesburg, MS 39401

RE: *Mosley v. MDOC*
      US District Court No. 2:98CV357PG

Dear Judge Pickering:

Enclosed please find Plaintiff's exhibits in quadruplicate. We have made copies of same for the jurors and will bring those to trial. Likewise, a copy of the exhibits has been mailed to Leonard Vincent

Respectfully yours,

Michael D. Cooke

MDC/dpd
Enclosure
cc: Leonard Vincent, Esquire
      Mr. Britton Mosley

UNITED STATES DISTRICT COURT
FOR THE SOUTHERN DISTRICT OF MISSISSIPPI
HATTIESBURG DIVISION

BRITTON MOSLEY   PLAINTIFF

V.   NO. 2:98CV357-P-G

MISSISSIPPI DEPARTMENT OF CORRECTIONS   DEFENDANT

PLAINTIFF'S EXHIBIT LIST

DATE	NUMBER	DESCRIPTION	SPONSOR	EVID.	I.D.
	P-1	Pertinent portions of Plaintiff's personnel file including Plaintiff's performance appraisals, correspondence to Plaintiff from Defendant, MDOC Summary of Employee Benefit Plans, Termination Slip, and Plaintiff's Letter of resignation			
	P-4	Plaintiff's earnings record including Plaintiff's 1996, 1997, and 1998 W-2s from Defendant, Plaintiff's 1998 and 1999 Income Tax Returns, and recent check stub from Marion County.			
	P-5	Incident Report dated November 5, 1996			
	P-6	Medical Records of Dr. Terry L. Jordan, M.D.			

CERTIFICATE OF SERVICE

I, Michael D. Cooke, do hereby certify that I have this day mailed by United States Mail, postage prepaid, a true and exact copy of the above and foregoing Plaintiff's Exhibit List to the following individuals at their respective addresses:

Leonard C. Vincent, Esquire
Post Office Box 38
Parchman, MS 38738

THIS 22ND day of December, 2000.

MICHAEL D. COOKE

Fabricating Evidence

AFFIDAVIT

STATE OF MISSISSIPPI
COUNTY OF MARION

Personally appeared before me, the undersigned, JIMMY FANCHER, who being by me first duly sworn on oath as follows:

1. I have personal knowledge of all the matters and things set forth in this affidavit.

On or about November or December of the year 2000, Leonard Vincent, attorney for the Mississippi Department of Corrections, came to my office at the Marion-Walthall Correctional Facility in Columbia, Mississippi. He came to discuss my testimony in the Brett Mosley case. Mr. Vincent asked me if I could testify to the fact that it was racially motivated. I replied, "I could not." He replied, "Well they tried to fuck him (B. Mosley), but it is not racially motivated."

JIMMY FANCHER

SWORN TO and subscribed before me, this ___ day of _____, 2002.

_____
Notary Public
My Commission Expires:_____

Britton Mosley, Sr.

AO 88 (Rev. 11/91) Subpoena in a Civil

United States District Court

SOUTHERN DISTRICT OF MISSISSIPPI

BRITTON MOSLEY
V.
MISSISSIPPI DEPARTMENT OF CORRECTIONS

SUBPOENA IN A CIVIL CASE

CASE NUMBER: 2:98CV357-P-G

TO: JIMMY FANCHER

☒ YOU ARE COMMANDED to appear in the United States District Court at the place, date, and time specified below to testify in the above case.

PLACE OF TESTIMONY	COURTROOM
William M. Colmer Federal Building & Courthouse 701 North Main Street, Hattiesburg, MS	No. 1
	DATE AND TIME 9/12/00 at 1:00 p.m.

☐ YOU ARE COMMANDED to appear at the place, date, and time specified below to testify at the taking of a deposition in the above case.

PLACE OF DEPOSITION	DATE AND TIME

☐ YOU ARE COMMANDED to produce and permit inspection and copying of the following documents or objects at the place, date, and time specified below (list documents or objects):

PLACE	DATE AND TIME

☐ YOU ARE COMMANDED to permit inspection of the following premises at the date and time specified below.

PREMISES	DATE AND TIME

Any organization not a party to this suit that is subpoenaed for the taking of a deposition shall designate one or more officers, directors, or managing agents, or other persons who consent to testify on its behalf, and may set forth, for each person designated, the matters on which the person will testify. Federal Rules of Civil Procedure, 30(b)(6).

ISSUING OFFICER SIGNATURE AND TITLE (INDICATE IF ATTORNEY FOR PLAINTIFF OR DEFENDANT)	DATE
Michael D. Cooke	8/9/00

ISSUING OFFICER'S NAME, ADDRESS AND PHONE NUMBER
Michael D. Cooke, Attorney at Law (662)423-2000
P.O. Box 625, Iuka, MS 38852

(See Rule 45, Federal Rules of Civil Procedure, Parts C & D on Reverse)

Fabricating Evidence

AO 88 (11/91) Subpoena in a Civil Case

PROOF OF SERVICE

	DATE	PLACE
SERVED	8/15/00	Columbia Ms.

SERVED ON (PRINT NAME)	MANNER OF SERVICE
Jimmy Fancher	Hand Served

SERVED BY (PRINT NAME)	TITLE
James Harvey	Deputy Warden

DECLARATION OF SERVER

I declare under penalty of perjury under the laws of the United States of America that the foregoing information contained in the Proof of Service is true and correct.

Executed on 8/15/00
           DATE

SIGNATURE OF SERVER: *James Harvey*

ADDRESS OF SERVER: Columbia Ms. 39429

Rule 45, Federal Rules of Civil Procedure, Parts C & D:

(c) PROTECTION OF PERSONS SUBJECT TO SUBPOENAS.

(1) A party or an attorney responsible for the issuance and service of a subpoena shall take reasonable steps to avoid imposing undue burden or expense on a person subject to that subpoena. The court on behalf of which the subpoena was issued shall enforce this duty and impose upon the party or attorney in breach of this duty an appropriate sanction, which may include, but is not limited to, lost earnings and a reasonable attorney's fee.

(2)(A) A person commanded to produce and permit inspection and copying of designated books, papers, documents or tangible things, or inspection of premises need not appear in person at the place of production or inspection unless commanded to appear for deposition, hearing or trial.

(B) Subject to paragraph (d)(2) of this rule, a person commanded to produce and permit inspection and copying may, within 14 days after service of the subpoena or before the time specified for compliance if such time is less than 14 days after service, serve upon the party or attorney designated in the subpoena written objection to inspection or copying of any or all of the designated materials or of the premises. If objection is made, the party serving the subpoena shall not be entitled to inspect and copy the materials or inspect the premises except pursuant to an order of the court by which the subpoena was issued. If objection has been made, the party serving the subpoena may, upon notice to the person commanded to produce, move at any time for an order to compel the production. Such an order to compel production shall protect any person who is not a party or an officer of a party from significant expense resulting from the inspection and copying commanded.

(3)(A) On timely motion, the court by which a subpoena was issued shall quash or modify the subpoena if it

(i) fails to allow reasonable time for compliance;
(ii) requires a person who is not a party or an officer of a party to travel to a place more than 100 miles from the place where that person resides, is employed or regularly transacts business in person, except that, subject to the provisions of clause (c)(3)(B)(iii) of this rule, such a person may in order to attend trial be commanded to travel from any such place within the state in which the trial is held, or
(iii) requires disclosure of privileged or other protected matter and no exception or waiver applies, or
(iv) subjects a person to undue burden.

(B) If a subpoena

(i) requires disclosure of a trade secret or other confidential research, development, or commercial information, or
(ii) requires disclosure of an unretained expert's opinion or information not describing specific events or occurrences in dispute and resulting from the expert's study made not at the request of any party, or
(iii) requires a person who is not a party or an officer of a party to incur substantial expense to travel more than 100 miles to attend trial, the court may, to protect a person subject to or affected by the subpoena, quash or modify the subpoena or, if the party in whose behalf the subpoena is issued shows a substantial need for the testimony or material that cannot be otherwise met without undue hardship and assures that the person to whom the subpoena is addressed will be reasonably compensated, the court may order appearance or production only upon specified conditions.

(d) DUTIES IN RESPONDING TO SUBPOENA.

(1) A person responding to a subpoena to produce documents shall produce them as they are kept in the usual course of business or shall organize and label them to correspond with the categories in the demand.

(2) When information subject to a subpoena is withheld on a claim that it is privileged or subject to protection as trial preparation materials, the claim shall be made expressly and shall be supported by a description of the nature of the documents, communications, or things not produced that is sufficient to enable the demanding party to contest the claim.

AO 88 (Rev. 11/91) Subpoena in a Civil

United States District Court

SOUTHERN DISTRICT OF MISSISSIPPI

BRITTON MOSLEY
V.
MISSISSIPPI DEPARTMENT OF CORRECTIONS

SUBPOENA IN A CIVIL CASE

CASE NUMBER: 2:98CV357-P-G

TO: MARVIN THOMAS

☒ YOU ARE COMMANDED to appear in the United States District Court at the place, date, and time specified below to testify in the above case.

PLACE OF TESTIMONY	COURTROOM
William M. Colmer Federal Building & Courthouse 701 North Main Street, Hattiesburg, MS	No. 1
	DATE AND TIME
	9/12/00 at 1:00 p.m.

☐ YOU ARE COMMANDED to appear at the place, date, and time specified below to testify at the taking of a deposition in the above case.

PLACE OF DEPOSITION	DATE AND TIME

☐ YOU ARE COMMANDED to produce and permit inspection and copying of the following documents or objects at the place, date, and time specified below (list documents or objects):

PLACE	DATE AND TIME

☐ YOU ARE COMMANDED to permit inspection of the following premises at the date and time specified below.

PREMISES	DATE AND TIME

Any organization not a party to this suit that is subpoenaed for the taking of a deposition shall designate one or more officers, directors, or managing agents, or other persons who consent to testify on its behalf, and may set forth, for each person designated, the matters on which the person will testify. Federal Rules of Civil Procedure, 30(b)(6).

ISSUING OFFICER SIGNATURE AND TITLE (INDICATE IF ATTORNEY FOR PLAINTIFF OR DEFENDANT) — DATE 8/9/00

ISSUING OFFICER'S NAME, ADDRESS AND PHONE NUMBER
Michael D. Cooke, Attorney at Law (662)423-2000
P.O. Box 625, Iuka, MS 38852

(See Rule 45, Federal Rules of Civil Procedure, Parts C & D on Reverse)

Fabricating Evidence

AO 88 (11/91) Subpoena in a Civil Case

PROOF OF SERVICE

	DATE	PLACE
SERVED	08-13-00	Newton MS
SERVED ON (PRINT NAME) Malvin Thomas		MANNER OF SERVICE Hand Service
SERVED BY (PRINT NAME) Sharon Seals		TITLE Bus Driver Newton School

DECLARATION OF SERVER

I declare under penalty of perjury under the laws of the United States of America that the foregoing information contained in the Proof of Service is true and correct.

Executed on 08-13-00
DATE

Sharon Seals
SIGNATURE OF SERVER

ADDRESS OF SERVER
Newton MS 39345

Rule 45, Federal Rules of Civil Procedure, Parts C & D:

(c) PROTECTION OF PERSONS SUBJECT TO SUBPOENAS.

(1) A party or an attorney responsible for the issuance and service of a subpoena shall take reasonable steps to avoid imposing undue burden or expense on a person subject to that subpoena. The court on behalf of which the subpoena was issued shall enforce this duty and impose upon the party or attorney in breach of this duty an appropriate sanction, which may include, but is not limited to, lost earnings and a reasonable attorney's fee.

(2)(A) A person commanded to produce and permit inspection and copying of designated books, papers, documents or tangible things, or inspection of premises need not appear in person at the place of production or inspection unless commanded to appear for deposition, hearing or trial.

(B) Subject to paragraph (d)(2) of this rule, a person commanded to produce and permit inspection and copying may, within 14 days after service of the subpoena or before the time specified for compliance if such time is less than 14 days after service, serve upon the party or attorney designated in the subpoena written objection to inspection or copying of any or all of the designated materials or of the premises. If objection is made, the party serving the subpoena shall not be entitled to inspect and copy the materials or inspect the premises except pursuant to an order of the court by which the subpoena was issued. If objection has been made, the party serving the subpoena may, upon notice to the person commanded to produce, move at any time for an order to compel the production. Such an order to compel production shall protect any person who is not a party or an officer of a party from significant expense resulting from the inspection and copying commanded.

(3)(A) On timely motion, the court by which a subpoena was issued shall quash or modify the subpoena if it

(i) fails to allow reasonable time for compliance;
(ii) requires a person who is not a party or an officer of a party to travel to a place more than 100 miles from the place where that person resides, is employed or regularly transacts business in person, except that, subject to the provisions of clause (c)(3)(B)(iii) of this rule, such a person may in order to attend trial be commanded to travel from any such place within the state in which the trial is held, or
(iii) requires disclosure of privileged or other protected matter and no exception or waiver applies, or
(iv) subjects a person to undue burden.

(B) If a subpoena
(i) requires disclosure of a trade secret or other confidential research, development, or commercial information, or
(ii) requires disclosure of an unretained expert's opinion or information not describing specific events or occurrences in dispute and resulting from the expert's study made not at the request of any party, or
(iii) requires a person who is not a party or an officer of a party to incur substantial expense to travel more than 100 miles to attend trial, the court may, to protect a person subject to or affected by the subpoena, quash or modify the subpoena or, if the party in whose behalf the subpoena is issued shows a substantial need for the testimony or material that cannot be otherwise met without undue hardship and assures that the person to whom the subpoena is addressed will be reasonably compensated, the court may order appearance or production only upon specified conditions.

(d) DUTIES IN RESPONDING TO SUBPOENA.

(1) A person responding to a subpoena to produce documents shall produce them as they are kept in the usual course of business or shall organize and label them to correspond with the categories in the demand.

(2) When information subject to a subpoena is withheld on a claim that it is privileged or subject to protection as trial preparation materials, the claim shall be made expressly and shall be supported by a description of the nature of the documents, communications, or things not produced that is sufficient to enable the demanding party to contest the claim.

Britton Mosley, Sr.

AO 88 (Rev. 11/91) Subpoena in a Civil

United States District Court

SOUTHERN DISTRICT OF MISSISSIPPI

BRITTON MOSLEY
V.
MISSISSIPPI DEPARTMENT OF CORRECTIONS

SUBPOENA IN A CIVIL CASE

CASE NUMBER: 2:98CV357-P-G

TO: DANIEL C. PAFF

☒ YOU ARE COMMANDED to appear in the United States District Court at the place, date, and time specified below to testify in the above case.

PLACE OF TESTIMONY	COURTROOM
William M. Colmer Federal Building & Courthouse 701 North Main Street, Hattiesburg, MS	No. 1
	DATE AND TIME 9/12/00 at 1:00 p.m.

☐ YOU ARE COMMANDED to appear at the place, date, and time specified below to testify at the taking of a deposition in the above case.

PLACE OF DEPOSITION	DATE AND TIME

☐ YOU ARE COMMANDED to produce and permit inspection and copying of the following documents or objects at the place, date, and time specified below (list documents or objects):

PLACE	DATE AND TIME

☐ YOU ARE COMMANDED to permit inspection of the following premises at the date and time specified below.

PREMISES	DATE AND TIME

Any organization not a party to this suit that is subpoenaed for the taking of a deposition shall designate one or more officers, directors, or managing agents, or other persons who consent to testify on its behalf, and may set forth, for each person designated, the matters on which the person will testify. Federal Rules of Civil Procedure, 30(b)(6).

ISSUING OFFICER SIGNATURE AND TITLE (INDICATE IF ATTORNEY FOR PLAINTIFF OR DEFENDANT) — DATE 8/9/00

ISSUING OFFICER'S NAME, ADDRESS AND PHONE NUMBER
Michael D. Cooke, Attorney at Law   (662)423-2000
P.O. Box 625, Iuka, MS 38852

(See Rule 45, Federal Rules of Civil Procedure, Parts C & D on Reverse)

Fabricating Evidence

AO 88 (11/91) Subpoena in a Civil Case

PROOF OF SERVICE

	DATE	PLACE
SERVED	08-13-00	Newton MS

SERVED ON (PRINT NAME): MARVIN Thomas

MANNER OF SERVICE: Hand Service

SERVED BY (PRINT NAME): Sharon Seals

TITLE: Bus driver Newton School

DECLARATION OF SERVER

I declare under penalty of perjury under the laws of the United States of America that the foregoing information contained in the Proof of Service is true and correct.

Executed on 08-13-00

SIGNATURE OF SERVER: Sharon Seals

ADDRESS OF SERVER: Newton MS 39345

Rule 45, Federal Rules of Civil Procedure, Parts C & D:

(c) PROTECTION OF PERSONS SUBJECT TO SUBPOENAS.

(1) A party or an attorney responsible for the issuance and service of a subpoena shall take reasonable steps to avoid imposing undue burden or expense on a person subject to that subpoena. The court on behalf of which the subpoena was issued shall enforce this duty and impose upon the party or attorney in breach of this duty an appropriate sanction, which may include, but is not limited to, lost earnings and a reasonable attorney's fee.

(2)(A) A person commanded to produce and permit inspection and copying of designated books, papers, documents or tangible things, or inspection of premises need not appear in person at the place of production or inspection unless commanded to appear for deposition, hearing or trial.

(B) Subject to paragraph (d)(2) of this rule, a person commanded to produce and permit inspection and copying may, within 14 days after service of the subpoena or before the time specified for compliance if such time is less than 14 days after service, serve upon the party or attorney designated in the subpoena written objection to inspection or copying of any or all of the designated materials or of the premises. If objection is made, the party serving the subpoena shall not be entitled to inspect and copy the materials or inspect the premises except pursuant to an order of the court by which the subpoena was issued. If objection has been made, the party serving the subpoena may, upon notice to the person commanded to produce, move at any time for an order to compel the production. Such an order to compel production shall protect any person who is not a party or an officer of a party from significant expense resulting from the inspection and copying commanded.

(3)(A) On timely motion, the court by which a subpoena was issued shall quash or modify the subpoena if it

(i) fails to allow reasonable time for compliance;
(ii) requires a person who is not a party or an officer of a party to travel to a place more than 100 miles from the place where that person resides, is employed or regularly transacts business in person, except that, subject to the provisions of clause (c)(3)(B)(iii) of this rule, such a person may in order to attend trial be commanded to travel from any such place within the state in which the trial is held, or

(iii) requires disclosure of privileged or other protected matter and no exception or waiver applies, or
(iv) subjects a person to undue burden.

(B) If a subpoena

(i) requires disclosure of a trade secret or other confidential research, development, or commercial information, or
(ii) requires disclosure of an unretained expert's opinion or information not describing specific events or occurrences in dispute and resulting from the expert's study made not at the request of any party, or
(iii) requires a person who is not a party or an officer of a party to incur substantial expense to travel more than 100 miles to attend trial, the court may, to protect a person subject to or affected by the subpoena, quash or modify the subpoena or, if the party in whose behalf the subpoena is issued shows a substantial need for the testimony or material that cannot be otherwise met without undue hardship and assures that the person to whom the subpoena is addressed will be reasonably compensated, the court may order appearance or production only upon specified conditions.

(d) DUTIES IN RESPONDING TO SUBPOENA.

(1) A person responding to a subpoena to produce documents shall produce them as they are kept in the usual course of business or shall organize and label them to correspond with the categories in the demand.

(2) When information subject to a subpoena is withheld on a claim that it is privileged or subject to protection as trial preparation materials, the claim shall be made expressly and shall be supported by a description of the nature of the documents, communications, or things not produced that is sufficient to enable the demanding party to contest the claim.

Britton Mosley, Sr.

AO 88 (Rev. 11/91) Subpoena in a Civil

United States District Court

SOUTHERN DISTRICT OF MISSISSIPPI

BRITTON MOSLEY
V.
MISSISSIPPI DEPARTMENT OF CORRECTIONS

SUBPOENA IN A CIVIL CASE

CASE NUMBER: 2:98CV357-P-G

TO: DANIEL C. PAFF

☒ YOU ARE COMMANDED to appear in the United States District Court at the place, date, and time specified below to testify in the above case.

PLACE OF TESTIMONY	COURTROOM
William M. Colmer Federal Building & Courthouse 701 North Main Street, Hattiesburg, MS	No. 1
	DATE AND TIME
	9/12/00 at 1:00 p.m.

☐ YOU ARE COMMANDED to appear at the place, date, and time specified below to testify at the taking of a deposition in the above case.

PLACE OF DEPOSITION	DATE AND TIME

☐ YOU ARE COMMANDED to produce and permit inspection and copying of the following documents or objects at the place, date, and time specified below (list documents or objects):

PLACE	DATE AND TIME

☐ YOU ARE COMMANDED to permit inspection of the following premises at the date and time specified below.

PREMISES	DATE AND TIME

Any organization not a party to this suit that is subpoenaed for the taking of a deposition shall designate one or more officers, directors, or managing agents, or other persons who consent to testify on its behalf, and may set forth, for each person designated, the matters on which the person will testify. Federal Rules of Civil Procedure, 30(b)(6).

ISSUING OFFICER SIGNATURE AND TITLE (INDICATE IF ATTORNEY FOR PLAINTIFF OR DEFENDANT)   DATE 8/9/00

ISSUING OFFICER'S NAME, ADDRESS AND PHONE NUMBER
Michael D. Cooke, Attorney at Law   (662)423-2000
P.O. Box 625, Iuka, MS 38852

(See Rule 45, Federal Rules of Civil Procedure, Parts C & D on Reverse)

Fabricating Evidence

AO 88 (11/91) Subpoena in a Civil Case

PROOF OF SERVICE

	DATE	PLACE
SERVED	8-22-00	Jugalis Yard PAS MS
SERVED ON (PRINT NAME)		MANNER OF SERVICE
PAUL McLENDON		HAND SERVICE
SERVED BY (PRINT NAME)		TITLE
Tyree Harris		Aligatech

DECLARATION OF SERVER

I declare under penalty of perjury under the laws of the United States of America that the foregoing information contained in the Proof of Service is true and correct.

Executed on 8-22-00
DATE

SIGNATURE OF SERVER

ADDRESS OF SERVER

Miss Point MS

Rule 45, Federal Rules of Civil Procedure, Parts C & D:

(c) PROTECTION OF PERSONS SUBJECT TO SUBPOENAS.

(1) A party or an attorney responsible for the issuance and service of a subpoena shall take reasonable steps to avoid imposing undue burden or expense on a person subject to that subpoena. The court on behalf of which the subpoena was issued shall enforce this duty and impose upon the party or attorney in breach of this duty an appropriate sanction, which may include, but is not limited to, lost earnings and a reasonable attorney's fee.

(2)(A) A person commanded to produce and permit inspection and copying of designated books, papers, documents or tangible things, or inspection of premises need not appear in person at the place of production or inspection unless commanded to appear for deposition, hearing or trial.

(B) Subject to paragraph (d)(2) of this rule, a person commanded to produce and permit inspection and copying may, within 14 days after service of the subpoena or before the time specified for compliance if such time is less than 14 days after service, serve upon the party or attorney designated in the subpoena written objection to inspection or copying of any or all of the designated materials or of the premises. If objection is made, the party serving the subpoena shall not be entitled to inspect and copy the materials or inspect the premises except pursuant to an order of the court by which the subpoena was issued. If objection has been made, the party serving the subpoena may, upon notice to the person commanded to produce, move at any time for an order to compel the production. Such an order to compel production shall protect any person who is not a party or an officer of a party from significant expense resulting from the inspection and copying commanded.

(3)(A) On timely motion, the court by which a subpoena was issued shall quash or modify the subpoena if it

(i) fails to allow reasonable time for compliance;
(ii) requires a person who is not a party or an officer of a party to travel to a place more than 100 miles from the place where that person resides, is employed or regularly transacts business in person, except that, subject to the provisions of clause (c)(3)(B)(iii) of this rule, such a person may in order to attend trial be commanded to travel from any such place within the state in which the trial is held, or

(iii) requires disclosure of privileged or other protected matter and no exception or waiver applies, or
(iv) subjects a person to undue burden.

(B) If a subpoena

(i) requires disclosure of a trade secret or other confidential research, development, or commercial information, or
(ii) requires disclosure of an unretained expert's opinion or information not describing specific events or occurrences in dispute and resulting from the expert's study made not at the request of any party, or
(iii) requires a person who is not a party or an officer of a party to incur substantial expense to travel more than 100 miles to attend trial, the court may, to protect a person subject to or affected by the subpoena, quash or modify the subpoena or, if the party in whose behalf the subpoena is issued shows a substantial need for the testimony or material that cannot be otherwise met without undue hardship and assures that the person to whom the subpoena is addressed will be reasonably compensated, the court may order appearance or production only upon specified conditions.

(d) DUTIES IN RESPONDING TO SUBPOENA.

(1) A person responding to a subpoena to produce documents shall produce them as they are kept in the usual course of business or shall organize and label them to correspond with the categories in the demand.

(2) When information subject to a subpoena is withheld on a claim that it is privileged or subject to protection as trial preparation materials, the claim shall be made expressly and shall be supported by a description of the nature of the documents, communications, or things not produced that is sufficient to enable the demanding party to contest the claim.

Britton Mosley, Sr.

AO 88 (Rev. 11/91) Subpoena in a Civil

United States District Court

SOUTHERN DISTRICT OF MISSISSIPPI

BRITTON MOSLEY
V.

SUBPOENA IN A CIVIL CASE

MISSISSIPPI DEPARTMENT OF CORRECTIONS

CASE NUMBER: 2:98CV357-P-G

TO: JOE BEARD

☒ YOU ARE COMMANDED to appear in the United States District Court at the place, date, and time specified below to testify in the above case.

PLACE OF TESTIMONY	COURTROOM
William M. Colmer Federal Building & Courthouse 701 North Main Street, Hattiesburg, MS	No. 1
	DATE AND TIME
	9/12/00 at 1:00 p.m.

☐ YOU ARE COMMANDED to appear at the place, date, and time specified below to testify at the taking of a deposition in the above case.

PLACE OF DEPOSITION	DATE AND TIME

☐ YOU ARE COMMANDED to produce and permit inspection and copying of the following documents or objects at the place, date, and time specified below (list documents or objects):

PLACE	DATE AND TIME

☐ YOU ARE COMMANDED to permit inspection of the following premises at the date and time specified below.

PREMISES	DATE AND TIME

Any organization not a party to this suit that is subpoenaed for the taking of a deposition shall designate one or more officers, directors, or managing agents, or other persons who consent to testify on its behalf, and may set forth, for each person designated, the matters on which the person will testify. Federal Rules of Civil Procedure, 30(b)(6).

ISSUING OFFICER SIGNATURE AND TITLE (INDICATE IF ATTORNEY FOR PLAINTIFF OR DEFENDANT)   DATE

Michael D. Cooke   8/9/00

ISSUING OFFICER'S NAME, ADDRESS AND PHONE NUMBER
Michael D. Cooke, Attorney at Law   (662)423-2000
P.O. Box 625, Iuka, MS 38852

(See Rule 45, Federal Rules of Civil Procedure, Parts C & D on Reverse)

Fabricating Evidence

AO 88 (11/91) Subpoena in a Civil Case

PROOF OF SERVICE

	DATE	PLACE	
SERVED	8-15-00	Leakesville MS	
SERVED ON (PRINT NAME) Joe Bean		MANNER OF SERVICE Hand Served	
SERVED BY (PRINT NAME) David Horatter		TITLE Builder	

DECLARATION OF SERVER

I declare under penalty of perjury under the laws of the United States of America that the foregoing information contained in the Proof of Service is true and correct.

Executed on 8-15-00
DATE

SIGNATURE OF SERVER David Horatter

ADDRESS OF SERVER
Lucedale MS 39452

Rule 45, Federal Rules of Civil Procedure, Parts C & D:

(c) PROTECTION OF PERSONS SUBJECT TO SUBPOENAS.

(1) A party or an attorney responsible for the issuance and service of a subpoena shall take reasonable steps to avoid imposing undue burden or expense on a person subject to that subpoena. The court on behalf of which the subpoena was issued shall enforce this duty and impose upon the party or attorney in breach of this duty an appropriate sanction, which may include, but is not limited to, lost earnings and a reasonable attorney's fee.

(2)(A) A person commanded to produce and permit inspection and copying of designated books, papers, documents or tangible things, or inspection of premises need not appear in person at the place of production or inspection unless commanded to appear for deposition, hearing or trial.

(B) Subject to paragraph (d)(2) of this rule, a person commanded to produce and permit inspection and copying may, within 14 days after service of the subpoena or before the time specified for compliance if such time is less than 14 days after service, serve upon the party or attorney designated in the subpoena written objection to inspection or copying of any or all of the designated materials or of the premises. If objection is made, the party serving the subpoena shall not be entitled to inspect and copy the materials or inspect the premises except pursuant to an order of the court by which the subpoena was issued. If objection has been made, the party serving the subpoena may, upon notice to the person commanded to produce, move at any time for an order to compel the production. Such an order to compel production shall protect any person who is not a party or an officer of a party from significant expense resulting from the inspection and copying commanded.

(3)(A) On timely motion, the court by which a subpoena was issued shall quash or modify the subpoena if it

(i) fails to allow reasonable time for compliance;
(ii) requires a person who is not a party or an officer of a party to travel to a place more than 100 miles from the place where that person resides, is employed or regularly transacts business in person, except that, subject to the provisions of clause (c)(3)(B)(iii) of this rule, such a person may in order to attend trial be commanded to travel from any such place within the state in which the trial is held, or

(iii) requires disclosure of privileged or other protected matter and no exception or waiver applies, or
(iv) subjects a person to undue burden.

(B) If a subpoena

(i) requires disclosure of a trade secret or other confidential research, development, or commercial information, or
(ii) requires disclosure of an unretained expert's opinion or information not describing specific events or occurrences in dispute and resulting from the expert's study made not at the request of any party, or
(iii) requires a person who is not a party or an officer of a party to incur substantial expense to travel more than 100 miles to attend trial, the court may, to protect a person subject to or affected by the subpoena, quash or modify the subpoena or, if the party in whose behalf the subpoena is issued shows a substantial need for the testimony or material that cannot be otherwise met without undue hardship and assures that the person to whom the subpoena is addressed will be reasonably compensated, the court may order appearance or production only upon specified conditions.

(d) DUTIES IN RESPONDING TO SUBPOENA.

(1) A person responding to a subpoena to produce documents shall produce them as they are kept in the usual course of business or shall organize and label them to correspond with the categories in the demand.

(2) When information subject to a subpoena is withheld on a claim that it is privileged or subject to protection as trial preparation materials, the claim shall be made expressly and shall be supported by a description of the nature of the documents, communications, or things not produced that is sufficient to enable the demanding party to contest the claim.

IN THE UNITED STATES DISTRICT COURT
FOR THE SOUTHERN DISTRICT OF MISSISSIPPI
HATTIESBURG DIVISION

BRITTON MOSLEY   PLAINTIFF

v.   NO. 2:98CV357-P-G

MISSISSIPPI DEPARTMENT OF CORRECTIONS   DEFENDANT

PLAINTIFF'S PRE-DISCOVERY DISCLOSURE OF CORE INFORMATION

Pursuant to the amendments to the Civil Justice Reform Act, the Plaintiff provides herewith the name and, if known, the address and telephone number of each individual likely to have discoverable information relevant to the claim of the Plaintiff, along with a short summary of the anticipated discoverable knowledge of each individual; however, these summaries do not purport to encompass the extent of each person's knowledge, but only what the Plaintiff now believes to be the extent of their knowledge. Information that is incomplete or unavailable at the time of this filing will be supplemented as same becomes available.

In addition to the Plaintiff, the following persons may have discoverable knowledge:

> Brenda Mosley (Plaintiff's wife) - is aware of the circumstances that lead to the Plaintiff's constructive termination from the MDOC.

Paul McLendon (address unknown*) - Sgt. McLendon is aware of a conversation between two MDOC officers relative to "getting rid of the Plaintiff." Upon information and belief, Sgt. McLendon gave a statement of these facts to FBI Special Agent Randall L. Nedecker.

David Turner (address unknown*) - upon information and belief, Supt. Turner was involved in a second attempted set-up of the Plaintiff.

Joe Errington (address unknown*) - Capt. Errington was one of the Plaintiff's superiors. Upon information and belief, Capt. Errington was involved in a second attempted set-up of the Plaintiff.

Joe Beard (address unknown*) - Mr. Beard is aware of a vendetta that Joe Errington had against the Plaintiff. Upon information and belief, Joe Beard gave a statement to the FBI relevant to the his knowledge of these facts.

Michael Miller (address unknown*) - on November 4, 1996, CO Miller participated in an attempt to frame the Plaintiff when he left a package with Sgt. Daniel Paff at the maintenance complex with instructions to give the package to the Plaintiff with instructions that it be given to an inmate. It was later discovered that the packaged contained two ounces of marijuana and other items.

Daniel Paff (address unknown*) - Sgt. Paff delivered the package left by Michael Miller with instructions that it be given to the Plaintiff to be given to inmate Mandell Walker. Sgt. Paff suggested to the Plaintiff that he search the contents of the package.

Johnny Denmark (address unknown*) - upon information and belief, Capt. Denmark[1] has knowledge of, and upon information and belief, had a part in the attempted set-up of the Plaintiff.

Larry Smith (address unknown*) - Internal Audit Investigator who investigated the incidents regarding the attempted set-up of the Plaintiff. Mr. Smith is aware of the circumstances of the attempted framing of the Plaintiff and, upon information belief, is aware of the participants in that attempted set-up.

Victor Brewer (address unknown*) - Lt. Brewer[2] has knowledge of, and upon information and belief, had a part in the attempted set-up of the Plaintiff. Lt. Brewer directed the Plaintiff to not write an incident report about the findings of the package delivered on November 4, 1996.

Malcolm McClendon (address unknown*) - Investigator McClendon[3] was called to the Central Security Office to investigate the marijuana findings of the package delivered on November 4, 1996. Upon information and belief, Investigator McClendon had prior knowledge of and a part in the attempted drug set-up of the Plaintiff.

Louis Kittrell (address unknown*) - CO Kittrell, upon information and belief has knowledge of and/or a part in the attempted set-up of the Plaintiff.

Terry Burgess (address unknown*) - Lt. Burgess, upon information belief, has knowledge of and/or a part in the attempted set-up of the Plaintiff. Lt. Burgess was another of Plaintiff's superiors.

---

[1] Johnnie Demark subsequently promoted to Deputy Warden

[2] Victor Brewer subsequently promoted to Captain.

[3] Malcolm McClendon subsequently promoted to Chief Investigator.

John Graham (address unknown*) - Sgt. Graham, upon information belief, has knowledge of and/or a part in the attempted set-up of the Plaintiff.

Danny Woodard (address unknown*) - CO II Woodard[4], upon information belief, has knowledge of and/or a part in the attempted set-up of the Plaintiff.

Jerry Dettman (address unknown*) - Internal Audit Investigator, upon information belief, has knowledge of and/or a part in the attempted set-up of the Plaintiff. Mr. Dettman also participated in the investigation of the incident concerning the attempted set-up.

Harold James (address unknown) - CO II James[5] was present when the marijuana was discovered and present when Investigator McClendon investigated the incident.

Nicole Pearson (address unknown*) - upon information and belief CO II Pearson has knowledge of the attempted set-up of the Plaintiff.

Randall L. Nedecker, Special Agent, FBI - Agent Nedecker investigated incidents related to the Plaintiff's being set-up while employed at the MDOC facility in _____.

Linton Rice, FBI Special Agent - the Plaintiff gave Agent Rice a statement regarding the incidence which are the subject of this lawsuit.

Mandell Walker, Inmate #78206, SMCI-I, Leaksville, MS - Mr. Walker has knowledge of the attempted set up of the Plaintiff.

---

[4]Danny Woodard was subsequently promoted to Sergeant.

[5]Harold James subsequently resigned from the MDOC.

Marvin Thomas, Inmate #79517, Greenwood, MS - Mr. Thomas has knowledge of the attempted set up of the Plaintiff.

Nicole Pearson, US Department of Justice, Washington, DC - Ms. Pearson has knowledge of the Department of Justice's investigation into the incidents at the SMCI in Leaksville.

Jacqueline Spratt, US Department of Justice, Washington, DC - Ms. Spratt has knowledge of the Department of Justice's investigation into the incidents at the SMCI in Leaksville.

Julius Gonzales, Regional Director, FBI - has knowledge of the Plaintiff's averments and the FBI's subsequent investigation.

*employed with the SMCI

Plaintiff's physicians who have seen him in connection with stress, trauma and emotional harm:

Alexis Polles, MD

Terry L. Jordan, MD

R.L. Douglas, PhD, PA

Tracey Yost, MSLPC

Steve Morris, MD

Charles Hornfort, MALCP
(address unknown at present time)

II.

A copy of, or a description by category and location of, all documents, data compilations, and tangible things in the possession, custody, or control of the party that are relevant to the claims asserted are as follows:

1. Personnel file of the Plaintiff in the possession of the Defendant.

2. Personnel policies/manuals of the Defendant in the possession of the Defendant.

3. Internal operating procedures policies and/or procedures in the possession of the Defendant.

4. EEOC investigative file to Charge Nos. 131-99-0192 and 131-98-1361 in the possession of the Equal Employment Opportunity Commission, Jackson, Mississippi.

5. Internal Audit Investigative Reports and/or recorded/transcribed statements concerning any incident which is the subject of this lawsuit, all in the possession of the Defendant.

6. FBI Investigative Reports and/or recorded/transcribed statements concerning any incident which is the subject of this lawsuit, all in the possession of the FBI.

7. US Department of Justice Reports and/or recorded/transcribed statements concerning any incident which is the subject of this lawsuit, all in the possession of the US Department of Justice.

Britton Mosley, Sr.

U.S. District Court for the Southern District of Mississippi Hattiesburg Division

Britton Mosley, Sr.
    Plaintiff
Vs.
    2:98CV357-PG
Mississippi Department of Corrections
    Defendant

1. U.S. District Judge
a. Charles W. Pickering, Sr., W/M
b. Margaret A. Kinchen, RMR, CRR, W/F

2. U.S. Attorney General of Mississippi
a. Jack Lacey, Assistant Attorney General, W/M

3. FBI
a. Lenton Rice, FBI Special Agent, W/M
b. Randall Neidecker, FBI Special Agent, W/M
c. Julius Gonzales, H/M

4. Attorney General State Of Mississippi
a. Mike Moore, Attorney General, W/M
b. Joe Goff, Assistant Attorney General, W/M
c. Lee Martin, Assistant Attorney General, W/M

5. 19 Circuit Court District
a. Keith Miller, District Attorney, W/M
b. Darren Versiga, Investigator

6. Mississippi Department of Public Safety
a. David Oubre, M/Sgt. B-47, W/M
b. Darrell Perkins, Investigator, W/M
c. Nelson Tate, Lt., B/M

7. Mississippi Department of Corrections Internal Audit Division
a. Malcolm V. McLendon, Former Chief (IAD), W/M
b. Larry Smith, Integrity Investigator, W/M

c. Johnny Covington, Integrity Investigator, W/M
d. Jerry Dettman, Integrity Investigator, W/M

8. Attorney for MDOC (Defendant)
a. Leonard C. Vincent, General Counsel

9. Attorney for Britton Mosley, Sr. (Plaintiff)
a. Michael D. Cooke, MSB #6503

Britton Mosley, Sr.

IN THE UNITED STATES DISTRICT COURT
FOR THE SOUTHERN DISTRICT OF MISSISSIPPI
HATTIESBURG DIVISION

SOUTHERN DISTRICT OF MISSISSIPPI
FILED
JAN 1 7 2001
J.T. NOBLIN, CLERK
BY _____ DEPUTY

BRITTON MOSLEY   PLAINTIFF

VERSUS   CIVIL ACTION NO. 2:98cv357PG

MISSISSIPPI DEPARTMENT OF CORRECTIONS   DEFENDANT

JUDGMENT ON JURY VERDICT

This matter came on to be tried before this Court in a jury composed of Jack W. Young and seven others and after the issues have been duly tried and due deliberations by the jury a verdict in favor of the Defendant was returned.

IT IS, THEREFORE, ORDERED AND ADJUDGED that judgment is entered in favor of the Defendant and this matter is dismissed with prejudice.

SO ORDERED AND ADJUDGED, this the ___17th___ day of ___January___, 2001.

CHARLES W. PICKERING, SR.
UNITED STATES DISTRICT JUDGE

CHAPTER NINE

Attorney Michael D. Cooke

After years of searching for an attorney to file a civil lawsuit against the Mississippi Department of Corrections (MDOC), Tony Plotketski, staff writer for *The Clarion-Ledger*, wrote a story about a trumped-up drug charge by two former sheriff deputies in Tishomingo County, Mississippi. Attorney Michael Cooke won the lawsuit for the man who accused authorities of planting drugs that led to his arrest. I contacted Attorney Cooke at his office in Luka, Mississippi, and after telling him my story he took my case.

On October 15, 1998, I signed an employment contract (his version of an attorney/client contract) with Attorney Cooke, stating that he would represent me in the lawsuit against MDOC, and I would pay him a contingency fee of 50% of any recovery.

In the beginning of our business relationship, Attorney Cooke was very impressive and appeared diligent. He kept me abreast of everything. However, after a year of working with Attorney Cooke, I became suspicious. He wouldn't conduct the one process that was extremely important to my case—a deposition of my list of witness I had given to him, which is a method often used in a lawsuit. He only took written statements (one of many red-flag moments). When Attorney Cooke wouldn't dispose SMCI staff that attempted to plant drugs on me or the list of witnesses I had given him, my suspicion heightened. Attorney Cooke's documentary evidence started to show a shift in his representation of my best interest. This was painful to watch. However, we both knew I wouldn't find another attorney in Mississippi to represent me in this case. Thanks to Judge Pickering and Attorney Cooke, MDOC had all the advantages in this case and they won the case easily.

Attorney Michael Cooke made a lot of promises he didn't keep, and in the middle of the river, he flip-flopped on me. He stopped communicating with me, and I was a year into the case with him and it took so long for me to get a court case, I didn't want to secure a new attorney.

Even though I had a signed employment contract based on a contingent fee, Attorney Michael Cooke sued me in the Justice Court of Greene County, Mississippi for $2,433.14. This was adding insult to injury, and downright arrogance. He should have sent that bill to MDOC, the client he helped to win their case. I fought the case against Attorney Michael Cooke in Justice Court and won. I never saw or heard from Attorney Michael Cooke after that day in court.

Fabricating Evidence

Michael D. Cooke
Attorney At Law

106 Front Street . Post Office Box 625 . Iuka, Mississippi 38852
Tel: (662) 423-2000   Fax: (662) 423-2052

January 22, 2001

Mr. Britton Mosley
Post Office Box 390
State Line, Mississippi 39362

CERTIFIED LETTER - RETURN RECEIPT REQUESTED

Re: *Mosley v. MDOC*
      US District Court No. 2:98CV257PG

Dear Britt:

Enclosed please find several documents which I am sending to you in order that you can continue with an appeal in your case. I am sending this to you "certified - return receipt requested" as we have had problems with the mail lately and I wanted to make certain that you get these documents as soon as possible.

I am ending my involvement in your case as of this date. I do not feel I can continue to put more time, money and effort into an appeal which I do not feel you can win. As I told you in Hattiesburg, after the trial, you need to move on with your life and forget this entire matter. We had our day in court and we lost.

You certainly have every right to an appeal, but you must remember that an appeal cannot be simply because you don't like the verdict. You have to find something that was done wrong by the Court at the trial level. It is my considered opinion that Judge Pickering conducted a very fair trial and bent over backwards in allowing us to go to a jury. Our evidence was very thin as to race discrimination and retaliation. I think that Judge Pickering could have very easily granted a judgment as a matter of law for the Defendant and not let the jury hear the case. I believe he would have been justified if he had ruled in that manner.

January 22, 2001
Page 2

Enclosed you will find the following documents:

1. The Court's Judgement
2. A copy of our Employment Contract dated October 15, 1998
3. Trial Exhibit P-1
4. Trial Exhibit P-4
5. Trial Exhibit P-5
6. Trial Exhibit P-6
7. All of the medicals I have in your file, including medicals from Dr. Douglas, Dr. Polles, Laurelwood Center, and Steve Morris.
8. Miscellaneous check stubs and a W-2.
9. A copy of your deposition in the workers' compensation claim.
10. A copy of Brenda's Amended Complaint and Motion to Enforce Settlement.
11. A copy of the Order from the Circuit Judge in the Errington land-line suit.
12. A copy of several Affidavits in Greene County Justice Court and an Indictment on Michael Miller
13. A copy of a letter from you to the United States Justice Department of August 15, 1997.
14. A copy of the transcript of the tape of inmate Marvin Thomas and others.
15. A copy of a newspaper article from the Washington County News of July 1, 1998.
16. A bound copy of the Mississippi Department of Public Safety Report of September 22, 1999 at the request of Judge Pickering.

Last, but not least, I have copied the entire Federal Rules of Appellate Procedure with the Fifth Circuit Rules attached thereto. You will note in Rule 4 that you must file an Appeal within thirty (30) days from the date of the Judgement which Judge Pickering signed. The rest of those Rules tell you what you must do. They are fairly basic and to the point.

January 22, 2001
Page 3

> I have also attached a sample Notice of Appeal. You can use the sample and just sign and file with the Clerk with the United States District Court in Hattiesburg, along with the filing fee.
>
> Finally, I have attached an itemized statement of my expenses and request that you reimburse me for those upon receipt of this letter. As you know, I spent a lot of time and effort in this matter with no fee pursuant to our Contract. However, in the third paragraph, the Contract does provide that you will reimburse any expenses that I have incurred in the case. I do expect payment of the expenses within the next thirty (30) days.
>
> I wish you the best of luck with this matter. If you have any questions, please call me.
>
> Sincerely yours,
>
>
> Michael D. Cooke
>
> MDC/dpd
> Enclosures

Michael D. Cooke
Attorney At Law

106 Front Street . Post Office Box 625 . Iuka, Mississippi 38852
Tel: (662) 423-2000 Fax: (662) 423-2052

April 25, 2000

Mr. Britton Mosley
Post Office box 390
State Line, MS 39362

Re: Mosley v. MDOC

Dear Britt:

Enclosed please find a copy of a Motion for continuance of the pretrial conference and trial of your matter, which I have filed due to other conflicts which I have.

For the present time, I am going to stay involved in the case. Let me tell you what I did on April 12th and 13th. I drove to Meridian after work on the night of the 12th.

I made arrangements to see Mandall Walker and did spend about an hour with him at 9:00 a.m. on April 13th at the East Mississippi Correctional Facility, just west of Meridian. He says that some white officers were racially motivated, but he could not give any specifics about whether your case was racially motivated. He did not think you or Michael Miller were involved in drugs in any manner. He knew nothing of the shower shoe incident. He knew nothing about a tape recording about you allegedly being set up on drugs. He felt that the white officers and other officers in the correctional facility did not like you because of your wife's lawsuit. He was questioned about two to three months after the incident happened with the shower shoes by an investigator from the Mississippi Department of Corrections. He indicates he told the investigator the same thing he told me. Basically, he would not be of any help in the lawsuit.

I then drove to Newton and met Marvin Thomas about 11:30 at the Hardee's restaurant. Marvin was very helpful. He indicated that Investigator McClendon talked to him about setting you up and gave him some marked

April 25, 2000
Page 2

money to buy drugs or either wanted drugs planted at the guard house for you to pick up. He said that Corrections Officer Kittrell came to him and promised to get him out of the penitentiary if he would set you up with drugs. He thinks it is race related. He talked to McClendon and Kittrell several times during a two-month time frame in 1997. They moved him to the Greenwood Correctional Facility because of this problem. He then talked to FBI agents while he was at Parchman. He talked to FBI Agent Randall Neddecker and Agent Gonzalez. He also talked to Jerry Dettman in McClendon's office on one occasion. They gave him $120 in marked money which he kept for several days and then returned to them saying he could not make a buy from you. He did not attempt to make a buy from you, because he thought you were clean. All the officers he talked to were white. Obviously, he will be of some help. In fact, my impression is that he is the only witness we have when we go to trial other than you.

I think the case is still very questionable because I do not think we can prove much. One witness is not necessarily going to prove everything, but Marvin Thomas is very positive towards your position. The problem that we have is that the jury is going to know that he is an ex-convict and that is going to taint his testimony.

On April 17th and 18th I called Keith Miller, the current District Attorney in Pascagoula. I had spoken with him previously several months ago. He says that the charges were ultimately dismissed Michael Miller because there was no evidence to support any allegations that he was involved in drugs or involved in any set up. Of course, this doe not help your case. Keith Miller was very cooperative. However, he did not think that Michael Miller would be willing to talk with me. I gave him my telephone number and he was going to call Michael and ask him to call me. If Miller was not willing to talk with me, He was going to get back with me. To date, neither has called.

I then called Agent Randall Neddecker at his office in Gulfport and left messages on two occasions. Neddecker called me while I was out of the office on the 24th and I have been unable to get with him as of the date of this letter.

April 25, 2000
Page 3

I will let you know when I hear from the court relative to my motion to continue the matter. Of course, any additional witnesses will be helpful, but remember, that I must provide their names to the defendant prior to trial.

Sincerely yours,

Michael D. Cooke

MDC/dpd
Enclosure

Fabricating Evidence

Michael D. Cooke
Attorney At Law

106 Front Street . Post Office Box 625 . Iuka, Mississippi 38852
Tel: (662) 423-2000 Fax: (662) 423-2052

February 10, 2000

Mr. Britton Mosley
P.O. Box 390
State Line, MS 39362

Re: Mosley v. MDOC

Dear Mr. Mosley:

I have read and re-reviewed the Mississippi Department of Public Safety report that you sent to me the first of December. After review of the report, realizing that you say that there are some major items not contained in the report, I am very concerned about our chances of success in this case.

First, let me say that Judge Pickering is going to take the position after reading this report that this is a lot of smoke and no fire.

Secondly, I am concerned about how we are going to prove these allegations. Not a single person that was interviewed has indicated that there was any conspiracy to set up anyone with drugs at the MDOC Correctional Facility in Greene County.

Upon receipt of this letter please contact me by telephone so that we may discuss this. We are at a juncture in this lawsuit that I need to be taking depositions. However, I have some serious reservations about expending large sums of money on depositions and other discovery when I don't see any way to prevail in this matter. I am sorry to be so candid with you in this letter, but I think you need to know my feelings without them being sugar coated.

I shall await your call.

Sincerely yours,

[signature: Michael D. Cooke]

Michael D. Cooke

MDC/bmz

Fabricating Evidence

Michael D. Cooke
Attorney At Law

106 Front Street . Post Office Box 625 . Iuka, Mississippi 38852
Tel: (662) 423-2000   Fax: (662) 423-2052

November 5, 1999

Mr. Britton Mosley
Post Office Box 390
State Line, Mississippi 39362

Re: Mosley v. MDOC

Dear Britt:

I talked with Joe Goff on Tuesday, November 2, 1999. He advised me that the investigative report is complete. However, Judge Pickering had not previously indicated that he was in receipt of the report. The reason for this, I do not know.

As you can see, I have requested a copy of the report from Judge Pickering. Once I receive same, I will provide you with a copy of same. Hopefully we can then start the discovery process within the next few weeks.

Sincerely yours,

Michael D. Cooke

MDC/dpd
Enclosure

EMPLOYMENT CONTRACT

THIS CONTRACT is between Michael D. Cooke ("Attorney") and _____ __BRITTON MOSLEY_____, ("Client").
Client employs Attorney to represent Client in a claim against _____ __MS. Dept. of CORRECTIONS_____ or any other person, firm, or entity for damages which occurred on or about __MAY 28__, 19__98__.

Client will pay and assign to Attorney a contingent fee as follows:

_____ (A) 40% OF ANY RECOVERY. By choosing this option, Client understands that Client will pay all costs and expenses of this case as they occur.

__Britton Mosley, Sr.__ (B) 50% OF ANY RECOVERY. By choosing this option, Client understands that Attorney will advance all costs and expenses of this case and that Attorney will be reimbursed at the conclusion of the case for all costs and expenses.

Client will pay all costs/expenses incurred by Attorney, who may incur such costs as he deems necessary. Attorney will provide an accounting of all costs/expenses at the close of the case. Attorney's fees will be deducted before expenses are reimbursed to Attorney. The payment of costs does not include costs incurred upon an appeal of this case, and Client will be responsible for any costs of an appeal.

Should Client decide to terminate this litigation prior to a conclusion of the case, Client shall owe Attorney a fee based upon the number of hours expended by Attorney at the rate of $125 per hour. Any fees and/or expenses not paid by Client to Attorney when due, shall incur one-half percent (½ %) interest per month. Client agrees to pay all costs of collection of fees and expenses, including reasonable attorney's fees.

Fabricating Evidence

WITNESS OUR SIGNATURES this 15th day of OCTOBER, 1998.

_____ Button Mosley, Sr.
ATTORNEY   CLIENT

[3] Joe Beard — Justice Ct. Judge, Greene County
P.O. Box 258
Leakesville, Ms. 39451
601-394-5900

race — no race related incidents

Retaliation — Joe Arrington's family had land dispute w/ Britt's family. He told Joe that he would take care of "that black son-of-a-bitch". He tried to get Beard to handle the land line suit but it was a Chancery suit. He wanted to file criminal charges against Britt. Judge Wizzell (Justice Ct. Judge) tried to rule against Britt. Judge Backstrom (Circuit Judge) ruled against Arrington.

Arrington was Captain & Britt's immediate boss.

Matter w/ Arrington went on for a couple of months — he was mad at Britt & told Judge that he would "take care of that black son-of-a-bitch; I know where he works". It was obvious that Arrington was mad at Britt.

When inmates file affidavits in Justice Ct., the justice ct. sends them to prosecuting atty, who forwards to MBI investigator (Malcolm McClendon) + there has never been

have probable cause in the eyes. That he has been Justice Ct. Judge.

see documents related to Justice Ct. and Circuit Court.

Nov. 1996 — Marijuana placed on Britt — attempted
July 1997 —   "   "   "   "   "
June 1998 — Britt resigned

Race discrimination + retaliation!

Daniel C. Paff
P.O. Box 538
Leakesville, Ms. 39451
601-394-4252 (H)
works at prison in Leakesville

worked since 4/3/89 — known Britt since he came to work. Doesn't know if it was race discrimination. He thinks they were after Britt because of wife's suit + Britt's EEOC filing.

Nov. 1996 — He was working maintenance — w/ Britt + Harold James — He gave DOC a taped statement the next day. Miller came in w/ black satchel — Miller is white — asked for #; gave it to him to give to Britt!! He put it beside desk. Britt returned; he told him about bag and signed out. Britt picked up bag & thought it felt heavy for shower shoes. After he left Officer James' & Britt discovered that marijuana was in bag.

He never heard anyone say that were going to set-up Britt —

2000 inmates — opened in 1989 — large ratio of blacks to whites — all types of prisoners.

Miller got fired over this incident; David identified him on tape to Malcolm McLendon, investigator.

[2] Harold James
P.O. Box 169
Buckatunna, Ms. 39322
601-648-2944

race — he is unsure
Retaliation — unsure

His story is the same as Daniel Paff's. Dunnahl + Victor Beaver came to check on marijuana; they then ended up talking to McClendon. They never asked he/him Britt to fill out a report.

He knows of no incidents toward Britt that were race related. He did not notice any change in attitude toward Britt after Britt's wife filed her lawsuit.

Fabricating Evidence

[5] PAUL McCLENDON
211 Pittman Dr., Apt 38
Columbia, Ms.
601-
Marion S.O. — work

race → wife's suit

retaliation → wife's suit; land line suit
w/ Erington's family.

Hattiesburg — in Court; he was a
witness — talking w/
Joe Erington
Steve Polchett
M.V. McClendon
David Turner

[4] Jimmy Fancher
P.O. Box 1187
Columbia, MS.
601-731-5319 (H)
Marion S.O. ~~736~~ 736-3621 (W)

※ he helped open
SMCI - Greene Co.

Race — not much except white supremacy
letters, etc.; all persons above
Britt were white.

retaliation — Britt's wife's suit
— law suit re: Arrington
Claudia Howell MDOC Sgt. living w/ Steve May, current + Aryan Brother
Charles Bailey   } 2 main players
Joe Errington

They went to Charles McClendon about
Britt, alleging he did drugs.

He never has heard Britt's name in any
capacity from inmates about trafficking
drugs or anything else bad.

Target list existed of officers to get rid of;
can be verified by M/W Mark Dickey
(he will get name to me). He has testified
in personnel board hearing to this.

Louis Kittrell → key to the Aryan Brotherhood

Fabricating Evidence

```
                JUSTICE COURT SUMMONS                    BOOK    7  PAGE  164

STATE OF MISSISSIPPI
TO ANY LAWFUL OFFICER OF GREENE COUNTY JUSTICE COURT
   THIS IS TO COMMAND YOU TO SUMMONS MOSELY,        BRITTON
                                 P.O. BOX 390
                          STATE LINE  MS       39362

TO APPEAR BEFORE A JUSTICE COURT JUDGE OF GATE COUNTY AT
LEAKESVILLE      ON THE   7TH DAY OF    October, 2002  01:00 p.m.
TO ANSWER THE SUIT OF:
COOKE, MICHAEL D.  VS MOSELY, BRITTON

AND HAVE THERE THIS WRIT.

      WITNESS MY HAND, THIS THE 27TH DAY OF   August ,2002.

NOTICE TO YOU THE DEFENDANT: YOU ARE BEING SUED. IT IS MANDATORY THAT YOU,
THE DEFENDANT, BE IN COURT ON THE DATE AND TIME YOU HAVE BEEN SUMMONED
IF YOU WISH TO CONTEST THIS SUIT.  IF YOU DO NOT WISH TO CONTEST THIS CASE,
IT IS NOT NECESSARY THAT YOU APPEAR IN COURT.  IF YOU DO NOT APPEAR AS YOU
HAVE BEEN SUMMONED, A DEFAULT JUDGMENT CAN BE RENDERED AGAINST YOU.  IT IS
IMPORTANT THAT YOU BE AWARE OF ALL OF THE ABOVE INFORMATION. IF YOU HAVE
ANY QUESTIONS ABOUT THIS SUMMONS, YOU MUST BE IN COURT ON THE DATE AND TIME
LISTED ABOVE.



                                      JUSTICE COURT CLERK
                                      _____
                                      DEPUTY JUSTICE COURT CLERK

==============================================================
                    CONSTABLE'S RETURN INFORMATION

____SERVED IN PERSON       DATE____/____/____
____POSTED AT RESIDENCE    _____
                           CONSTABLE

**************************************************************

        LEFT SUMMONS WITH
        _____
        A MEMBER OF DEFENDANTS FAMILY WHO IS
        16 YEARS OF AGE OR OLDER
        _____
```

Britton Mosley, Sr.

IN THE JUSTICE COURT OF GREENE COUNTY, MISSISSIPPI

MICHAEL D. COOKE   PLAINTIFF

V.   CAUSE NO. 7-164

BRITTON MOSLEY   DEFENDANT

DECLARATION

1. The plaintiff's name, address and telephone are:
   Name: Michael D. Cooke
   Street: 106 Front Street; Post Office Box 625
   City & Zip Code: Iuka, MS 38852

2. The defendant's name and address are:
   Name: Britton Mosley
   Street: Post Office Box 390
   City: State Line, MS 39362

3. The defendant's place of business and address are:
   Place of Business:
   Street:
   City:

4. The defendant(s) is indebted to the plaintiff in the amount of $ 2,433.14 plus court costs.

5. The basis for the plaintiff's claim against the defendant is:
   Breach of Contract; expenses and costs incurred while representing Defendant in a lawsuit. The Defendant has refused to pay the expenses and costs pursuant to the contract. See contract attached hereto as exhibit "A". See itemized expenses attached hereto as exhibit "B".

   PLAINTIFF: *Michael D. Cooke*

Sworn to and subscribed before me, this 22nd day of August, 2002.

Pamela Sue Eaton

Fabricating Evidence

Michael D. Cooke
Attorney At Law

106 Front Street . Post Office Box 625 . Iuka, Mississippi 38852
Tel: (662) 423-2000   Fax: (662) 423-2052

August 16, 2001

Mr. Britton Mosley
P.O. Box 390
State Line, MS 39362

RE: Mosley vs. Mississippi Department of Corrections

FOR SERVICES RENDERED:

Filing Fee	$150.00
Long Distance Charges	$131.50
Copying Costs	$328.80
Postage and Delivery Fee	$34.79
Mileage	$921.94
Lodging	$156.18
Meals	$120.61
Process Server's Fee	$25.00
Witness Checks	$423.00
TOTAL EXPENSES	$2,291.82

Thank you!

Britton Mosley, Sr.

JUSTICE COURT SUMMONS   BOOK   7 PAGE   164

STATE OF MISSISSIPPI
TO ANY LAWFUL OFFICER OF GREENE COUNTY JUSTICE COURT
   THIS IS TO COMMAND YOU TO SUMMON: MOSELY,   BRITTON
                              P.O. BOX 390
                              STATE LINE MS   39362

TO APPEAR BEFORE A JUSTICE COURT JUDGE OF SAID COUNTY AT
*LEAKESVILLE   ON THE 7thDAY OF   October   2002   01:00 p.m
TO ANSWER THE SUIT OF:
COOKE, MICHAEL D.   VS MOSELY, BRITTON

AND HAVE THERE THIS WRIT.

    WITNESS MY HAND, THIS THE 27thDAY OF   August ,2002.

NOTICE TO YOU THE DEFENDANT! YOU ARE BEING SUED. IT IS MANDATORY THAT YOU,
THE DEFENDANT, BE IN COURT ON THE DATE AND TIME YOU HAVE BEEN SUMMONED
IF YOU WISH TO CONTEST THIS SUIT. IF YOU DO NOT WISH TO CONTEST THIS CASE,
IT IS NOT NECESSARY THAT YOU APPEAR IN COURT. IF YOU DO NOT APPEAR AS YOU
HAVE BEEN SUMMONED, A DEFAULT JUDGEMENT CAN BE RENDERED AGAINST YOU. IT IS
IMPORTANT THAT YOU BE AWARE OF ALL OF THE ABOVE INFORMATION. IF YOU HAVE
ANY QUESTIONS ABOUT THIS SUMMONS, YOU MUST BE IN COURT ON THE DATE AND TIME
LISTED ABOVE.

                                    JUSTICE COURT CLERK
                                    _____
                                    DEPUTY JUSTICE COURT CLERK

================== CONSTABLE'S RETURN INFORMATION ==================

____ SERVED IN PERSON   DATE ___/___/___
____ POSTED AT RESIDENCE   _____
                             CONSTABLE

****

         LEFT SUMMONS WITH
         _____
         A MEMBER OF DEFENDANTS FAMILY WHO IS
         16 YEARS OF AGE OR OLDER

         ___/___/___ DATE

CHAPTER TEN

The Appeal Process

In January 2001, approximately one week after the jury verdict in my lawsuit, I received a certified return receipt requested letter from Attorney Michael Cooke. Enclosed was documentary evidence that was given to Attorney Cooke prior to the lawsuit trial. This documentary evidence was also given to Judge Pickering prior to the trial. If the jurors had been permitted by Judge Pickering and Attorney Cooke to review this evidence, the verdict might have been different. It might have been in my favor.

In his letter dated January 22, 2001, Attorney Cooke stated, *"I am ending my involvement in your case."*

He also stated,

"You need to move on with your life and forget this entire matter. We had our day in court and we lost. You certainly have every right to an appeal, but you must remember that an appeal cannot be simply because you don't like the verdict. You have

to find something that was done wrong by the Court at the trial level. It is my considered opinion that Judge Pickering conducted a very fair trial and bent over backwards in allowing us to go to a jury. Our evidence was very thin as to race discrimination and retaliation. I think that Judge Pickering could have very easily granted a judgment as a matter of law for the Defendant and not let the jury hear the case. I believe he would have been justified had he ruled in that manner."

Now you see why I lost this case.

On February 5, 2011, I filed a Notice of Appeal to the United States Court of Appeals for the Fifth Circuit from the judgment on the jury verdict.

Britton Mosley, Sr.

vs.

Mississippi Department of Corrections
(No. 2:98CV357-P-G)

The appeals process was very challenging for I knew it would be an uphill battle. The three panel judges on the Fifth Circuit Appeals Court were White men, like the White men who attempted the drug set-up. Judge Pickering was being considered for judgeship on the Fifth Circuit Court and very conservative.

However, I needed this attempt at justice. Attempting an appeal without an attorney to coordinate with me would have been hard.

When former President George W. Bush nominated Judge Charles W. Pickering, Sr. to the United States Court of Appeals for the Fifth Circuit, it ended my attempt at an appeal. Former Mississippi Attorney General Mike Moore endorsed Judge Pickering. Attorney General Mike Moore was the attorney for the Mississippi Department of Corrections (MDOC). Mike Moore and Judge Pickering needed to protect MDOC from the embarrassment of my case. I allowed the appealed to be dismissed. I am not a quitter. However, some fights are unnecessary.

Britton Mosley, Sr.

CERTIFICATE OF SERVICE

I, Britton Mosley, do hereby certify that I have this day mailed by United States Mail, postage prepaid, a true and exact copy of the above and foregoing Objection to the following:

> Leonard Vincent, Esquire
> General Counsel, Mississippi Department of Corrections
> Post Office Box 38
> Parchman, MS 38738
>
> Honorable Charles W. Pickering, Sr.
> United States District Judge
> 701 North Main St., Suite 228
> Hattiesburg, MS 39401

THIS 5 day of Feb, 2001.

Britton Mosley, Sr.
BRITTON MOSLEY

Fabricating Evidence

Michael D. Cooke
Attorney At Law

106 Front Street . Post Office Box 625 . Iuka, Mississippi 38852
Tel: (662) 423-2000   Fax: (662) 423-2052

February 19, 2001

Office of the Clerk
US District Court
701 Main Street, Suite 200
Hattiesburg, MS 39403

RE: Mosley v. Mississippi Department of Corrections
      US District Court No. 2:98CV357-P-G

Dear Madam/Sir:

I am in receipt of a copy of the "filed" stamped Notice of Appeal filed by my former client in the above matter. I will not be representing Mr. Mosley in his appeal and I have advised him accordingly. Please note this in your records.

Sincerely yours,

Michael D. Cooke

MDC/dpd
cc: Mr. Britton Mosley

Britton Mosley, Sr.

IN THE UNITED STATES COURT OF APPEALS
FOR THE FIFTH CIRCUIT

No. 01-60152

BRITTON MOSLEY

        Plaintiff - Appellant

v.

MISSISSIPPI DEPARTMENT OF CORRECTIONS

        Defendant - Appellee

U.S. COURT OF APPEALS
FILED
MAY 7 2001
CHARLES R. FULBRUGE III
CLERK

Appeal from the United States District Court for the
Southern District of Mississippi, Hattiesburg

CLERK'S OFFICE:

Under 5TH CIR. R. 42.3, the appeal is dismissed as of May 7, 2001, for want of prosecution. The appellant failed to timely make financial arrangements with the court reporter.

                                 CHARLES R. FULBRUGE III
                                 Clerk of the United States Court
                                 of Appeals for the Fifth Circuit

                       By: _____
                             Linda Miles, Deputy Clerk

                              FOR THE COURT - BY DIRECTION

Fabricating Evidence

United States Court of Appeals

FIFTH CIRCUIT
OFFICE OF THE CLERK

CHARLES R. FULBRUGE III
CLERK

TEL: 504-589-6514
600 CAMP STREET
NEW ORLEANS, LA 70130

February 28, 2001

Mr Britton Mosley
PO Box 390
State Line, MS 39362

      No. 01-60152 Mosley v. MDOC
      USDC No. 2:98-Cv-357-PG

We have docketed the appeal and ask you to use the case number above in future inquiries.

You must first complete the transcript order form the district court clerk provided you. When completed, this meets your obligation to order the necessary portion(s) of the court reporter's transcript, see FED. R. APP. P. 10(b). Second, you must make financial arrangements with the court reporter to pay for the transcript. If you are pro se and unable to afford payment, you must file a motion with the district court requesting a transcript at government expense, and notify this court of the filing. We will then coordinate with the court reporter for a time to file the transcript. After January 1, 2001, the court reporter should contact you directly if an extension of time is granted to file the transcript. If you do not order or make arrangements to pay for the transcript within the 15 days, we will dismiss your appeal without further notice, unless the case is a criminal appeal and you are proceeding In Forma Pauperis, see 5TH CIR. R. 42.3.

We will provide information concerning the briefing of this appeal to all parties at a later date. If a transcript is unnecessary, notify us and we will start the briefing schedule. Please note that effective January 1, 2001, 5TH CIR. R. 31.4 and the Internal Operating Procedures following rules 27 and 31 state the court's sense that except in the most extraordinary circumstances, the <u>maximum</u> extension for filing briefs is 30 days in criminal cases and 40 days in civil cases.

All counsel who desire to appear in this case must sign and return the attached appearance form, naming each party you represent, within 15 days from this date, see FED. R. APP. P. 12(b) and 5TH CIR. R. 12. If you fail to do so we will remove your name from our docket in this case. We cannot release official records on appeal unless you have entered an appearance. Pro se parties do not need to file an appearance form.

Racism tactic is cheap shot, tiring

Concerning the confirmation of U.S. District Judge Charles Pickering, Mississippians of all races and political stripes should feel demeaned and betrayed.

To push the political leaning of the 5th U.S. Circuit Court of Appeals to the left, groups such as People for the American Way and the National Abortion and Reproductive Rights Action League have resorted to the character assassin's bullet of choice, the charge of racism.

These leftist groups find a man from the South and let fly with allegations of complicity with the Klan and ties to various other dens of disgusting bigotry.

If the above were the only facts in this instance, it would be so unfortunately common as to not even be news. But in one of the more shocking and tragic happenings so far this year, the Mississippi NAACP has entered the fray, to its eternal shame and our state's great loss. Its press conference was a vivid display of how far that once-important organization has fallen, resorting now to attacking a man who has done so much for black Mississippians.

The true facts about Judge Pickering have been reprinted hundreds of times, so there's no need to use ink on them here.

The real issue is how you cannot be a conservative white man from the South and expect to enter public life without being branded a racist, however unfair the charge.

It's way past time for Mississippians to forgo these tactics and the politicians, like 2nd District U.S. Rep. Bennie Thompson, who practice them.

Matt Eichelber

U.S. District Judge Charles Pickering (left) and state Attorney General Mike Moore meet with President Bush last week.

Pickering's pro-life stance real issue

This concerns the nomination of U.S. District Judge Charles Pickering by President Bush to the 5th U.S. Circuit Court of Appeals in New Orleans.

He has been accused of being a racist, at least of being insensitive to civil rights.

I understand that Mississippi Attorney General Mike Moore endorses him and that Charles Evers, the brother of slain civil rights leader Medgar Evers, is very much in favor of the nomination. But you haven't heard the whole story — and this one statement is why so many are ... Judge Pickering.

He is pro-life.

If you agree with him, please contact our senators at 1-202 224-3121.

Mildred Smith
Quitman

GOP can dish it out, so now take it!

Now that the Democrats are in control of the Senate, when they oppose our president's choice for a federal judge, it is called a lynching.

But when the Republicans were in control, it was OK that they stonewalled President Clinton's judicial appointments.

It seems like a double standard to me. I think that if they can dish it out, they should be able to take it, without crying like a bunch of babies.

Johnny Smith
P...

Thompson no better than Bilbo was

2nd District U.S. Rep. Bennie Thompson's use of lies and half- in the state's Capitol — right next to Sen. Bilbo's in the basement

U.S. District Judge Charles Pickering meets with President Bush.

Charles Pickering man of character

I continue to be interested in the bickering over the nomination of Charles Pickering to the 5th U.S. Circuit Court of Appeals. The liberals blatantly label Pickering as a racist. This is a ploy that they use to appeal to their constant base, black Americans. The liberals assume that black Americans do not read and listen for themselves. Today, a growing number of black Americans are refusing to take the Democrat/liberal word on issues.

A glaring example of the above is Charles Evers. In an article, "Black leaders spar over Pickering," so-called black leaders asked Judge Pickering to withdraw his name from nomination. Pickering did not comment — a show of character in my opinion. However, Evers did comment. Sen. David Jordan, a Democrat, said, "Charles is a good fruit gone bad as far as the civil rights movement."

Mr. Evers had a few choice comments in rebuttal. The translation of Sen. Jordan's comments is that Evers is a Republican so he doesn't count. The fact is that it takes a real leader and a man of character and principles to speak out on what he believes and knows to be truth. Anyone can, as Mr. Cooper, president of the Magnolia Bar Association, and Sen. Jordan have done, go with the flow and do what is expected rather than what is based on fact and truth.

President Bush has more real black leaders in his administration than any other President. Of course, like Mr. Evers, Dr. Condoleezza Rice and Colin Powell are, I assume, "good fruits gone bad"as well in the eyes of Cooper and Jordan.

What this boils down to is political partisanship. Racism is the tool, not the issue. For the liberals, the abortion issue is the driving force. I believe that most black Americans are against abortion.

I have always admired Charles Evers. He believes what he says and stands by it. That is leadership.

Charles Pickering is a man of character and principles. He will follow the law and not make or change the law. This the liberals' greatest fear.

Think about it, fearing following the law. That is a scary thought.

Debbie Gamblin
Brandon

CHAPTER ELEVEN

National Association for the Advancement of Colored People (Mississippi State Conference)

One year had passed since the unjust verdict in my civil lawsuit, and former President George W. Bush had nominated US District Judge Charles S. Pickering to the 5th US Circuit Court of Appeals. The State National Association for the Advancement of Colored People (NAACP) was against Judge Pickering's nomination because he had consistently shown a "hostile attitude" toward civil rights cases in Mississippi by manipulating and suppressing evidence. L.A. Warren (now deceased), Legal Redress Committee Chair NAACP, was leading this movement. When I'd learned of the NAACP's plans, I was sure that my case would help to prove their case. My opposition to Judge Pickering's nomination was neither politically nor racially motivated. His judicial integrity in the way he handled my case was the issue. I met with L.A. Warren and gave him all documentation and audiotape pertaining to my case to assist with keeping Judge Charles Pickering from being appointed to the 5th US Circuit Court of Appeals. Also, present at the meeting was Derrick Johnson, 4th Vice President and NAACP attorney. During my meeting with L.A. Warren and Derrick Johnson, and after listening to the audio tape of Inmate Marvin Thomas and Lieutenant Louis Kittrell, it was established that there was, in fact, a drug set-up, and it was clearly suppressed by Judge Pickering. I was assured that once the nomination hearings were completed, the NAACP would help me get the justice I was denied at the hands of Judge Pickering. My case was one of six cases involving discrimination, labor and women's rights used by the NAACP to deny Judge Pickering's nomination.

On January 3, 2002, the Mississippi State NAACP called a press conference to release the second in a series of cases that would show the continuing conspiracy between local, state and federal officials to cover up long standing civil rights violations. Prior to the press conference, I spoke with Hillary Shelton, Director of the NAACP's Washington Bureau and Senior Vice President for Advocacy and Policy, by phone and she thanked me for giving them my documentation and audio tape.

After the failed nomination attempt of Judge Pickering, the NAACP did not keep their promise of helping me get justice. The Mississippi State Conference of the NAACP refused to talk about my case. One of the NAACP's stated goals is to secure for all people their guaranteed right under the Fourteenth Amendment to the United States Constitution, which promises equal protection of the law. Being betrayed by the oldest civil rights organization for ethnic minorities in the United States was painful. After over a decade, the pain and disappointment has never left. The NAACP never gave me a reason as to why they betrayed me. My speculations are there connections with the Mississippi Department of Corrections (MDOC) and the Attorney General's office. Chris Epps, former commissioner of the MDOC was often honored by local branches of the NAACP. The social/economic class systems within the NAACP in Mississippi rivals that of Jim Crow.

Fabricating Evidence

NATIONAL ASSOCIATION FOR THE ADVANCEMENT OF COLORED PEOPLE
MISSISSIPPI STATE CONFERENCE

EUGENE BRYANT, SR.
President

George Roberts
1st Vice President

Curvy Clark
2nd Vice President

Melvin Hollins
3rd Vice President

Derrick Johnson
4th Vice President

Kelvin Buck
5th Vice President

Eddie Smith
6th Vice President

Janette Self
Secretary

Dorothy Isaac
Asst. Secretary

James Crowell
Treasurer

James Creer
Asst. Treasurer

For Immediate Release: January 31, 2002

For more information, contact:
L. A. Warren
Legal Redress
Committee Chair
(601) 353-6906

PRESS STATEMENT

January 31, 2002—The Mississippi State Conference of the NAACP calls this press conference to release the second in a series of audio tapes that will show the continuing conspiracy between local, state, and federal officials to cover-up and prolong the instances of longstanding civil rights violations.

On July 20, 2001, there was a state investigation of the Marion-Walthall Correctional Facility conducted by the AG's office. According to Attorney General Mike Moore's office, the state investigator assigned to investigate the MWCF was identified as Roger Cribbs. Mr. Cribbs was interviewing Major Johnnie Glover of the MWCF.

Others present at this interview, according to the AG's office, were Chief Deputy Rocky Williamson and Detective Tim Singley. Investigator Cribbs stated that this interview was part of a state criminal investigation, "and if anyone talked about it, they could be charged."

Investigator Cribbs then proceeded to make a graphic sexual comment too obscene to print. It appears that Major Johnny Glover made a racial slur, as well. It also appears that either Chief Deputy Rocky Williamson or Detective Tim Singley made racial slurs, too.

The racial slurs also continued with Roger Cribbs, using the old racial slur that says, "I'd rather be red on the head like the dick of a dog, than brown on the crown like shit on the ground."

Investigator Cribbs racially profiled former black Deputy Warden James Harvey and all other black officers at Unit 29 at Parchman prison as being "gang bangers" when he stated, "that's not out of the ordinary though for them."

We are waiting for the AG's explanation as to why Chief Deputy Rocky Williamson and Detective Tim Singley of the Marion County Sheriff's Department were present at the interview of the investigation of MWCF by Roger Cribbs. We are also waiting on the AG's report of the investigation of the prior allegations of misconduct made by

1072 West Lynch Street • Suite 310 • Jackson, Mississippi 39203 • (601) 353-6906 • 1-800-80NAACP • FAX (601) 353-1565

the NAACP against Sheriff Rip Stringer and Chief Deputy Rocky Williamson. We are also awaiting Investigator Roger Cribbs' explanation as to _why_ he can't remember _who_ said _what_ and _why_ the interview was not recorded.

It appears that Agent Cribbs uses double standards when interviewing whites and blacks. When interviewing whites, the process was done collectively and not recorded; however, when interviewing blacks, it was individually and recorded.

The web of conspiracy appears to evolve from the Marion County Sheriff's Office to possibly, the federal bench.

On December 28, 2000, there was a failed attempt of entrapment against former Deputy Warden James Harvey by Marion County Sheriff Richard "Rip" Stringer and Chief Deputy Rocky Williamson. _(See tape and transcript)_

The Marion-Walthall Correctional Facility is a county owned facility that houses state inmates. There appears to be a pattern of conspiracy and cover-up involving Mississippi Department of Corrections and the AG's office. The MDOC _claims_ that they are unaware of who was present at this investigation of MWCF.

The NAACP investigation reveals that Captain Britton Mosley, Sr., who was fired from Marion/Walthall Correctional Facility, appears to have also been a victim of an earlier drug setup and conspiracy by MDOC, the AG's office, and a federal judge.

Drugs were planted on Mosley by former staff member Michael Miller at South Mississippi Correctional Institution, who hired then-attorney Keith Miller, who is now District Attorney for Jackson, George and Green counties. Upon Miller becoming District Attorney, he dismissed the charges on his client without prejudice. When affidavits in the case were filed, he promised to appoint a special prosecutor— which never occurred.

Approximately a month ago, Mississippi State Conference NAACP Second Vice-President Curley Clark took eleven affidavits back to District Attorney Miller, who told him he would again appoint a special prosecutor; to our knowledge, this has not occurred.

The Attorney General's office also failed or refused to investigate the Mosley case. From this inaction, Mosley filed a lawsuit in U.S. District Court. The case was presided over by Federal Judge Charles W. Pickering, Sr.

Before hearing the case, Judge Pickering ordered a state agency to investigate another state agency—instead of asking the FBI (a federal agency) to investigate Mosley's

Fabricating Evidence

FEB 01 '02 12:12 FR ASSOCIATED PRESS   601 948 7975 TO 8995879   P.01/02

899 5879

Page 1   M6239 msba- r nbx

^BC-MS--Pickering Nomination, Bjt,520<
^Second Pickering hearing slated; NAACP questions record<
^AP Photos<
^Eds: PMs<
^js/stf/fcn/tb<
^By JASON STRAZIUSO=
^Associated Press Writer=
¶ JACKSON, Miss. (AP) _ State NAACP leaders will attempt to prove Judge Charles Pickering has shown a "hostile attitude" toward civil rights cases at the district judge's second nomination hearing next week.
¶ Pickering, the father of Rep. Chip Pickering, R-Miss., has been nominated for a seat on the 5th U.S. Circuit Court of Appeals in New Orleans.
¶ He had his first hearing in October. A second hearing has been set for Feb. 7, Senate Judiciary Committee spokeswoman Mimi Devlin said.
¶ Democrats insisted on a second hearing to review the Mississippi judge's unpublished opinions.
¶ L.A. Warren of the Mississippi branch of the National Association for the Advancement of Colored People said Thursday his organization has forwarded six Pickering decisions to the Judiciary Committee for review.
¶ Warren said the six cases involve discrimination, labor and women's rights issues and will likely be brought up at next week's hearing.
¶ "There's a pattern of a hostile attitude," Warren said. "It's the way he handled those cases by prolonging them. He controls the evidence that gets to the table. In a sense, that affects the outcome of the case."
¶ Pickering said Thursday he looked forward to testifying before the committee, but he won't comment on specific issues until then.
¶ A spokesman for Sen. Trent Lott, R-Miss., said that Pickering has broad support.
¶ 'The people in Mississippi that know Judge Pickering know his integrity and understand that he is a well-qualified judicial nominee," Lee Youngblood said.
¶ The Judiciary Committee has received 37 support letters for Pickering, including letters from former Democratic Gov. William Winter and 10 former presidents of the Mississippi Bar Association, Senate records show.
¶ The committee has received 26 letters in opposition, mainly from women's and civil rights groups, including the Magnolia Bar Association, a mostly black lawyer's group.
¶ In highlighting one of the six cases, Warren said Pickering heard a case in 2001 brought by Britton Mosley Sr., a black man, who alleged in a federal lawsuit that he was set up on drug charges and wrongly dismissed by the Mississippi Department of Corrections.
¶ The alleged drug setup was caught on tape by Mosley, Warren said.
¶ Warren said that Pickering heard the Mosley tape outside the courtroom and then didn't allow the tape into evidence.
¶ Another issue that groups opposed to Pickering have raised is his 1990 testimony to become a U.S. district judge.
¶ According to Senate records, Pickering testified he "never had any contact with the Sovereignty Commission," Mississippi's now-defunct

segregation watchdog agency.

However, a 1972 letter in the commission's files said Pickering, while a state senator, had "requested to be advised" by the commission about a group organizing pulpwood workers.

NAACP: Tape to damage Pickering

■ Supporters say substance lacking, they can't respond

From staff and wire reports

NAACP officials said Thursday all the information needed to keep U.S. District Judge Charles Pickering from being appointed to the 5th U.S. Circuit Court of Appeals is on a cassette tape. Only they didn't play the tape, nor did they say what was said on it.

Instead, L.A. Warren, chairman of the Mississippi NAACP Legal Redress Committee said, national NAACP officials have decided to let the tape be played for the first time at Pickering's Feb. 7 hearing before the Senate Judiciary Committee during which Democrats are expected to question the judge again.

Pickering

Warren

Warren said his organization has forwarded six opinions involving discrimination, labor and women's rights issues to the committee. "There's a pattern of a hostile attitude," he said. "It's the way he handled those cases by prolonging them."

Pickering said Thursday he looked forward to testifying to the committee but couldn't comment on specific issues until then.

A spokesman for Sen. Trent Lott, R.-Miss., said Pickering has broad support. "The people in Mississippi that know Judge Pickering know his integrity and understand that he is a well qualified judicial nominee," said Lott spokesman Lee Youngblood.

The Judiciary Committee has received 37 support letters for Pickering, including letters from former Democratic Gov. William Winter and 10 former presidents of the Mississippi Bar Association, Senate records show.

The committee has received 26 letters in opposition, mainly from women's and civil rights groups, including the Magnolia Bar Association.

Pickering supporters planned and then cancelled an afternoon news conference to rebut NAACP allegations because they said they felt there was nothing of substance to respond to.

In highlighting one of the six cases sent to the Judiciary Committee, Warren said Pickering heard a case in 2001 brought by Britton Mosley Sr., who alleged in a federal lawsuit he was set up on drugs and wrongly dismissed by the state Department of Corrections because of his race. Mosley is black. The alleged setup, Warren said, was caught on tape by Mosley.

He said Pickering heard the Mosley tape outside the courtroom and then didn't allow the tape into evidence.

After the news conference, Mosley said of the tape, "I think it's going to have a profound effect."

Britton Mosley, Sr.

Home | Mississippi News | Story

February 1, 2002

NAACP: Tape to damage Pickering

• Supporters say substance lacking, they can't respond

From staff and wire reports

NAACP officials said Thursday all the information needed to keep U.S. District Judge Charles Pickering from being appointed to the 5th U.S. Circuit Court of Appeals is on a cassette tape.

Only they didn't play the tape, nor did they say what was said on it.

Instead, L.A. Warren, chairman of the Mississippi NAACP Legal Redress Committee said, national NAACP officials have decided to let the tape be played for the first time at Pickering's Feb. 7 hearing before the Senate Judiciary Committee during which Democrats are expected to question the judge again.

Warren said his organization has forwarded six opinions involving discrimination, labor and women's rights issues to the committee. "There's a pattern of a hostile attitude," he said. "It's the way he handled those cases by prolonging them."

Pickering said Thursday he looked forward to testifying to the committee but couldn't comment on specific issues until then.

A spokesman for Sen. Trent Lott, R.-Miss., said Pickering has broad support.

"The people in Mississippi that know Judge Pickering know his integrity and understand that he is a well qualified judicial nominee," said Lott spokesman Lee Youngblood.

The Judiciary Committee has received 37 support letters for Pickering, including letters from former Democratic Gov. William Winter and 10 former presidents of the Mississippi Bar Association, Senate records show.

The committee has received 26 letters in opposition, mainly from women's and civil rights groups, including the Magnolia Bar Association.

Pickering supporters planned and then cancelled an afternoon news

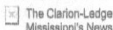

Fabricating Evidence

conference to rebut NAACP allegations because they said they felt there was nothing of substance to respond to.

In highlighting one of the six cases sent to the Judiciary Committee, Warren said Pickering heard a case in 2001 brought by Britton Mosley Sr., who alleged in a federal lawsuit he was set up on drugs and wrongly dismissed by the state Department of Corrections because of his race. Mosley is black. The alleged setup, Warren said, was caught on tape by Mosley.

He said Pickering heard the Mosley tape outside the courtroom and then didn't allow the tape into evidence.

After the news conference, Mosley said of the tape, "I think it's going to have a profound effect."

Send this article as a postcard

[an error occurred while processing this directive]

MOSS POINT-JACKSON COUNTY BRANCH OF NAACP
Christopher Epps to speak at Freedom Fund banquet

Submitted by Julia Holmes

Jackson County Branch of the NAACP will host its annual Freedom Fund banquet at 7 p.m. Friday at Pelican Landing in Moss Point.

The banquet will honor individuals and organizations for their outstanding service to the community. Recipients for the Outstanding Achievement, Humanitarian of the Year, Outstanding Community Service and Volunteer of the Year awards will be recognized.

The theme will be "NAACP: One Nation, One Dream."

Guest speaker will be Christopher Epps, commissioner for the Mississippi Department of Corrections.

Epps was appointed commissioner by former Gov. Ronnie Musgrove in 2002 and reappointed to his post by Gov. Haley Barbour in 2004. He has held various leadership positions throughout his career in corrections and in the military. He entered military service in 1984 and when he received his honorable discharge from the Mississippi Army National Guard, he was a lieutenant colonel.

Epps

In 2009, Epps was presented a concurrent resolution from the Mississippi House of Representatives for outstanding service to the Mississippi Department of Corrections and upon being the longest serving commissioner in the history of the agency.

Tickets are $30 per person. Contact Julia Holmes at 228-475-6432 or Curley Clark at 228-762-9692 for details.

CHAPTER TWELVE
Protecting the Whistleblower

It is worth remembering that in 1619, my descendants of Africa and Europeans were the original immigrants that came to America. However, my descendants were slaves, and this was the beginning of the European and African rivalry in America. The slaves were told by their masters to be penitence, which is where the word penitentiary originated. Centuries later, this slavery doctrine is still maintained on people of African descent in America. This doctrine is now called "mass incarceration," slavery's new name.

Fabricating evidence and by law enforcement personnel and being sent to prison was common in Mississippi. Motivation, in most cases, was racial hate, and the fact that they could get away with it, and it almost happened to me.

The phrase "all politics is local" is a common phrase in United States' politics. However, the former Speaker of the U.S. House of Representative Tip O'Neal is closely associated with this phrase. The phrase motivated me to request help from local politicians. Former Representative (Democrat) Billy Broomfield and I met at his home in Moss Point, Mississippi. We attended the same high school.

During the meeting with Broomfield (now Mayor of Moss Point), documentary and audio evidence was given to him. Broomfield assured me that he had the power to correct this broken system. I was persuaded. However, after that meeting, Broomfield refused to talk with me at all. Mississippi's Senate Corrections Committee Members—Senator Willie Lee Simmons and Senator Sampson Jackson—and House Committee Member former Representative Frances Fredericks and former Representative Randy "Bubba" Pierce (now Mississippi Supreme Court Justice) were given complaints about the climate of corruption at South Mississippi Correctional Institution (SMCI). The lawmakers' non-action was "extremely distressing." In R. L. Nave article, "In Prison Reform, Will Racism Persist?" in the *Jackson Free Press*, Nave stated that "Racial and economic disparities that persist in the criminal-justice system concerned other lawmakers, such as Rep. Charles Young Jr., D-Meridian. Of the approximately 25,980 men and women in MDOC's custody, 65 percent are African American, MDOC information shows. Mississippi has a Black population of 37.4 percent." It is alleged that Mississippi has the highest number of elected lawmakers in the United States; four of the five lawmakers I reported the problems to were African Americans.

The phrase "all politics is local" works inside the Mississippi Department of Corrections.

According to the United States Department of Labor's OSHA Whistleblower's website, "OSHA's Whistleblower Protection Program enforces the whistleblower provisions of more than twenty whistleblower statutes protecting employees who report violations of various workplace safety, airline, commercial motor carrier, consumer product, environmental, financial reform, food safety, health insurance reform, motor vehicle safety, nuclear, pipeline, public transportation agency, railroad, maritime, and securities laws. Rights afforded by these whistleblower acts include, but are not limited to, worker participation in safety and health activities, reporting a work related injury, illness or fatality, or reporting a violation of the statutes."

I was not protected under this act.

Being a law enforcement officer and whistleblower would black ball you, which is why many Blacks are deterred from joining law enforcement. As a loyal, upstanding law enforcement officer, I witnessed unjust behavior against prison inmates and reported it. Being a prison inmate does not mean you are below protection of the law, and it certainly does not mean you are automatically subjected to brutal physical, mental and emotional abuse by the same people who were hired to assist with an inmate's rehabilitation. Yes, I blew the whistle on unjust behavior by law enforcement officers, and as a law enforcement officer, I was not protected under the Whistleblower Act. It was impossible for me to ignore the cruel and usual punishments of inmates that violates the Constitutional ban; however, bringing attention to this injustice almost cost me my freedom.

Fabricating Evidence

THE RESOURCE

HOUSE CONCURRENT RESOLUTION 114

A CONCURRENT RESOLUTION COMMENDING COMMISSIONER CHRISTOPHER B. EPPS ON HIS DEDICATED AND OUTSTANDING SERVICE TO THE DEPARTMENT OF CORRECTIONS AND UPON BEING THE LONGEST SERVING COMMISSIONER IN THE HISTORY OF THE DEPARTMENT.

WHEREAS, Commissioner Christopher Bernard Epps is being honored for his stellar and dedicated service to the Mississippi Department of Corrections, where he has served as a guiding force for the department in its efforts to rehabilitate offenders; and

WHEREAS, in addition to being an outstanding leader for the department, Commissioner Epps has the notable distinction of being the longest serving commissioner in the department's history; and

WHEREAS, a native of Tchula, Mississippi, Commissioner Epps, knowing the importance of receiving an education, received his bachelor's degree in 1982 from Mississippi Valley State University and in 2001, he received his master's in guidance and counseling from Liberty University; and

WHEREAS, after receiving his undergraduate degree, Commissioner Epps embarked upon his career with the Mississippi Department of Corrections in 1982, where he began as a corrections officer and later serving in the following positions with the department before being appointed as commissioner: correctional case manager, acting disciplinary investigator/hearing officer, director of treatment services, case management supervisor, executive 3/deputy superintendent/chief of security, director of offender services, chief of special staff, chief records officer, deputy commissioner of community services, and deputy commissioner of institutions; and

WHEREAS, due to Commissioner Epps' extensive work ethic, knowledge, expertise and dedication to the Mississippi Department of Corrections, he was appointed as commissioner of the department in 2002 by former Governor Ronnie Musgrove; and

WHEREAS, as a testament of his outstanding performance as Commissioner of the Department of Corrections under the Musgrove administration, Commissioner Epps was reappointed to this position in 2004 by the then newly elected Governor Haley Barbour; and

WHEREAS, Commissioner Epps, as one who knows the importance of being active in his profession, where ideas are shared and implemented, is an active member of the following: Association of State Correctional Administrators (ASCA), where he serves on the Correctional Industries, Research & Technology, Re-entry & Community Corrections, Racial Issues and Program & Training Committees; the Southern States Correctional Association, where he served as vice president in 2008; the American Correctional Association (ACA), where he serves as an auditor and in 2008, where he was elected to a two-year term as treasurer; and

WHEREAS, also, Commissioner Epps, the ultimate corrections professional, was elected in 2006 to serve on the ACA Nominating Committee, and in June 2004, he was elected to the Commission on Accreditation for Corrections of the ACA for a four-year term, which speaks volumes of the commissioner's knowledge and expertise in corrections as a whole; and

WHEREAS, Commissioner Epps also serves on the following boards, committees and task force: Alcohol Services, Mississippi Prison Industries, Mississippi Drug Court Advisory Committee, Council of Advisors for the College of Public Service at Jackson State University, State Workforce Investment Board, Joint Terrorism Task Force, Interstate Commission for Adult Offender Supervision, and as Chairman of the Mississippi Wireless Communications; and

WHEREAS, due to his public service, Commissioner Epps has received numerous awards, some of which are as follows: 2007 "Humanitarian of the Year" by the Mississippi Association of Professionals in Corrections and the 2000 and 2004 "Professional of the Year" by that same organization; the 2007 Distinguished Alumni Award from the National Association for Equal Opportunity in Higher Education; named one of the "50 Most Influential African Americans in Mississippi" by BlackMississippi.com and the 2004 "Distinguished Public Service Award" by the University of Southern Mississippi's Department of Criminal Justice; and

WHEREAS, in addition to his multiple accolades and awards and his service to the department, Commissioner Epps is a man who loves and has served this country, more specifically, he was honorably discharged in March 2008, from the Mississippi Army National Guard after attaining the rank of Lieutenant Colonel and after 24 years of valiant service; and

WHEREAS, Commissioner Epps has received the following awards and honors for his stellar military service career: Army Commendations Medal; Army Achievement Medal with Oak Leaf Cluster; Army Reserve Component Achievement Medal with Oak Leaf Cluster; National Defense Service Medal; NCO Professional Development Ribbon; Army Service Ribbon, Mississippi Medal of Efficiency; Mississippi War Medal; Mississippi Longevity Medal with Oak Leaf Cluster and the honorary title of the 2007 "Kentucky Colonel" by former Kentucky Governor Ernie Fletcher; and

WHEREAS, throughout his military and public service career Commissioner Epps has been supported by his loving wife, Catherlean, and their two caring sons, Chris and Tracey; and

WHEREAS, it is the policy of this Legislature to commend an outstanding public servant, such as Commissioner Chris Epps, whose vast contributions to the Department of Corrections, as its leader, is a superb example of state government working at its best:

NOW, THEREFORE, BE IT RESOLVED BY THE HOUSE OF REPRESENTATIVES OF THE STATE OF MISSISSIPPI, THE SENATE CONCURRING THEREIN, That we do herby commend and congratulate Commissioner Christopher B. Epps on his outstanding service to the Mississippi Department of Corrections and on making history by being the longest serving commissioner in the history of the department, and we wish him continued success in all his future endeavors.

BE IT FURTHER RESOLVED, That copies of this resolution be furnished to Commissioner Christopher B. Epps, the Office of the Governor and to the members of the Capitol Press Corps.

MISSISSIPPI
DEPARTMENT OF CORRECTIONS

PRESS RELEASE

Date: June 15, 2012
Contact: Jasmine C. Cole
Phone: (601) 359-5689
Fax: (601) 359-5738

MDOC Commissioner Christopher Epps Selected to Present Before United States Senate Judiciary Committee

Jackson—The United States Senate Judiciary Subcommittee on the Constitution, Civil Rights and Human Rights today announced the selection of witnesses for a hearing on "Reassessing Solitary Confinement: The Human Rights, Fiscal and Public Safety Consequences." Mississippi Department of Corrections Commissioner and president-elect of the American Correctional Association, Christopher Epps, was selected to present testimony at the hearing which will take place at the Dirksen Senate Office Building on June 19, 2012 in Washington, D.C.

The witnesses are:

The Honorable Charles Samuels
Federal Bureau of Prisons, Director
Washington, DC

Christopher Epps
Mississippi Department of Corrections, Commissioner
Jackson, MS

Stuart M. Andrews, Jr.
Nelson Mullins Riley & Scarborough LLP, Partner
Columbia, SC

Anthony Graves
Anthony Believes, Founder
Houston, TX

Dr. Craig Haney
University of California, Santa Cruz,
Professor of Psychology
Santa Cruz, CA

Pat Nolan
Justice Fellowship/Prison Fellowship Ministries, President
Leesburg, VA

The hearing will take place on Tuesday, June 19, 2012 at 10:00 a.m. and may be viewed via webcast at:
http://www.judiciary.senate.gov/hearings/hearing.cfm?id=6517e7d97c06eac4ce9f60b09625ebe8

###

Fabricating Evidence

3/10/2015   FBI — Former Commissioner of Mississippi Department of Corrections and Local Businessman Plead Guilty in Federal Court

Jackson Division

Home · Jackson · Press Releases · 2015 · Former Commissioner of Mississippi Department of Corrections and Local Businessman Plead Guilty in Federal Court

Former Commissioner of Mississippi Department of Corrections and Local Businessman Plead Guilty in Federal Court

U.S. Attorney's Office   **Southern District of Mississippi**
February 25, 2015   (601) 965-4480

Jackson Division Links
Jackson Home

Contact Us
· Overview
· Territory/Jurisdiction

News and Outreach
· Press Room | Stories
· In Your Community

About Us
· Our People & Capabilities
· What We Investigate
· Our Partnerships
· Jackson History

Wanted by the FBI - Jackson

FBI Jobs

JACKSON, MS—Christopher B. Epps, former Commissioner for the Mississippi Department of Corrections, and Cecil McCrory, a former Mississippi legislator, former Justice Court Judge, former Chairman of the Rankin County School Board, and a local businessman, entered guilty pleas today before U.S. District Judge Henry Wingate, announced Acting U.S. Attorney Harold Brittain, FBI Special Agent in Charge Donald Alway, IRS-Criminal Investigation Acting Special Agent in Charge Jerome R. McDuffie, U.S. Postal Inspector in Charge Robert Wemyss, and Mississippi State Auditor Stacey Pickering.

Christopher Epps pled guilty to one count of money laundering conspiracy and one count of filing a false tax return. Cecil McCrory pled guilty to one count of money laundering conspiracy.

Epps will be sentenced on June 9, 2015 at 9:30 a.m. and McCrory will be sentenced on June 10, 2015 at 9:30 a.m. The maximum penalty for money laundering conspiracy is 20 years in prison and a $500,000 fine or twice the value of the property involved in the transaction. The maximum penalty for filing a false tax return is three years in prison and a $250,000 fine.

This case was investigated by the FBI, IRS-Criminal Investigation, U.S. Postal Inspection Service, Mississippi State Auditor's Office, and the Leake County Sheriff's Office.

Assistant U.S. Attorneys Mike Hurst, Darren LaMarca, and Scott Gilbert, as well as financial analyst Kim Mitchell, are prosecuting the case.

This content has been reproduced from its original source.

Accessibility | eRulemaking | Freedom of Information Act | Legal Notices | Legal Policies and Disclaimers | Links | Privacy Policy | USA.gov | White House
FBI.gov is an official site of the U.S. government. U.S. Department of Justice

Close

http://www.fbi.gov/jackson/press-releases/2015/former-commissioner-of-mississippi-department-of-corrections-and-local-businessman-plead-guilty-in-feder...   1/2

CONCLUSION

As a Black male born and raised in the Jim Crow era in Mississippi, the fear of wrongful convictions based on fabricated evidence was always present in my mind. In most cases, law enforcement personnel was motivated by racial hate, and the fact that they could get away with this crime. Too often these crimes were covered up.

However, in the so-called "post Jim Crow era" drug set-ups are still happening in Mississippi, a state that ranks number 2 in the United States with the highest numbers of inmates housed in its facilities. Most of them are people of color and are incarcerated for a drug-related offense. Staff members at South Mississippi Correctional Institution (SMCI) are law enforcement, convicting me on a fabricated drug possession charge that would have been successful in Mississippi's criminal justice system. Today in law enforcement, most Blacks are still a segregated group, needing to always watch their backs.

This book shows and explains the integrity melt down inside the Mississippi Department of Corrections (MDOC). *Webster Dictionary* defines the word integrity as *firm adherence to a code of ESP; moral or artistic values; incorruptibility; soundness, honesty.* However, MDOC personnel found a way to redefine integrity. MDOC has the power to work collectively with other law enforcement agencies in order to successfully ensure the outcome of an investigation. MDOC's Internal Audit Division (IAD) Investigators are called "Integrity Investigators."

The injustice by the officials of the court and law enforcement personnel put me and my family in harm's way and caused great financial and emotional hardship to befall us. I was forced to file bankruptcy twice, and denied employment because I was black-balled by former SMCI Superintendent C. David Turner, who stated in my personnel file, "made unfounded allegations toward administration prior to resignation," making it extremely difficult for me to secure gainful employment. A prime example is Transportation Security Administration (TSA). After successfully passing all the assessments for consideration for an appointment as transportation security screener with TSA, a background check was conducted. One aspect of the background check was former employment. Of course, my former employer is Mississippi Department of Corrections. After the background check was completed, I was informed that I was denied employment.

Exposing corruption at SMCI was economic suicide. The people that committed malfeasance against me are enjoying a state paid retirement. Meanwhile, it's social security retirement for me…unequal protection of the law.

At the end of the day, I survived the malicious acts against me, and so did my family. But, it is disheartening that with all the evidence I had against MDOC that, as a citizen of the United States of America, I was not able to have an unbiased trial, with a jury of my peers.

My intention was to share my experience as correctional officer in Mississippi. I hope to convince the American people the need for criminal justice reform. Hopefully my story will start an intense national movement to fix the broken system. Prison reform and sentencing reform will improve the United States criminal justice system. I hope this book will show Mississippi should be ground zero for prison reform.

Fabricating Evidence

U.S. DEPARTMENT OF TRANSPORTATION
TRANSPORTATION SECURITY ADMINISTRATION
400 7TH STREET
WASHINGTON, D.C. 20590

Date: 09/03/2002 Testing Location: JACKSON Airport: PIB

Name: MOSLEY BRITTON

SSN: _____

Candidate ID #: 352 2538

Congratulations! You successfully passed Phase 1 of the assessment process. The next step of the process, Phase 2, includes an interview, physical and medical assessment, and the collection of additional information for completion of the background investigation. This Phase will require another four to six hours of your time on another day and you need to schedule it now. **Please go to the scheduling table before you leave the center today for further direction and scheduling.** Any member of the assessment center staff can direct you to this area.

Successful candidates will receive either an immediate offer of employment or placement in the Ready Pool (a pool of candidates from which TSA can make additional offers of employment). If you do not schedule the next and final portion of the assessment today, your chances for immediate employment with TSA are greatly diminished.

_____
Human Resources Representative

REMINDER

Date and time scheduled: 10 AM 09/05/2002
Phase 2 requires a physical assessment; please wear comfortable shoes and clothing.

Revised 7/20/02

Britton Mosley, Sr.

U.S. DEPARTMENT OF TRANSPORTATION
TRANSPORTATION SECURITY ADMINISTRATION
400 7th STREET
WASHINGTON, D.C. 20590

Date: 09/05/2002   Testing Location: JACKSON, MS

Name: Mosley Britton SR

SSN: _____

Candidate ID #: 352 2538

Congratulations! You have successfully passed all of the assessments for consideration for an appointment as a Transportation Security Screener in the Department of Transportation, Transportation Security Administration.

At this time, you will be placed in a **Ready Pool** of candidates. This Ready Pool will provide the Department of Transportation (DOT), Transportation Security Administration (TSA) with individuals who can be rapidly trained and placed at the airports. As positions and training dates become available, TSA will draw first from the Ready Pool to fill these positions. The order of filling these jobs from the Ready Pool will be based on selective factors required to meet TSA staffing needs. These factors include workforce requirements and job-related experience and certifications. We will continue to process your background investigation for the necessary security clearance. **It is recommended that you NOT resign or give immediate notice to resign from your current place of employment until you receive an official offer of employment.**

An appointment to this position is contingent upon the successful results of your security background investigation, urinalysis drug test, any outstanding medical information results, and the successful completion of the required training.

Frequently, applicants ask questions about the nature of the background investigation and about problems that may surface in it. The following information is intended to answer the questions, which are asked more often:

- The purpose of the background investigation is to ensure that applicants meet the TSA's personnel security standards. Background investigations are extremely thorough. At a minimum, the TSA will ensure that your credit history is satisfactory and that you do not have a criminal history. We will contact regional credit bureaus where you have lived, and conduct checks of local law enforcement agencies for jurisdictions in which you have resided, attended school, or been employed. Also, if you have served in the military, we will review your military records.

Fabricating Evidence

- We will withdraw an employment offer if the investigation reveals information that precludes a security and/or suitability clearance (e.g., serious credit problems, abuse of alcohol, history of illegal drug use outside of TSA guidelines, misrepresentations during the application process, etc.) In addition, applicants who have been convicted of a felony or domestic violence charge or who display a lack of candor during any phase of the hiring process will be automatically disqualified from further consideration.

- The TSA, which is firmly committed to a drug-free society and work place, realizes that qualified individuals may have used illegal drugs at some point in their past. It is the policy of the TSA that prospective employees will be required to pass a urinalysis test, which screens illegal drug use prior to final appointment.

It creates significant hardship for both the TSA and the candidate, who has passed all of the assessments, if the offer must be withdrawn at the end of the background process. To prevent such hardship, we want to alert you to these potential problems now, at the outset, and invite you to discuss any concerns you may have. If you have any concerns you wish to discuss, please contact a Human Resources staff member at the TSA Assessment Center immediately.

If you find that you are no longer interested in this position or unable to meet the conditions of employment, please notify a Human Resources staff member at 1 (888) 218-1555.

Thank you for your interest in employment with TSA. Should you be called for an appointment, you should find here a great opportunity for public service and a distinguished career in transportation security.

Jonn R.
Human Resources Representative

Accepted: *Brittan Mosley, Sr.* 09/05/2002
 (Applicant Signature)

Britton Mosley, Sr.

TERMINATION SLIP

EMPLOYEE: Mosley, Britton   SSN: _____   PIN: _____
DEPARTMENT: SMCI   POSITION TITLE: Corr Officer II

TERMINATION DATE: 06/01/98
[X] RESIGNED [ ] DISMISSED [ ] DEATH
[ ] RETIRED   [ ] RIF   [ ] OTHER

REASON FOR TERMINATION: Resigned

LAST DAY WORKED: 1-Jul-97
LAST DAY VAC /COMP /MAJOR MEDICAL (if applicable): NA
RDO'S: Wednesday/Thursday

RECOMMEND FOR REHIRE: [ ] YES [✓] NO   IF NO, EXPLAIN:
Made unfounded allegations toward administration prior to resignation.

OTHER COMMENTS:

RECEIVED JUN 09 1998 PERSONNEL MDOC-SMCI

Signature of Supervisor/Dept Head: C. David Turner, Superintendent   (Date): 06/08/98

LEAVE TAKEN DURING CALENDAR MONTH IN WHICH TERM FALLS

		UNUSED LEAVE HOURS	
PERSONAL TAKEN	0	PERSONAL	8.5
MAJOR MEDICAL TAKEN	0	MAJOR MEDICAL	4.2
COMP TIME TAKEN	0	COMP - FLSA	0
OTHER (Explain)	0	COMP - OTHER	0
LWOP	0		
TOTAL # OF HRS. PHYSICALLY WORKED	0	REMARKS:	
HOLIDAY HOURS	0		

(Signature and Title): Lisa Bivens, Personnel Officer III   (Date): 06/05/98

PEP FORM PROCESSED ON _____ BY _____
TERM-DATA ENTERED INTO SYSTEM ON _____ BY _____

PAYROLL USE ONLY

TO BE PAID _____ Hrs Base for(Mo.,Yr.) _____ (regular salary) $_____
TO BE PAID _____ Hrs Personal Leave $_____
TO BE PAID _____ Hrs FLSA Overtime (Non-Exempt Employees Only) $_____

(Signature) _____   (Date) _____   00918

Original: Personnel File
CC: Payroll

gmb/forms/term slip/10-22-97

"SUPPORTING DOCUMENTATION"

PRESENTED BY THE FOLLOWING WITNESSES:

PAUL McCLENDON, W/M (hire date unknown)
Home #
Sgt. McClendon over heard a conversation outside Federal Court in Jackson, MS, March 23, between Supt. David Turner and Captain Joe Errington about getting rid of me. This conversation heard by Sgt. Paul McClendon was told to Randall L. Nedecker, special agent with the FBI.
This plot to get rid of me discussed by Supt. David Turner and Capt. Joe Errington prompted me to resign my position at South MS Correctional Institute. I held this position for over six (6) years, and for fear of my life, I resigned June 1998.

JOE BEARD, W/M
Home #
Joe Errington had a vendetta against me due to a land dispute wherein Joe Errington told Joe Beard he wanted him to do something with me regarding the land dispute. Joe Beard gave a statement to the FBI relevant to the dispute described as follows:
Joe said "I know where the Black Son of a Bitch works". I'll get him my way. Shortly afterwards, the two attempts to set me up transpired.

As to my character and work performance, Jimmie Fancher could be considered a witness.
JIMMIE FANCHER, W/M Correctional Institute
Phone #
Jimmie Fancher is a Captain with eighteen (18) years of experience with the department.

Prison official claims conspiracy forced his resignation

■ Proceedings scheduled this week in Hattiesburg

By BRAD CROCKER
George County Bureau

STATE LINE — A former correctional officer at the South Mississippi Correctional Facility in Leakesville claims he was the victim of a personal vendetta and forced to resign.

Britton Mosley Sr., 50, of State Line, claims in a federal lawsuit filed last March against the state Department of Corrections that his supervisors and fellow officers conspired to plant drugs on him on two different occasions. He was forced to resign.

Discovery proceedings are scheduled to be held in U.S. District Court in Hattiesburg this week, with a pretrial conference set for March.

Ken Jones, public relations director for the department of corrections, said the department would not comment on the case because it is pending.

Mosley, who is 50 and black, claims conspiracies began prior to a settlement of a 1996 federal lawsuit against the Department of Corrections filed by his wife, Brenda, who also works at the Leakesville prison. Brenda Mosley filed a discrimination lawsuit after she was not promoted to a telecommunications job for which she applied. She was awarded that position following the settlement and is still employed there, Britton Mosley said.

"This is not a race issue," Mosley said. "It's a justice issue."

Mosley claims that in November 1996 a plot was devised to have him found with two ounces of marijuana in his possession, a drug trafficking offense for which he could have received 30 years imprisonment, he said.

On Nov. 4, 1996, Mosley said an inmate, escorted by a correctional officer trainee, asked him how a prisoner could obtain shower shoes.

Later that same day, Mosley said he returned from a work detail outside the facility, and a small carrying bag was left with a sergeant by the trainee. The trainee allegedly told the sergeant that Mosley "would know what to do with (the bag)," he said.

Mosley claims he called another officer in the room, opened the bag and inspected it. He said he found size 8 shower shoes, hair, moisturizer and a container of baby powder.

Mosley assumed the products were for the prisoner seen with the trainee earlier but said he became suspicious because the prisoner who had requested the shower shoes wore size 14 shoes, and was also bald.

Mosley alleges that two ounces of marijuana wrapped in black tape inside of a plastic bag fell out of the powder container when he dumped it. He said he called the watch commander to investigate the findings.

After waiting several minutes, Mosley said he walked to the west end of the maintenance building and discovered his two superiors were inside the office with the door locked and the lights turned out. He claims they were normally at home at this time of day.

He believes he was supposed to be caught with the bag, which would have been searched, and the marijuana would have appeared to belong to him.

The second alleged plant conspiracy occurred in July 1997. Mosley contends that an inmate approached him and said that several of Mosley's behalf asked the inmate to plant drugs in Mosley's office.

Mosley said the prisoner did not want to participate. He said the inmate agreed instead to wear a "wire" on Mosley's behalf to prove wrongdoing. The taped conversation between the inmate and one of Mosley's co-workers is expected to be used as evidence to support the alleged conspiracy.

Following this incident, Mosley alleges that two state investigators offered him "any job I wanted" if he promised not to file a lawsuit. "It was insulting," Mosley said.

In his lawsuit, Mosley claims he learned that some of his superiors "made threats to get rid" of him. He said he resigned on June 1, 1998, because of a hostile work environment.

"I'm not motivated by money. I'm motivated by justice," he said. "I want the DOC to write a letter verifying that I didn't do anything wrong," he added. "Having the respect of my kids means more than money ... that's priceless."

> "I want the DOC to write a letter verifying that I didn't do anything wrong. Having the respect of my kids means more than money ... that's priceless."
>
> — Britton Mosley Sr.

Fabricating Evidence

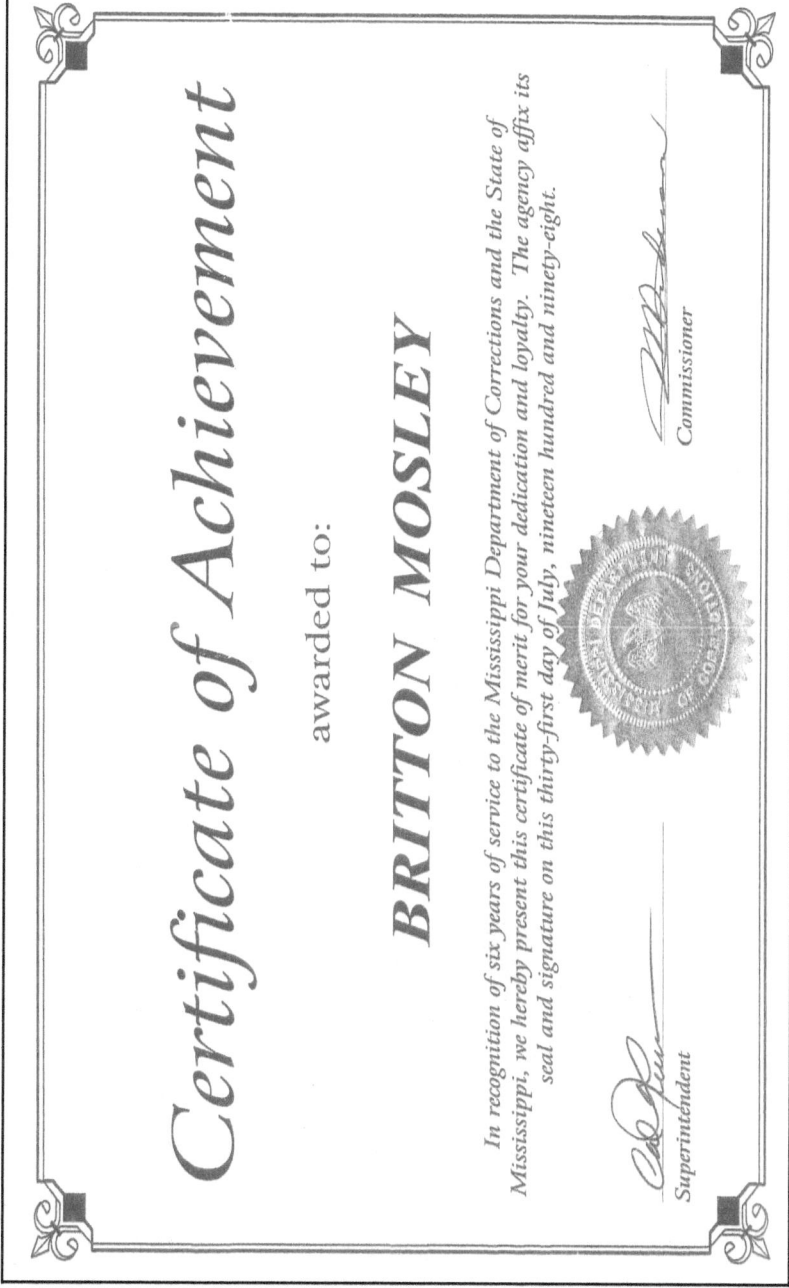

Britton Mosley, Sr.

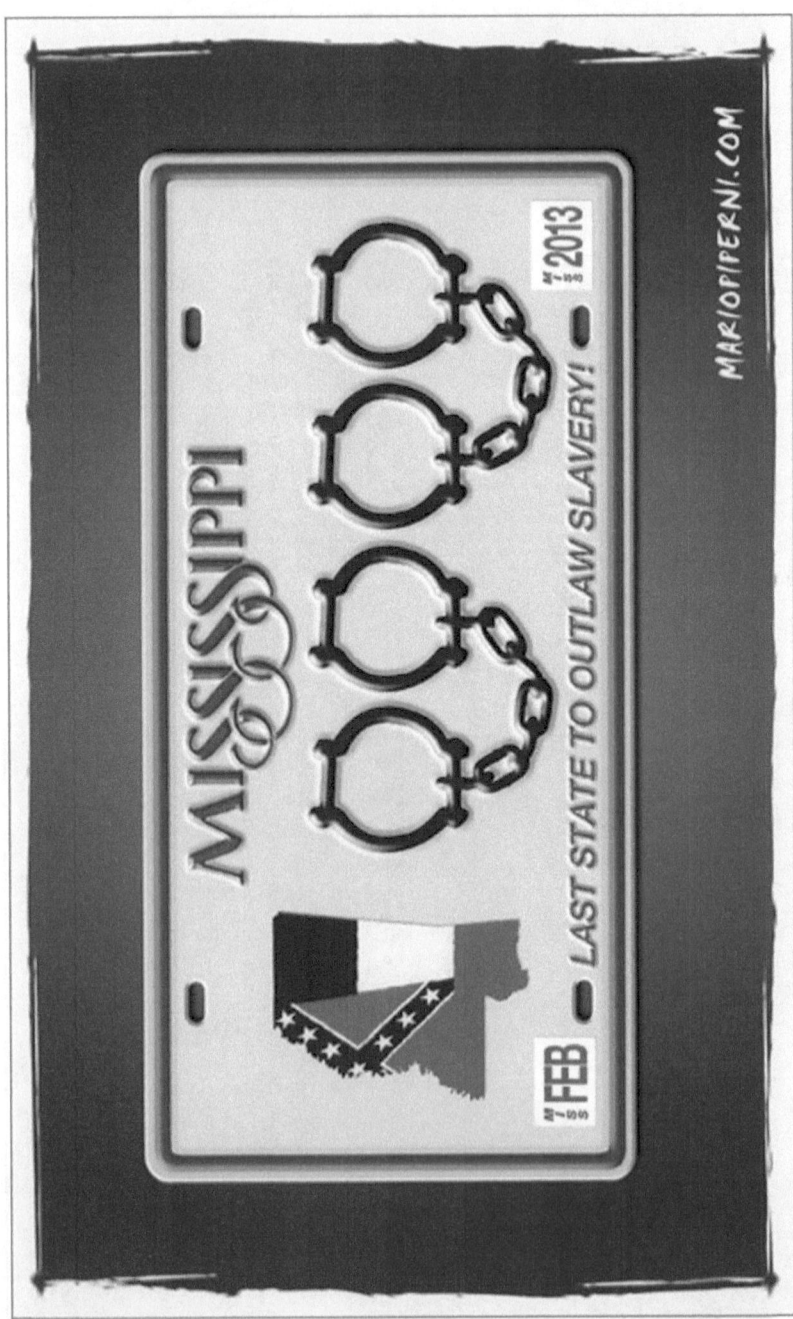

ABOUT THE AUTHOR

Britton Mosley, Sr. was born in Mississippi in the late forties, and grew up during the civil rights era. In his early years, he became a strong civil rights advocate and attended many marches, boycotts, meetings and various advocacy events. Later in life, he joined the Mississippi Department of Corrections as a Correctional Officer. During his almost eight years with MDOC, he was an advocate of prison reform and stood up against brutality and excessive forward toward inmates.

Mr. Mosley has appeared on a television documentary, and has hosted and appeared on many radio shows pertaining to the advocacy of prison reform. He currently resides in Northern Virginia.

www.ingramcontent.com/pod-product-compliance
Lightning Source LLC
Chambersburg PA
CBHW020642300426
44112CB00007B/212